Ireland and the Great War

Ireland and the Great War

'A war to unite us all'?

EDITED BY
ADRIAN GREGORY AND
SENIA PAŠETA

MANCHESTER
UNIVERSITY PRESS
MANCHESTER AND NEW YORK

distributed exclusively in the USA by Palgrave

Published by Manchester University Press
Oxford Road, Manchester M13 9NR, UK
and Room 400, 175 Fifth Avenue, New York, NY 10010, USA
www.manchesteruniversitypress.co.uk

Distributed exclusively in the USA by
Palgrave, 175 Fifth Avenue, New York NY 10010, USA

Distributed exclusively in Canada by
UBC Press, University of British Columbia, 2029 West Mall,
Vancouver, BC, Canada V6T 1Z2

British Library Cataloguing-in-Publication Data
A catalogue record for this book is available from the British Library

Library of Congress Cataloging-in-Publication Data
A catalog record for this book is available from the Library of Congress

ISBN: 0 7190 5925 9 paperback

ISBN 13: 9780719059254

First edition published 2002 by Manchester University Press

First digital, on-demand edition produced by Lightning Source 2006

Contents

List of tables

Acknowledgements

We would like to thank the friends and colleagues who supported this project from the outset and listened to our (no doubt tedious) descriptions of its progress. We are especially grateful to: Sarah Cohen, Roy Foster, Marc Mulholland, Katarina Pašeta, Simon Riley and Charles Townshend. Alan O'Day gave useful advice, and Roy Foster deserves special mention for his suggestion of the title. Thank you, one and all.

Thanks also to the staff at Manchester University Press who displayed exemplary patience and professionalism, often in the face of delays and procrastination, and to the archivists at the Imperial War Museum who responded so promptly to our request for photographs. Senia Pašeta is particularly grateful to Kevin Myers and Esther Murnane who generously allowed access to a valuable collection of Kettle letters; and to Peter Martin who replied speedily and with good humour to numerous requests for information.

Finally, we would like to thank all the contributors who responded so enthusiastically to our proposal. While we may not agree with all their opinions, we have learned much from their articles and remain grateful for their input.

Adrian Gregory
Senia Pašeta
Oxford

Notes on contributors

Joanna Bourke is Professor of History at Birkbeck College, London. She has published widely on aspects of the social, economic and political history of modern Britain and Ireland, as well as cultural studies of masculinity and modern warfare. Her publications include *Husbandry to Housewifery: Women, Economic Change and Housework in Ireland, 1890–1914* (1993), *Dismembering the Male: Men's Bodies, Britain, and the Great War* (1996), and *An Intimate History of Killing: Face-to-Face Killing in Twentieth Century Warfare* (1999).

D. George Boyce holds a personal chair in the Department of Politics and International Relations, the University of Wales, Swansea. He is the author of many books on modern Irish and British history including *Englishmen and Irish Troubles: British Public Opinion and the Making of Irish Policy* (1972), *Nationalism in Ireland* (1982/1991), *The Irish Question and British Politics, 1868–1996* (1996), and *The Making of Modern Irish History* (1996).

Adrian Gregory is a Fellow in Modern History at Pembroke College, Oxford. He is the author of *The Silence of Memory: Armistice Day, 1919–1946* (1994), and is currently working on a history of the British Home Front during the First World War.

James Loughlin is Reader in History at Magee College, University of Ulster. He has published widely on British and Irish history in the nineteenth and twentieth centuries; his books include *Gladstone, Home Rule and the Ulster Question, 1882–93* (1986); *Ulster Unionism and British National Identity since 1885* (1995); and *The Ulster Question Since 1945* (1998).

Peter Martin completed an M.A. on Irish Peers, 1909–1924 at University College, Dublin in 1998. He is presently a postgraduate and Government of Ireland Scholar at Trinity College, Dublin, where he is working on a comparative analysis of censorship in Northern Ireland and Southern Ireland between 1922 and 1939.

Theresa Moriarty is a researcher and project supervisor at the Irish Labour History Museum and Archive, Dublin. Her main area of research is women's labour history. She has published 'Work in Progress: Episodes from the History of Irish Women's Trade Unionism' (1994), and articles on Delia Larkin and Mary Galway.

Ben Novick is a graduate of the Universities of Michigan and Oxford. He is currently teaching history at Oakland University and the University of Michigan. He has written *Conceiving Revolution: Irish Nationalist Propaganda during the First World War* (2001), and a number of articles on aspects of modern Irish history.

Philip Orr read English at the University of East Anglia and currently teaches Theatre Studies at Down High School, Downpatrick. His contributions to Irish military and social history include *The Road to the Somme: Men of the Ulster Division Tell their Story* (1987). He is chairman of The New Ireland Group, an autonomous Belfast-based political think-tank.

Senia Pašeta is a Fellow in Modern History at St Hugh's College, Oxford. Her publications include articles on the social and political history of late nineteenth- and early twentieth-century Ireland, and *Before the Revolution: Nationalism, Social Change and Ireland's Catholic Elite, 1879–1922* (1999). She is currently working on a history of Irish women in the twentieth century.

Eileen Reilly is the Associate Director of Glucksman Ireland House, the Center for Irish Studies at New York University. Her main research interests are nineteenth- and twentieth-century politics and culture, specifically debates conducted through the medium of popular literature. She is currently finishing a book entitled *Taking Up the Cudgels: Political Debate in the Irish Novel 1880–1914*.

List of abbreviations

ASE	Amalgamated Society of Engineers
ASTT	Amalgamated Society of Tailors and Tailoresses
BEF	British Expeditionary Force
Bodl	Bodleian Library, Oxford
CCWPC	County Cavan Women's Patriotic Committee
DMP	Dublin Metropolitan Police
DORA	Defence of the Realm Act
DSO	Distinguished Service Order
HML	His Majesty's Lieutenant
IL HSM	Irish Labour History Society Museum and Archive
IPP	Irish Parliamentary Party
IRA	Irish Republican Army
ITGWU	Irish Transport and General Workers' Union
ITUC	Irish Trade Union Congress
IWHSD	Irish War Hospital Supply Depot
IWM	Imperial War Museum
IWWU	Irish Women Workers' Union
NAM	National Army Museum
NFWW	National Federation of Women Workers
NLI	National Library of Ireland
PRO	Public Record Office (Kew)
PRONI	Public Record Office, Northern Ireland
RIC	Royal Irish Constabulary
RIFM	Royal Irish Fusiliers' Museum
TCD	Trinity College, Dublin
TOSI	Textile Operatives Society of Ireland
UCD	University College, Dublin
UDC	Urban District Council
UVF	Ulster Volunteer Force
UWUC	Ulster Women's Unionist Council
VAD	Voluntary Aid Detachment
WNHA	Women's National Health Association
WTUL	Women's Trade Union League

Introduction

ADRIAN GREGORY
AND SENIA PAŠETA

Ireland has not been immune from the recent upsurge of interest in the First World War. The end of the twentieth century was marked by a veritable deluge of books, films and plays which focused on the war experiences of numerous individuals and nations, the vast majority of which stressed the futility, corruption and offence to humanity which that war has come to represent. What this literary and cinematic fascination seems to suggest above all else is that the Great War continues to matter, even eighty years after its end.

Why this should be the case has given rise to much debate and, in the case of Ireland, to soul-searching about the place in the country's history and contemporary life of the First World War. Much of this was spear-headed by a generation of historians who sought to integrate Irish experiences of the war into broader historical studies. It is now unthinkable that a general history of Ireland would fail to devote a significant section to the Great War and to its effect on the momentous events of 1914–1922. As Keith Jeffery has recently noted, enough work has now been done to enable us to 'look intelligently and with a more informed perspective than hitherto on the period'.[1] There is no need here to rehearse his comprehensive overview of the work which has been done, but it is important to bear in mind that First World War scholarship suffers from the same omissions and prejudices as wider Irish historiography. Given the tendency of historians of early twentieth-century Ireland to explore conflict above all else, it is unsurprising that civilian responses to and experiences of the war remain shadowy. The same may be said of war experiences which do not always fit neatly into the mainly political studies of unionist and nationalist responses to the Great War.

This collection includes chapters on both broadly social and political analyses of Ireland's war years. The enormous impact of the First World War on Ireland cannot hope to be summarised in one volume, but we set out to include articles on some lesser-known aspects of Ireland's war years as well as including studies of what might be termed more traditional areas. Though these articles cover diverse topics, two related themes emerge: the politicisation of almost every facet of civilian and military involvement in the war effort, and the augmentation of already existing political tensions under wartime conditions.

This dynamic was not of course uniquely Irish, but the long-term consequences of the intensification of political differences during the Great War have had a particularly powerful effect on twentieth-century Ireland. The upheavals of a major war generate two contradictory tendencies which exist in an uneasy dialogue. War serves to unite a combatant society against an external enemy, whilst at the same time the unequal pressures of mobilisation can exacerbate existing fault lines, whether of class, gender or nationality. In the British Isles in the early summer of 1914 each of these fault lines already appeared to be particularly acute and, as Ben Novick's article demonstrates, national division was the most acute of them all. The initial impact of war was the creation of an unprecedented unity, both within the island of Ireland and between Ireland and Great Britain. It is tempting to attribute this to an irrational 'war enthusiasm' and the dissenting minority in both islands did exactly that.

Such an interpretation misses the point. As in all European countries, the war was perceived as essentially defensive. In the case of Britain and Ireland it was seen as a necessary evil in order to check unprovoked German aggression. But the strange fact of unity in itself created enthusiasm. In Great Britain, the reports of Redmond and Carson standing together in support of the Empire transformed perceptions of Ireland overnight. The 'loyal Irish' suddenly became popular with the British; the green flag was cheered on the streets of London. There was relief at the avoidance of civil war and the hope predominated that a new unity would be forged. But the unity which emerged in Ireland was suspicious and conditional. Old antagonisms were not buried overnight, but the practical needs of war none the less drew nationalists and unionists together. In the epoch of volunteer action Ireland behaved in ways that were recognisable in the rest of the United Kingdom, establishing a plethora of small bodies keen to do their bit. Whilst men joined the armed forces, as Eileen Reilly illustrates, women mobilised to support them.

Unprecedented levels of agricultural prosperity and vastly improved employment possibilities meant that for non-combatants, the war, even if not exactly popular, was certainly tolerable. Theresa Moriarty's article on Irish trade unionism describes some of the economic advantages conferred by wartime demands and conditions. Advanced nationalists sniped continually and wittily in print at the local nationalist establishment and the British government, but faced with effective censorship and the ineptitude of the German government they were little more effective than their dissenting British counterparts. German atrocities against Catholic clergy in Belgium and the sinking of the *Lusitania* off the Irish coast were powerful arguments for the constitutional nationalist cause. The suspension of Home Rule was an irritant, but it remained on the statute books and the Redmondite assumption that a display of unconditional Imperial loyalty would render implementation inevitable was perfectly logical.

It was, of course, too good to last. As in all European states, the fault lines persisted and national 'questions' remained at the very heart of the war. The multi-national United Kingdom was far from unique in this respect. The fragile unity of the Hapsburg Empire was exposed almost from the outset. Conscripted Czechs surrendered and deserted *en masse* and were quickly persuaded to form military units to take the field against their rulers. By contrast the early efforts by Roger Casement to form anti-British units from volunteer Irish prisoners of war were a dismal failure. Polish 'legions' were formed by both sides as the Entente and Central powers engaged in a bidding war for Polish national sentiment, conducted largely in bad faith. In Belgium, the Germans cultivated Flemish separatism, whilst fearing the unreliability of their own conscripts from Alsace and Schleswig. When Italy entered the war, the inchoate separatism of the south led to substantial localised passive and occasionally armed resistance to impositions from Rome. As the strains mounted, Hungary practically stopped co-operating with Vienna, cutting off food supplies and interfering with military dispositions. In the United States there was an upsurge of nationalist sentiment amongst immigrants and *émigrés* and a multiplication of 'national committees' supporting one or other side in the war. Irish America, the groundbreaker in this respect, found itself flattered by a host of imitators.

Where Ireland was almost unique was that advanced nationalism led to an uprising against the government whilst the war was in progress.[2] The reflex of the conspiratorial physical force tradition, that British involvement in war was 'Ireland's opportunity', meant that such a rising was undertaken despite its military hopelessness and lack of active widespread support. In republican mythology, the Rising was the true expression of the essential Ireland. The blood sacrifice of Pearse and his fellow rebels reawakened Irish opinion to the essence of their colonial subjugation. Easter 1916 simply removed the veil of legitimacy disguising the brute facts of British rule. Revisionism, that crude term for a complex process of historical reassessment, has problematised this. At the most extreme, the events of Easter have been presented as a historical aberration, an outbreak of atavistic and even fascistic violence designed to thwart a peaceable and democratic settlement of affairs. The Republic was born in the fevered imagination of Patrick Pearse and history was derailed.

A broader perspective helps provide balance. The obsession of Pearse with redemptive blood sacrifice was far from unique; indeed he was speaking the common tongue of Europe in 1914–18. His views were no more intrinsically perverse or distasteful than those of Peguy, Brooke or D'Annunzio. The 'student' volunteers who died at 'Langemarck' and were mythologised by German nationalists were in essence very similar to those who fought and died at the Post Office. Raymond Asquith's condescending characterisation of 'The Volunteer' as a bored clerk dreaming chivalric daydreams who finds redemption in heroic death, applied as well to republican volunteers as to the millions who died on the Western Front. Nor were the Irish Volunteers the only unrepresentative armed minority to launch an urban coup in the name of great historical forces; the enterprise was undertaken successfully in Petrograd in 1917 and unsuccessfully in Berlin in 1918.[3] That these rebellions were undertaken in the name of a Utopian socialism rather than nationalism might once have made them appear more 'progressive'. A longer perspective of the twentieth century shows this to be illusory. Pearse was far less of an intellectual than Lenin, but ultimately he read history better. Poets, even bad poets, sometimes do. The mysterious conversion of James Connolly from pragmatist to martyr is less mysterious in this light. The Irish Republic endures; the Soviet Union does not, brought down in part by the forces that Pearse represented. The war itself was an essential context. The European empires had gone to war to defend the *ancien régime*, but a people's war unleashed forces they could not control. Of these forces nationalism proved more formidable than communism. Of the nine new nations created by the war in November 1918, seven have ultimately endured and the two that did not – Czechoslovakia and Yugoslavia – were themselves broken by further nationalistic forces.

In Ireland the war ultimately cemented the notion of 'two Irelands'. That one of these has often been described as a 'statelet' should not blind us to the nationalistic forces that helped to build it. It is impossible to ignore this ultimate polarisation, nascent in 1914, formalised in 1920. But Ireland was never a simple dichotomy and the war played on a wide range of competing ideologies and agencies. Constitutional nationalism had initially harnessed itself to the war effort. As Senia Pašeta's article on Tom Kettle demonstrates, this association became increasingly problematic as the costs of war mounted and the demands increased. Unionists, north and south, paid an even greater price, but loyalty to the Imperial cause came much more naturally to them and they gained more obvious rewards from the British government. For that government, Ireland was becoming an increasingly unwelcome complication in the larger business of defeating Germany. The impact of casualties and conscription, of industrial discontent and food shortages in Great Britain in 1917–18 made that government's responsibility of distributing sacrifices equitably intensely difficult. Ireland, by contrast, was tarred with the impression of being both disloyal and sheltered. People who had cheered the green flag in 1914 shunned the shamrock in 1917. In British opinion, the nationalist Irish were not only seditious, they were apparently profiteers and shirkers as well.

The abandonment of American neutrality removed an inhibiting influence on the British government, and the incorporation of unionist leaders into the cabinet hardened attitudes. By 1918 a peaceable solution to the historic problems of Ireland was far less important than winning the war. The resulting division, both of the United Kingdom and of Ireland, was not simply an outcome of long-term trends or of the bloody mindedness of one side or the other. Counterfactual speculations aside, the reasons were specific, contingent and war related. Eoin MacNeill tried to halt the Rising, but Pearse and Connolly made a conscious decision to proceed and in terms of their own agenda were ultimately largely vindicated. As Adrian Gregory argues, two years later Lloyd George similarly ignored expert advice and achieved his real goal of maintaining British consensus. Republican intransigence, unionist obstruction and Westminster indifference have been historical constants; in wartime this cocktail was peculiarly lethal.

D. G. Boyce's article shows how the experience of the war for the majority of Irish people turned out to be much more complex, subtle and ambiguous than later mythologies would acknowledge. Unionist loyalty often carried a high price in familial or personal catastrophe. In Ulster there was the cold comfort of vindication. Widows in Belfast or Portadown who might have wondered whether the cost of the Union had been too high were unlikely to be heard. James Loughlin demonstrates the process by which Ulster Protestants assimilated the war into a discourse of sacrificial loyalty. The Ulster Volunteer Force (UVF) was characterised by its losses on 1 July 1916; the fact that two years earlier it had been threatening armed rebellion against the British government utilising German-supplied rifles was conveniently forgotten. Southern unionists could perhaps take some comfort in duty fulfilled to compensate for finding themselves side-tracked by political developments. As Peter Martin argues, for the Irish aristocracy, like their British counterparts, the war was in some respects a last hurrah. Agricultural depression, land redistribution and the greening of local and national politics had been eroding their power for a generation, but the old bargain of the nobility, their justification by taking up the sword for King and Country still held. It would hold even for another generation and in a second war; the Anglo-Irish aristocracy – unionist 'Wild Geese' – reflexively fought and died for a country that had lost interest in them.

For constitutional nationalists and for the apolitical Southern Catholics who had served, even the consolations of duty were denied. The glorification of the republican minority left the far larger numbers who had served in good faith and fought for 'the cause of small nations', tainted with the stain of collaboration. At best they were frequently discriminated against, at worst they could be murdered. Joanna Bourke explains how those who had been physically or mentally maimed by the war could prove an embarrassment to all the governments concerned. For bereaved families, the rituals and monuments which assuaged grief elsewhere in the United Kingdom were often denied them.

History takes strange turns. In the 1980s and 1990s, as Ireland as a whole began to rediscover the First World War, it took on a new symbolic importance as counterpoint to assumptions of inevitable and immutable animosities and divisions. For a brief moment in 1914, Ireland had apparently been genuinely united and long animosities with Great Britain dissolved in a common cause. As the Northern Ireland peace process gathered momentum, the commemoration of the Great War, which had frequently been symbolic of the massive gulf between and within each of 'the two Irelands', became a forum for dialogue and reconciliation. In 1987 the IRA had perpetrated one of its most striking human and symbolic atrocities by bombing the war memorial at Enniskillen on Remembrance Day. Eleven years later the Queen and the President of the Republic joined together in unveiling a memorial to the joint martyrdom of the 16th and 36th Divisions at Messines in 1917. Catholic, nationalist and southern Ireland could apparently link hands with northern Protestant unionists over the grave of William Redmond. The spirit of 1914 could be reborn, the clock turned back.

But, as Philip Orr argues in his article on the 10th Division, the notion that these are the right grounds for reconciliation ought to be questioned. Can a conditional symbolic *détente* between traditions be built on celebrating common participation in a general European catastrophe which embodied nationalistic violence at its most extreme? If those who utilised guns in the belief that they were serving the freedom of Ireland at home once overshadowed those who did so in the belief they were serving the cause overseas, then it is not self-evident that simply reversing the polarity is a firm basis for the future. Wherever they fought and for whatever cause, the Irish of 1914–22 were both killers and victims and the circle of suffering spread well beyond the combatants. The events of those years which embraced the whole United Kingdom and the whole of Europe possessed no 'terrible beauty'; they were simply terrible. We can and should acknowledge the idealism involved – those who resorted to arms did so with real conviction and some justification – but in the end the only appropriate reaction is to remember them, to write about them and to mourn them.

Notes

1 K. Jeffery, *Ireland and the Great War* (Cambridge, Cambridge University Press, 2000), p. 1.
2 The nearest analogy is the Armenian uprising against the Ottomans in 1915. By comparison the horrors of Dublin fade into insignificance. The Armenian case was a much more genuinely widespread revolt, but it was also reactive in its nature, a response to a government-sponsored genocide.
3 Lenin noted the 1916 Rising with approval as an example of socialists and nationalists combining against 'imperialism'.

1

Thomas Kettle: 'An Irish soldier in the army of Europe'?

SENIA PAŠETA

Those who have lived through more years of this bloodstained century than Kettle was given to see, have witnessed cruelties and destruction more monstrous by far than those that shocked the innocence of 1914. The swelling generation who do not remember even a second war have horizons wider than those of Europe and face engines of annihilation more powerful than the mad guns of the Somme. Only the few who were young fifty years ago and have preserved some remembrance of what hopes and principles moved them then, can fully understand why Irishmen should have felt bound in honour to volunteer for war. So much has happened in Ireland in the years between that a gulf has opened between the generations.[1]

Thomas Kettle had a more immediate and intimate knowledge of the outbreak of the Great War than any of his political colleagues, and more indeed than most British commentators. Not only did he witness its commencement, he had also long been a keen observer of European affairs. As his wife later stated, 'He was deeply steeped in European culture. He was *au courant* with European politics. He knew his France, his Germany and his Russia as well as we know our Limerick, Cork and Belfast.'[2] His deep – and as he saw it – personal involvement in the hostilities must not be under-estimated and his advocacy of Ireland's involvement in the war must not, as has so often been the case, be attributed solely to the connection the war came to have with Home Rule, the alliance of nationalists and unionists or the increasing spectre of militarism. Kettle's support for the allied war effort was sparked by his genuine horror at the events he witnessed in Belgium, but it was buttressed primarily by wider ideological considerations: 'I have a confession', he declared in 1915. 'I care for liberty more than I care for Ireland.'[3]

The willing involvement of Irish nationalists in the British war effort has recently become the subject of much historical research, and a consideration of Kettle's endorsement of the allied war effort has received some scholarly attention. But historians have largely failed to investigate Kettle's motivation beyond a narrow consideration of temporal nationalist concerns. To analyse his wartime career solely in relation to the question of how Irish participation in the war might affect the uncertain Home Rule settlement, leads to an incomplete understanding of Kettle's motivations and ideas, both about Ireland and a wider Europe. This chapter will explore his internationalist reaction to the outbreak of war, the impact of the war on his developing political philosophy, and his ongoing attempts to justify Irish participation in the war effort.

Kettle was an extraordinarily gifted man who was frequently described as the greatest mind of his generation of Irish men. It is not, therefore, my intention to argue for his typicality or representativeness. This is very much a study of one political mind and one highly personal crusade. But an examination of both his intellectual reaction to the outbreak of war and his subsequent career as a recruiter and soldier reveals much about Irish politics in the early years of the century. The Great War had a profound influence on Kettle's political rhetoric and his literary output; it also cost him dearly in terms of his health, reputation and career. Ultimately, it claimed his life, but it was a life he gave willingly, not because he harboured a death wish, but because he genuinely believed the rhetoric he employed when encouraging young Irish men to enlist. Even if one considers his pro-allied stance to be foolish or naïve, such a condemnation should not detract from an understanding of the very real conviction with which it was articulated and, more importantly, from an acknowledgement that Kettle represented an important early twentieth-century political mentality which vanished alongside the memory of the Irish war dead.

Kettle was sent to Belgium on a gun-buying mission for the Volunteers in 1914. An ideal candidate for the mission, he spoke several European languages, had travelled widely on the continent, and was a trusted member of the Volunteers and confidant of Redmond. The sought-after guns were procured, as evidenced by Redmond's letter of congratulation to Kettle,[4] but the weapons never reached Ireland, being first detained by the Belgian government and eventually handed over by the Irish Party to the Belgians.[5] But gun-running quickly lost its urgency in the face of the events which unfolded before Thomas Kettle. He witnessed the build-up to war, and the gloomy indications that a terrible calamity was about to engulf Belgium and the wider continent. He was among the crowd at the Brussels Gare du Nord on 4 August which heard the news of the German invasion and he remained in Belgium as a war correspondent for the *Daily News* for the next two months. His immediate response to the German incursion was as vivid as it was unambiguous: 'Belgium,' he declared, 'is in agony.' He demanded that it be given immediate support, both financial and military.

In an article which seemed to anticipate the claim – so often subsequently made in Ireland's radical press – that war correspondents and the allied powers accepted as true atrocity stories which were in fact exaggerated for propaganda purposes, Kettle drew on his own experiences in Belgium and his training as a lawyer to present a catalogue of eye-witness accounts. These which were drawn from the evidence collected by a Belgian Committee which met shortly after the German invasion. He divided his report into three investigative sections, presenting evidence for: the use of explosive bullets and the dropping of bombs; murder and mutilations; and the destruction or confiscation of private property.[6] Though his language was unequivocal, he was uninterested in sensationalism, condemning journalistic extravagance and framing his support for the Belgians in moral and legal language. In one piece written shortly after the outbreak of war, he outlined what was to become the basis of his support for the allied war effort:

> It is impossible not to be with Belgium in the struggle. It is impossible any longer to be passive. Germany has thrown down a well-considered challenge to all the deepest forms of our civilization. War is hell, but it is only a hell of suffering, not a hell of dishonour. And through it, over its flaming coals, Justice must walk, were it on bare feet.[7]

The destruction of the University of Louvain, which housed an Irish seminary and a collection of Celtic manuscripts, touched an especially raw nerve in Kettle, who witnessed the ruins, and in the Irish population which was fed an increasingly potent anti-German diet by the Irish press and Catholic clerics. Reports of the rape of nuns and the shelling of churches and cathedrals only heightened pro-war sentiment. Kettle's anti-German rhetoric may, in the light of an enormous body of scholarship which has emphasised the futility of the Great War, the dishonesty with which it was promulgated and the ineptitude with which its battles were planned, appear inexcusably naïve to the contemporary reader. But the impact on the Irish population of what quickly became known as the 'rape of Belgium' has been underestimated and under-explored. Leaving aside Irish parallels and temporal needs for the moment, it is essential to recognise the very real antipathy and the faith with which news of the German assault was greeted in Ireland.[8] 'Little Belgium' – with its largely Catholic government – was held in high esteem before the war and parallels with 'Catholic Ireland' were already well established.[9] 'War fever' swept over Ireland, not only because of the excitement generated by the Home Rule crisis and the attendant spread of militarism, but also because of a genuine sense of outrage at German actions in Belgium and a sympathy for the country's plight.

While stationed with the 16th Division in France in 1916, Kettle claimed that Ireland had always been his 'centre of reference' when writing about the war, but this statement is not obviously borne out by his initial despatches in which Ireland had no explicit place. Absent from Kettle's early analysis of the war was any discussion of high European politics or diplomacy. He did not seem to consider the impact of war on the European balance of power or – until 1916 – on trade interests. His analysis clearly stemmed from his personal experience of the Belgium of 1914 and the Belgium he had so often visited before that fateful year. But, more importantly, it owed much to both the Christian humanist ideology which had underpinned much of his writing since the early years of the century, and his deep attachment to what he described as European civilisation. Kettle had travelled to the continent as a university student, acquainting himself with the geography and languages of Germany, France and Belgium. Europe became for him a sanctuary and a retreat, especially in times of physical and emotional distress. He spent a year reading philosophy and history at Innsbruck University, having been devastated by the death of a favourite brother in 1903 and suffering a breakdown in health in 1904. His stay in Germany also had a profound influence on his developing philosophical and political thought.

No mere dilettante, he became immersed in European literature and philosophy and was later to translate L. F. A. Paul-Dubios's *Contemporary Ireland* and contribute an introduction to the translation from French of Daniel Halévy's *Life of Frederick Nietzsche*. He enjoyed a mild flirtation with Nietzsche in his youth, but soon denounced him and subsequently saw in German militarism the excesses of his philosophy made real. As he viewed the ruins of Malines Cathedral in 1914, for example, he asserted, 'this is how Nietzsche has, from his grave, spat, as he wishes to spit, upon Nazareth'.[10] With Bismarck and the historian, Treitschke, Neitzsche came to embody what Kettle described as 'the gospel of the devil', a doctrine which was composed in equal parts of 'violence, intellect and a certain malign splendour of domination'.[11] Though perhaps intellectually crude and hardly unusual in the early years of the war, such analysis reflects his genuine anguish and his attempt to intellectualise the spectacle of the 'Europe which carried the fortunes and hopes of all mankind – degraded to a foul something which no image can so much as shadow forth'.[12]

Kettle's dedication to European political thought was well developed and well known by 1914. A large component of his enthusiasm for cosmopolitanism was purely cerebral: a deeply scholarly man, he found no Irish equivalent to Hegel or Goethe. But more important was his conviction that Europe represented progress towards democracy and sovereignty, a progress in which Ireland could participate, and a progress which was gravely threatened by German actions in Belgium. Though intellectually interesting, such sentiment might at first appear to be remarkably inappropriate. Home Rule was after all, an intrinsically imperial concept which seemed to bear little resemblance to political arrangements found on the continent, and Britain in

1912 surely offered more democracy and prosperity to Ireland than ever before.[13] The key to understanding Kettle's political philosophy lies in recognising that his dedication to continental thought was complementary rather than absolute, and that his own outlook was international rather than insular.

This view informed his impatience with parochial Irish nationalism and with the denunciation of continuing close relations between Ireland and England. He despaired of futile anglophobia, insisting that 'a natural alliance' existed between England and Ireland and that the gulf between the two nations was born of little more than misunderstanding. This natural alliance was to a large part based on the similar cultural, political and social organisations of the two countries, for Kettle an entirely natural and acceptable situation. As he told a London audience, 'our civilisation is substantially the type of civilisation here'. Moreover, he maintained that, 'We Irish are realists, and we hold the problems of the present as of more account than any agonies or tyrannies of the past.'[14] The tendency of Irish-Irelanders to look to the past and – increasingly – to assert that 'if a thing is English it is necessarily vile', had no place in his thinking. The maintenance of the Anglo-Irish relationship was thus central to Kettle's vision for a free and sovereign Ireland, but only, ideally, in a wholly reconstructed form. He argued that the 'inevitableness' of Home Rule, 'resides in the fact that it is ... a biped among ideas. It marches to triumph on two feet, an Irish and an Imperial foot'.[15] But the 'Imperial foot' required serious modernisation: 'The foolishness of England in Ireland', he claimed, 'finds an exact parallel, although on a smaller scale and for a shorter period, in the early foolishness of England in her own colonies.'[16] A Dublin parliament which would govern rather than administer, would, he claimed, furnish the 'germ of a reorganisation of the Empire'.[17]

Kettle remained, at the same time, one of the most acerbic critics of British policy in Ireland, and he wrote widely on aspects of British mismanagement and misappropriation of Irish resources. Crucially, however, his critique was based – inevitably – on what he described as 'realism in politics' and not on sentimental denunciations of English oppression. 'In order to understand Ireland,' he argued, 'we must begin by understanding England.'[18] 'Any fool in a crowd can raise cheers and ruin throughout the country by shouting "What about '98?" "Who murdered Wolfe Tone?" and so on',[19] but he maintained that the problematic nature of the Anglo-Irish relationship could only be understood if one accepted that it was as much a product of 'all the folly of Ireland' as 'all the folly of England'.[20] But critical of British policy in Ireland and in the wider Empire as he was, Kettle's vision of Home Rule Ireland rested absolutely on the willing maintenance not only of the British connection, but of British parliamentary traditions functioning in College Green.

This was in part a product of his pragmatic approach to politics – devolved government would, he maintained, lead to the disappearance of 'home-rulers' and unionists and to the development of a fully functioning multi-party political system – but it also depended on his broader world-view which eschewed insularity and embraced cosmopolitanism. He denied the notion that Irish identity could or should rest entirely on 'native' influences and feared that Irish-Irelandism would force the exclusion of European ideas from Ireland. He also denounced the backward-looking and un-intellectual way in which polemicists like Arthur Griffith approached such complex issues as economic rejuvenation and cultural development. As he told an audience in 1905:

> Ireland, a small nation, is, none the less, large enough to contain all the complexities of the twentieth century. There is no ecstasy and no agony of the modern soul remote from her experience; there is none of all the difficulties which beset men, eager to build at last a wise and stable society, that she has not encountered. In some of them she has even been the forerunner of the world. If this generation has, for its first task, the recovery of old Ireland, it has, for its second, the discovery of the new Europe. Ireland awaits her Goethe – but in Ireland he must not be a Pagan – who will one day arise to teach her that while a strong people has its own self for centre, it has the universe for circumference. All cultures belong to a nation that has once taken sure hold of its own culture. A national literature that seeks to found itself in isolation from the general life of humanity can only produce the pale and waxen growths of a plant isolated from the sunlight. In gaining her own soul Ireland will gain the whole world ... My only programme for Ireland consists, in equal parts, of Home Rule and the Ten Commandments. My only counsel to Ireland is, that in order to become deeply Irish, she must become European.[21]

But how could Ireland 'become European' and what did Kettle mean by this? The first point to be made is that he looked to Europe in an effort to internationalise Irish nationalism. Ireland could and should retain its strong links with the rest of the United Kingdom, but it should also acknowledge its role in the larger course of continental European history. Given that, as he saw it, 'the two supreme facts, the shaping forces of the nineteenth century were Nationality and Democracy', Ireland could not but be considered to be in the mainstream of recent European political developments.[22] Kettle maintained that Ireland's struggle for democracy and progress – the benefits of which included Catholic Emancipation and the abolition of tithes – was comparable to similar campaigns in countries including Belgium, Italy and Germany. Thus, he argued that 'whatever gloomy mood we fall into in the struggle for autonomy we have certainly no justification for feeling lonely'.[23]

The history of Ireland's struggle for Home Rule could, perforce, be viewed in a grander international context; such political concepts as liberalism, nationalism and democracy which shaped Europe in the nineteenth century and early twentieth century had similarly influenced the development of modern Ireland. European history thus provided Kettle with a historical framework in which to analyse the development of Irish statehood and progress towards sovereignty. For Kettle, the recognition and exposition of similarities between Irish and continental political struggles strengthened both Ireland's claim to nationhood and his conviction that the sometimes slow and disappointing constitutional path towards Home Rule was legitimate. This view was particularly relevant in the context of the wartime challenges of advanced nationalism to the Irish Party and its political programme. Crucially, it also underpinned his argument that European citizenship carried obligations as well as privileges and political and historical fellowship; refusing to participate in the allied war effort was tantamount to relinquishing any claim to such communion. As his wife later wrote, 'It was as an Irish soldier in the army of Europe and civilisation that he entered the war.'[24]

The Great War both transformed and fortified many of Kettle's ideas about Ireland, England, the Empire and Europe, and allowed him to draw together various of the ideological threads which had been woven through his numerous and wide-ranging publications. It is only through recognising the interplay between these strands of thought that we can begin to understand why he was such a fervent advocate of Ireland's participation in the war effort. Kettle's reports from Belgium convey both dismay and a deep sense of disbelief; but, as the Europe he knew fell apart before his eyes, many of his political assumptions and priorities were actually strengthened. His commitment to Irish membership of a community of European nations was, if anything, fortified, and he held that the war actually offered a valuable opportunity for Ireland to prove its European credentials. In common with many other constitutional nationalists, he believed that the European war held out to Ireland 'fair and high promise for the future', arguing, for example:

> the separate existence of the Irish Brigades is a thing to dwell on, for they are the living symbol of the truth that this war is Ireland's war, and that Ireland for the first time in the passage of long centuries sends out her sons fully accredited to fight for the sake of Ireland and for Ireland's cause.[25]

The urgency and severity of the situation in 1914 ensured that some old enmities and quarrels paled into insignificance as the war ushered in new political alignments which he would once have been the first to condemn. Though a supporter of their campaigns, Kettle had condemned, for example, the violence of both the suffragettes and Dublin's striking workers in 1913. He had also protested against the Boer War by distributing anti-recruiting leaflets and had, in 1906, tried to persuade John Redmond to include anti-enlistment in the Irish Party's programme.[26] But he showed no such opposition to British militarism in 1914. 'England,' he claimed in September of that year, 'is as right now as she was wrong in the Boer War.'[27]

> The England that made the Boer War was, perhaps, the greatest menace in the world at that time to freedom and justice. I fought against her with such poor weapons – alas! Only of controversy – as came to hand: I rejoiced in her defeats, and cried shame on Irishmen who enlisted under her flag. That England is dead. The Poles have changed place, the North has become South. Bad as it was, it was less menacing because less scientific, but it bore a strong resemblance to the Prussia of to-day. Jingoism was not so mystical as Kaiserism, but it was very like it. Were you to search all literature for the typical poet of Prussianism you would find it difficult to pass over Mr Rudyard Kipling.[28]

In Kettle's mind, England's difficulty became Ireland's opportunity, but not in the way in which this aphorism is usually understood. Most importantly, it presented the inauguration of a new basis on which the Anglo-Irish relationship would henceforth be conducted. England had rehabilitated itself – first by passing the third Home Rule Bill in 1912 and then by taking up the Belgian cause – and by doing so had purged itself of many of its past sins: Britain had begun to 'cleanse' itself.[29] Moreover, British policy in Ireland appeared increasingly benign in comparison with German policy on the continent and, in any case, old disputes had to be buried in the face of a much more potent threat than English tyranny:

> If we take our stand against Prussia we have got to take our stand with England. No man could condemn more strongly than myself the weary centuries of English blackguardism in Ireland. But the poisoners of Owen Roe O'Neill are dead, and the hangers of Emmet are dead. Even in our own time, and in the last ten years of it, a new world has come into existence. The England of 1914 is on the side of the Ten Commandments, and it does not reside in the spiritual tradition of Ireland to desert the Ten Commandments in order to gratify a hatred of which the mainsprings have disappeared. Therein lies the mistake of this whole school of interpretation. Its disciples go on a hatred, not a principle. And they have failed to observe that this is a world of change.[30]

The war also exposed Kettle to many of the same dilemmas faced by British liberals as they attempted to articulate their responses to British participation in a continental war, but for Kettle the war promised as much hope as despair. In the first instance, it allowed him to link his liberal Catholicism with a broader cause, important for a man who had long attempted to harness the two doctrines despite the very obvious and considerable ideological distance between them. This was an especially difficult task on an island which was largely Catholic, and increasingly suspicious of liberalism and its alleged association with anti-clericalism, secularism and socialism.

Kettle's papers reveal little anti-clericalism, though he did on one occasion claim that his career as an Irish Party MP had been blighted by 'noisy priests'.[31] The son of a loyal Parnellite, he was critical of clerical interference in politics, but he nevertheless enjoyed cordial relations with a number of prominent clerics, many of them Jesuits, and a number of them former teachers and mentors at the prestigious Clongowes Wood College and University College, Dublin. He remained a devoted Catholic all his life, surprising some of his friends who wondered how he managed to reconcile his Catholicism with his liberal ideals. Shane Leslie, for example, claimed that 'it was a miracle of intellect that he kept the Catholic faith'.[32] Though in no way in sympathy with the Easter rebels, Kettle was similarly prepared to sacrifice his life for his cause and to enlist the support of his fellow nationalists in this endeavour. His commitment was no doubt influenced by the militarism which had begun to sweep through Ireland even before the outbreak of hostilities and which subsequently flourished through the long war years, but it was also influenced by his Catholic faith and the doctrine of sacrifice which underpinned it. This was best demonstrated in his 1915 article on the 'Worker-Priests of France', an exposition of the heroic deeds and religious duties of priests who were actively involved in the allied effort; in Kettle's words 'a rich, even inexhaustible repository of Catholic heroism'.[33] He maintained the religious theme in much of his wartime writing, linking in particular German philosophy with anti-clericalism and atheism.[34]

Like his fellow Irish Party colleagues, Kettle also emphasised the Irish aspect of the war at every possible opportunity. In 1914, for example, he insisted that 'the future and expansion of the Home Rule Act are inseparably bound up with the European settlement that will follow the war'.[35] In his determination to attract recruits, he used a language of both duty and opportunity, arguing that the war was as much about nationhood as it was about ideology. This of course chimed well with the 'small nation' rhetoric adopted by William Redmond, Stephen Gwynn and their fellow recruiters. But Kettle's appeal was more strongly steeped in older preoccupations about the meaning and validity of nationhood. He had long despaired of the British tendency to view Ireland as 'a question rather than a nation'. The Third Home Rule Bill had added weight to his claim that the 'open secret of Ireland is that Ireland is a nation'; the war provided another opportunity to demonstrate Ireland's claim to that nationhood. While Kettle claimed to despise war and later came to question some British war aims, he never doubted that the challenge to European freedom must be faced down in the strongest possible way and that Ireland must play a role in the crusade against 'Prussian tyranny'. As his wife later wrote, 'I postulate that Tom Kettle died most nobly for the cause of Irish Nationality, in dying for the cause of European honour.'[36]

Kettle fought three wars between 1914 and 1916: a war against German aggression, a war against advanced Irish nationalists and a war against alcoholism. His notes reveal that he was deeply tormented by all three crises which became increasingly entwined as the war dragged on. With his brother, Laurence, he had presided over the establishment of the provisional committee of the Volunteers and become a leading propagandist for the organisation. He continued to condemn violence, but argued that Ulster resistance must be met with what he termed 'self-defence'. He considered the spilt in Volunteer ranks to be the first major blow to the Irish war effort and one which confirmed his worst suspicions about advanced nationalists. His earlier efforts to draw various schools of nationalism into one inclusive movement were abandoned as a journalistic war of words erupted between the prolific Kettle and the burgeoning anti-war press. Kettle was unquestionably in dispute with Sinn Féin by 1914, but his relations with the Gaelic League had been largely conciliatory, though by no means unambiguous. His identification of members of Sinn Féin, the Gaelic League and the Gaelic Athletic Association as the leading instigators of the Volunteer split led to some of his most hostile articles, most notably one entitled 'Why Kill the Gaelic League?'.[37]

As mentioned, Kettle had long objected to the provincial and inward-looking tendencies of Irish-Ireland organisations, but their alleged abandonment of the Volunteers and establishment of a rival, anti-war organisation represented their most direct threat to constitutional politics and to the fragile alliance which seemed to have been formed between rival nationalist groups. Thinking no doubt of the mayhem provoked by the disaster of 1891, he despaired of the 'desperate homesickness for a Split' so often displayed by Irish nationalists.[38] This fed his long-standing antipathy towards Sinn Féin, the Gaelic League and advanced nationalism in general, confirming his oft-stated claim that such organisations contained elements which were 'a subtler enemy of freedom than Dublin Castle'.[39] *Sinn Féin* had previously been as dismissive of Kettle as it had of his constitutional nationalist colleagues, but Kettle had been singled out for special attention. The newspaper had printed poor reviews of his publications and had condemned as an Irish Party sinecure his appointment to the Chair of National Economics at University College, Dublin. But Kettle's support for the war provoked an even more bitter dispute in which each side showed that it could give as good as it got. The harshest abuse Kettle could hurl was to denounce the '"physical force" school of Irish nationalist thinking' as 'naïve and Prussian',[40] and he condemned Sinn Féiners in particular for their moral and military cowardice:

The Sinn Féin Volunteer will not fight German invaders, or, indeed, invaders of any kind because they are bound to be enemies of England ... He will not fight England because 'the time has not yet come'. The only people he will fight are the elected representatives of the Irish nation. Into these he will discharge valiant volleys of adjectives, brightening up his performance by an occasional theft of rifles.[41]

Kettle understood the value of propaganda. He vowed in 1915 to 'lecture anywhere in Ireland on the agony of Belgium, showing plates from photos'.[42] He was also a keen critic of the radical press which flourished at the outset of the war under the benign eye of a distracted government, warning British officials of the potential impact of this anti-war bloc and advising countermeasures:

The first thing I noticed on coming back to Ireland was the absence of cheap literature on the right side. You have a daily, a weekly, and a monthly all chorusing the praises of Germany, and denying her barbarities in Belgium. Our decenter press, of course, explained at the beginning the justice of the cause of the Allies, *but they don't keep rubbing it in.* Now the problem in Ireland is to get at the individual conscience ... What has to be done is to put in the field a cheap counter-literature.[43]

A seasoned journalist and pamphleteer, Kettle then turned his attention to producing this cheap counter-literature and became one of the most prolific of all pro-war Irish writers. His output included pamphlets, numerous articles and, with Stephen Gwynn, *Battle Songs for the Irish Brigades*, a collection of ballads, some composed by Kettle and Gwynn, others by nationalist favourites including Davis and Mangan. But Kettle's greatest impact was probably as a recruiter. According to his wife, he made close to 200 speeches in 1914–15, both in England and in Ireland, and by becoming so closely and publicly associated with the allied cause, he once again invited the ridicule of what he described as 'the chattering gutter idealists'.[44] Despairing of Kettle's constant appearance on recruiting platforms and his tendency to talk on any number of issues, *Éire-Ireland*, for example, asked, 'Will any man of character help Mr. T. M. Kettle by standing on a platform and discussing any subject under heaven with that notorious person?'[45]

Kettle's invective was no doubt fuelled by a genuine concern about the impact on recruitment of these organisations, but it was also driven by the malicious way he was portrayed in the advanced nationalist press. He complained about the attacks on his character which appeared with increasing regularity as the war dragged on. As a devotee of the Irish Parliamentary Party (IPP), a supporter of Irish involvement in the war and as a critic of separatist organisations, he was an obvious target. His activities as a recruiter also provided a useful opening for his journalistic enemies who claimed that he hid behind recruitment in an effort to avoid active service.[46]

But Kettle himself courted ridicule, and it is difficult to comprehend some aspects of his behaviour in 1914–16 unless one takes into account his alcoholism. His excessive drinking was no secret and it impinged increasingly on his professional and personal life. Two incidents, in particular, became notorious: the first was his ill-judged decision to offer himself as a candidate for the East Galway by-election of November, 1914; the second was his appearance – in uniform and 'gloriously drunk'[47] – at the Thomas Davis Centenary Meeting in late 1915.

Kettle offered himself as a pledge-bound candidate for East Galway on the condition that he be allowed a 'short lease' of eleven months; after that time he would join the army. His campaign began and ended with the war and he offered little more than a defence of the allied cause to the electorate; he did not even offer to serve a parliamentary term. Unsurprisingly, neither his wife nor his friends referred to this incident in their reminiscences and this election bid remains one of the most shadowy episodes of his political career. He did not receive the nomination and was parodied mercilessly by the advanced nationalist press:

> When Colonel Moore reviewed his tour
> He bravely showed his mettle;
> And facts leaked out which plugged the spout
> Of Mr. 'Em'ty' Kettle.
> In days of old, this patriot bold
> Was 'guilty' of sedition!
> Now, out of a job, the Saxon bob
> Has changed his mind's condition.
>
> And since we find he changed his mind
> And twisted his old 'handle'
> Those German spies – so 'Em'ty' lies
> They cannot hold a candle.
>
> The Galway seat (who said defeat?)
> Will put him in good fettle,
> And then he'll sing 'God Save the King' –
> Brave Tommy Atkins Kettle.[48]

But by far the most damaging criticism was the increasingly frequent accusation that Kettle lacked the courage to volunteer for active service while sending Irish men in their thousands to die in France and Flanders: this was a charge regularly levied at Irish Party recruiters, Stephen Gwynn and William Redmond included. Kettle was in an unenviable situation: he was distressed by the attacks on his public and 'private character',[49] but he was unlikely to reveal that his applications to see immediate active service had been turned down, time and time again. Such a disclosure would amount to an admission of alcoholism, already a subject of gossip. From November 1914, he had argued that to encourage others to go while he remained at home was immoral,[50] but the army would not have him.

While he was being caricatured, Kettle did in fact attempt on several occasions to have himself sent to the Front, but his frequent applications were turned down on the grounds of poor health. The details of Kettle's enlistment and service are vague. He applied for but was refused an immediate commission as he passed through London on his way home from Belgium, but he was subsequently given the rank of Lieutenant and assigned to recruitment duties.[51] Time and time again, poor health stood between Kettle and the battlefield. Allusions to Kettle's 'ill-health' and 'nerves' were in fact oblique references to his alcoholism which became increasingly obvious during the war. In 1913 Kettle had addressed the problem of his alcoholism by submitting to a period of what appeared to be self-imposed exile in London.[52] In 1914 he was sent to a private hospital in Kent to be treated for 'dipsomania'; he believed that he had been 'cured', but his recovery was in fact short-lived and his health continued to deteriorate. According to T. P. O'Connor's biographer, attempts were made to have Kettle honourably discharged when Kettle 'proved to be unfit for army life'.[53] Kettle seemed to have reached the same conclusion in early 1915 when he decided 'after many sleepless nights which have made a nervous wreck of me that there is no course possible except for me to ask leave to resign as physically unfit'.[54]

But despite his ill-health, he seemed to have assumed in 1914 that his applying for active service was a mere formality, and that despite his age (34), he would be welcomed into the army before too long. But by early 1915 he had become so pessimistic about his chances of a commission and so worn-down by the constant journalistic attacks on his character and motivation that he claimed he could not appear in the streets of Dublin in the daytime, and wondered if he could continue to bear the jeers of the 'gutter press'.[55] His enthusiasm for active service was, however, renewed the following year when he asked to be accepted into 'any unit' on the condition that he was never again compelled to do any 'recruiting work whatever'. He told Lawrence Parsons that he 'meant to get out to the war' and that he wanted 'no interpretership, staff post, or anything else provided I can carry through my training'.[56] He begged to be allowed to leave with 'any division', but his requests were refused once again.[57]

Kettle finally received his commission in 1916, having been sent away to recuperate and to wean himself off alcohol. Interventions were also made on his behalf by his brother who argued that Kettle's recruiting work had thrown him 'into temptation he should have been kept from', and that he was sure to redeem himself if given an active commission.[58] His request was duly granted and Kettle was sent on active duty with the 16th Irish Division's 9th Royal Dublin Fusiliers, sailing for France on 14 July.

Kettle's two months in France coincided with one of the most productive periods of his short life. He filled the long hours between battles with intense periods of writing, producing some of his most moving letters and compact political compositions. Although his letters and prose do not seem to suggest that he welcomed death, they do reveal a man who began to prepare himself and his family and close friends for the possibility that he would not survive; hardly surprising in the context of one of the bloodiest battles of the war. Settling personal debts and begging forgiveness for past sins were high on his agenda, but perhaps more important was his desperate attempt to put down on paper a series of outlines of planned work and thoughts about the way the war had impacted upon his hopes for Ireland in the new century.

This overwhelming desire to both explain and justify his involvement in the war featured strongly in much of the writing he produced in the trenches, unsurprising for a man who knew his very existence was far from assured. It would be possible to dismiss his final pronouncements as frantic attempts to justify his involvement in a war whose legitimacy he came to doubt, but this would constitute a serious misreading of both the documents in question and of his political and moral world view. Any analysis of his final essays and correspondence must take into account a number of factors which undoubtedly coloured his final work. These include his very serious health and emotional problems, the new political climate suggested by the Easter Rising and his own strong disapproval of the insurrection. The rebels, as he told his wife, 'spoiled it all'. The murder of his brother-in-law, Francis Sheehy Skeffington, further deepened his despair, but, importantly, it did not threaten his resolve. If anything, the Rising strengthened his determination to both reiterate the opinion of the 'sane people of Ireland', and to emphasise the righteousness of the allied war effort. He thought it imperative that the propaganda generated by the events of Easter week should not be allowed to eclipse the far more important questions of the legitimacy of the allied war aims and constitutional Home Rule.

The difficult and tumultuous circumstances in which found himself certainly lent some of his prose a melancholy tone, but if, as some historians have suggested, Kettle had grown disillusioned with the war and weary of living, he kept these sentiments from the people to whom he wrote shortly before his death. He did, in his last letter to his wife, write, 'I think even that it is perhaps better that I should not see you again', but this was more likely due to the socially embarrassing and financially precarious situation in which his excessive drinking had placed his family before he left for France, than to a longing for death.[59] Certainly, as Patrick Maume has suggested, his desire to see active duty, his refusal to accept a safe position just before his Division's assault on Ginchy, and his apparent belief that his death might influence the Home Rule settlement point to 'some self-conscious collusion with the hoped-for-cult'.[60] What must be remembered, however, is that none of the sentiments he expressed from the trenches were new; rather, they were all reiterations of well-worn themes. It must also be emphasised – yet again – that Kettle did not volunteer for active duty in response to the Easter Rising. He was neither embarrassed nor shamed by the actions of the rebels into committing a similarly self-sacrificial act. As we have seen, Kettle had attempted on numerous occasions before 1916 to enlist, and none of his final correspondence suggests that he had changed his mind about his decision to see active duty.

Kettle freely admitted that conditions in the trenches were abominable and that he experienced episodes of fear, but, as he wrote to his brother, 'I am calm and happy, but I desperately want to live'. To his old political colleague, W. V. McLaughlin, he wrote: 'I myself am quite extraordinarily happy. If it should come my way to die I shall sleep well in the France I always loved, and shall know that I have done something towards bringing to birth the Ireland one has dreamed of.'[61] His final communications were full of plans for future work, both literary and political. The fact that he wore a steel waistcoat when he went into battle suggests that he was a man who desperately wanted to survive.

His faith in his mission clearly remained strong, but it was tempered with what appeared to be a growing realisation that it was increasingly threatened by the political programmes he had opposed during his career. Kettle's surviving letters contain few references to the political situation in Ireland itself, but what does survive is a strange combination of foresight and gloom at the direction Irish politics might take. His famous comment that 'these men [the Easter rebels] will go down to history as heroes and martyrs, and I will go down – if I go down at all – as a bloody British officer'[62] anticipated the changing allegiances of nationalist Ireland and the subsequent negation of the nationality of the Irish men who fought. His composition in 1916 of three articles entitled 'Why Ireland Fought' similarly suggested his awareness of the beginnings of this shift. He wrote these articles as the introductory section to *The Ways of War*, a collection of his war-related articles dating from 1914. Kettle's request to have such a volume published was due in part to his desperate concern for the financial plight of his family. But it was also motivated by his desire to pre-empt the allegations of disloyalty which he anticipated would be levied at the Irish men like himself who fought with the allies:

In this book – pieced together amid preoccupations of a very different kind – I have reprinted certain articles on various aspects of the war published in its earlier stages. I have done so not out of vanity, the reader may rest assured, but to repel an imputation. It has been charged against us who have taken our stand with the Allies that we were merely dancing to the tune of Imperialism, that our ideas came to us from London, that we hated Prussia and Prussianism not honestly but simply to order. Our recruiting appeals have been twisted from their plain utterance and obvious meaning. Wordy young men with no very notable public services to their record, have 'stigmatised' ... us all from Mr. Redmond down as renegades to Irish nationalism. What we have said and done is to be remembered against us in the new Ireland that is coming.[63]

In another of his final articles he returned to militant separatism, this time with a vigour no doubt prompted by what he perceived to be the misguided and even treacherous attitude displayed by some advanced nationalists towards Germany. Kettle typically condemned both their betrayal of the Irish men who sacrificed their lives to stop German aggression and their attempt to win German support for their brand of nationalism. But most of all, he denounced their intellectual bankruptcy, their 'infantile vision' of 'Ireland as a free Republic' under German protection and their adoption of Bismarck's 'Blood and Iron' mentality.[64] Advanced nationalism had committed the ultimate crime in colluding with Germany; it is hardly surprising that Kettle should have reacted so strongly.

Kettle's final pronouncements on the war assumed a new urgency after he witnessed first-hand just what he had urged young Irish men to endure. It is possible too that having at last secured his own active commission, he felt less inhibited both about extolling the virtues of sacrifice for a noble cause and about urging still more young men to join the colours. He continued to applaud the bravery of his men, but having experienced the 'chalk, lime, condensed milk, diabolical torturings of the air with unimaginable noises, and blood', he pledged to dedicate the rest of his life to preventing war. The actual practicalities of war weighed heavily on him and his descriptions of the horrors of war were a product of his commitment to 'see that it [the war] is not slurred over, but written and remembered'.[65] But they were also prompted by a genuine horror of what he witnessed in the trenches.

There is no hint, however, that he came to doubt his original belief that German aggression must be defeated. As he claimed shortly before his death, 'Until the objects for which the allies went into the war are achieved, it must go, and we mean it to go on, regardless of any waste of life or substance.'[66] Although he claimed that Ireland had been his priority, and that he behaved as any nationalist 'who had been at the trouble of thinking for himself' would, the defence of Europe remained for him not merely a worthy ideal, but the main justification for Irish participation in the war effort. As discussed, he did make genuine efforts to link Ireland's plight with Belgium's, and he attempted on numerous occasions to present the war as an opportunity to bring together nationalists and unionists, largely on the grounds that Irish problems would seem increasingly small and senseless in comparison with the enormity of the European conflict. But his Ireland-centred rhetoric never assumed the potency of his arguments about German aggression and its impact on democracy and progress on the continent. The European dilemma became his priority almost as soon as hostilities broke out. Even within the context of the excitement generated by the third Home Rule Bill and the subsequent establishment of unionist and nationalist militias, Kettle's attention turned resolutely and immediately towards the continent. Although he was one of the staunchest early advocates of the Volunteers and a member of its provisional committee, he claimed in 1916, 'When the war had broken out all volunteering in Ireland appeared to me to be a great deal of theatrical humbug.' He had been a bitter opponent of the men who split the Volunteers, but he emphasised that his primary reason for disassociating himself from the organisation was the spectacle of 'what had been done by the Germans in Belgium'.[67]

To claim, however, that he was uncritical about the war and about war in general, and that he welcomed its potential for sacrifice would be to miss the point entirely. Although he considered warfare to be an insult to 'simple men', he maintained that it was a price worth paying for the sake of a greater objective. Neither did his support for the war render him blind to the injustices he had come to associate with it. He insisted that a new article 'protesting against the transformation of a war for honour into a war for trade' be included in The Ways of War.[68] The war, he argued, was a struggle to end Prussian militarism, and not to establish British protectionism, and he claimed that, 'the tone of some of the English papers, and the attempt to transform this from a war of honour into a war for trade, are unholy things, and breakers of faith, for Irish comrades at any rate, did not die that new Birminghams might arise'.[69] 'No statesman,' he argued, had 'the right to change, behind the backs of the fighting men, the aim and purpose of the war. No government had a mandate to substitute markets for justice.'[70]

Such pronouncements suggest that he had become more critical of some aspects of British war policy, and it is interesting to speculate about how he might have reacted to the subsequent denunciation of the men who presided over the Battle of the Somme. But his was a short war and it is important to remember that Kettle's death in battle in September 1916 coincided with the unfolding of two major political shifts. He, like so many of his contemporaries, could hardly have imagined the degree of this change: the growing anti-war movement, both in Ireland and in wider Europe, the British government's handling of the Easter Rising, the threatened conscription crisis, the rise of Sinn Féin and the hardening of unionist attitudes in the aftermath of the Rising and the Battle of the Somme had yet to make their indelible marks on Irish history. Kettle, perched precariously on the cusp of two distinct periods of Irish history, belonged very firmly to the older tradition of constitutional nationalism, a tradition whose initial support for the war must not be overlooked. It is within this context – and within the context of his own cosmopolitan and humanist outlook – that his enduring support for the war may be best understood.

Notes

1 J. Meenan, introduction to T. M. Kettle, *The Day's Burden* (Dublin, Gill and Macmillan, 1968), p. 9.
2 M. Kettle, 'Memoir', in T. M. Kettle, *Ways of War* (London, Constable, 1917), p. 4.
3 T. M. Kettle, quoted in J. B. Lyons, *The Enigma of Tom Kettle: Irish Patriot, Essayist, Poet, British Soldier* (Dublin, Glendale Press, 1983), p. 278.
4 UCD, LA34/135, J. Redmond to T. M. Kettle, 25 August 1914, T. M. Kettle Papers.
5 P. Maume, *The Long Gestation: Irish Nationalist Life, 1891–1918* (Dublin, Gill and Macmillan, 1999), p. 148.
6 T. M. Kettle, 'An examination of the Belgian evidence', *Bristol Magazine*, vol. 8 (1914), p. 359.
7 T. M. Kettle, 'A world adrift', in *Ways of War*, p. 104.
8 See K. Jeffery, *Ireland and the Great War* (Cambridge, Cambridge University Press, 2000), pp. 9–12; and Maume, *Long Gestation*, pp. 147–8, for two of the few discussions of this kind.
9 Maume, *Long Gestation*, p. 148.
10 T. M. Kettle, 'Malines', in *Ways of War*, p. 123; and R. S. Sunderland, 'The life and times of Thomas Kettle' (Unpublished PhD thesis, University of Dublin, 1980), pp. 297–300 for an informative discussion of this issue.
11 T. M. Kettle, 'The gospel of the devil', in *Ways of War*, p. 206; and Sunderland, 'Life and times', pp. 297–300.
12 UCD, LA34/390, T. M. Kettle, 'Why Ireland fought' (draft notes), T. M. Kettle Papers.
13 Sunderland, 'Life and times', pp. 203–4.
14 T. M. Kettle, 'History' in his *The Open Secret of Ireland* (London, W. J. Ham-Smith, 1912), p. 23.
15 T. M. Kettle, 'The mechanics of Home Rule', *ibid.*, p. 120.
16 T. M. Kettle, 'The obviousness of Home Rule'. *ibid.*, p. 55.
17 T. M. Kettle, 'The mechanics of Home Rule', *ibid.*, p. 128.
18 T. M. Kettle, 'An exercise in humility', *ibid.*, p. 1.
19 T. M. Kettle to Hammond, 15 November 1915. I am grateful to Esther Murnane and Kevin Myers for bringing this small collection of letters to my attention. When I consulted them, they were uncatalogued and in private hands, but were subsequently deposited in the National Library of Ireland. All subsequent references to letters between Kettle and Hammond and Kettle and Parsons refer to letters in this collection.
20 UCD, LA34/399, T. M. Kettle 'Political', 3 September 1916, T. M. Kettle Papers.
21 T. M. Kettle, 'Apology' in his *The Day's Burden: Studies, Literary and Political* (London, T. Fisher Unwin, 1910), pp. xi–xii.
22 T. M. Kettle, 'The philosophy of politics', *ibid.*, pp. 12–13.
23 *Ibid.*, p. 14.
24 M. Kettle, 'Memoir', p. 3.

25 S. Gwynn and T. M. Kettle, *Battle Songs for the Irish Brigades* (Dublin, Maunsel, 1915), p. v.
26 T. Denman, '"The red livery of shame": the campaign against army recruitment in Ireland, 1899-1914', *Irish Historical Studies*, vol. 26 (November 1994), pp. 228–9.
27 UCD, LA34/367 (i), *Daily News*, 26 September 1914, cutting in T. M. Kettle Papers.
28 *Ibid.*, LA34/394(I), T. M. Kettle, draft notes.
29 T. M. Kettle, 'Why Ireland fought – I', in *Ways of War*, p. 70.
30 UCD, LA34/394(I), T. M. Kettle, 'Chapter II', draft notes, T. M. Kettle Papers.
31 NLI, Ms. 15081(8), T. M. Kettle to A. Stopford Green, 28 December 1909, Alice Stopford Green Papers.
32 S. Leslie, *The Irish Issue in its American Aspect: A Contribution to the Settlement of Anglo-American Relations During and After the Great War* (New York, C. Scribner's, 1918), p. 95.
33 T. M. Kettle, 'The soldier-priests of France', in *Ways of War*, p. 204; originally published in the *Hibernian Review* (November 1915).
34 See, for example, T. M. Kettle, 'Why Ireland fought – I', in *Ways of War*, p. 59, and Sunderland, 'Life and times', pp. 312–13.
35 *Freeman's Journal*, 3 November 1914; cited in Sunderland, 'Life and times', p. 304.
36 M. Kettle, 'Memoir', p. 6.
37 T. M. Kettle, 'Why kill the Gaelic League?', *National Volunteer*, vol. 1 (October 1914).
38 *National Volunteer*, vol. 1 (October 1914); see also T. M. Kettle to Hammond, n.d.
39 *Freeman's Journal*, 19 November 1914.
40 UCD, LA34/394, T. M. Kettle, draft article, T. M. Kettle Papers.
41 *Ibid.*, LA 34/395(3), T. M. Kettle, notes.
42 T. M. Kettle to Hammond, 15 November 1914.
43 *Ibid.*
44 *Freeman's Journal*, 19 November 1914.
45 *Éire-Ireland*, 14 November 1914. I am indebted to Ben Novick for this and subsequent references to *Éire-Ireland*.
46 *Éire-Ireland*, 23 and 30 November 1914.
47 D. Ryan, *Remembering Sion* (London, A. Barker, 1934), pp. 164–5.
48 *Éire-Ireland*, 24 November 1914.
49 *Freeman's Journal*, 19 November 1914.
50 T. M. Kettle to Hammond, 15 November 1914.
51 There is only very sketchy information pertaining to his pension entitlement in Kettle's war file in PRO, WO 339/13445.
52 Sunderland, 'Life and times', p. 260.
53 *Ibid.*, p. 307.
54 T. M. Kettle to Hammond, 11 January 1915.
55 *Ibid.*
56 T. M. Kettle to Parsons, 25 October 1915.
57 T. M. Kettle to Hammond, 30 October 1915.
58 L. Kettle to Hammond, 4 April 1916.
59 UCD, LA34/402, T. M. Kettle to Mary Kettle, 3 September 1916, T. M. Kettle Papers.
60 Maume, *Long Gestation*, p. 185.
61 UCD, LA34/397, T. M. Kettle to H. McLaughlin, 7 August 1916, T. M. Kettle Papers.
62 Lyons, *The Enigma of Tom Kettle*, p. 293.
63 T. M. Kettle, 'Why Ireland fought – I', in *Ways of War*, pp. 71–2.
64 UCD, LA34/394(3) and LA34/395(1), T. M. Kettle Papers.
65 T. M. Kettle, 'Why Ireland fought – I', in *Ways of War*, p. 63.
66 T. M. Kettle, 'Trade or honour', in *Ways of War*, p. 232.

67 Lyons, *The Enigma of Tom Kettle*, pp. 290–1.
68 UCD, LA34/400, T. M. Kettle, 'Literary', 3 September 1916, T. M. Kettle Papers.
69 T. M. Kettle to Hammond, 28 July 1916.
70 T. M. Kettle, 'Trade or honour', in Ways of War, p. 232.

2

Dulce et Decorum: Irish nobles and the Great War, 1914–19

PETER MARTIN

By 1914, the two hundred or so families which composed the Irish nobility represented a class firmly in decline. Their lands had been reduced by decades of debt, falling rents and purchase by tenants. They were not uniformly rich: for every plutocrat like Londonderry there was a peer like Fingall whose title and residence were all that distinguished him from the ordinary gentry. They were almost all Protestant and unionist with at least a small 'u', but their political theatre, the House of Lords, had been curtailed in 1910 and they had been powerless to stop the Home Rule Bill.

The Great War was both a tragedy and an opportunity for the Irish nobility. As a class which was dependent on the success of the British Empire for its wellbeing and which had a small population, war was a matter of the utmost seriousness. As this chapter will show, however, many of them, including Donoughmore, Dunraven and Fingall, hoped that the war would unite nationalists and unionists and would bring the volunteer movement back to the cause of the empire. For men like Lord Dunsany, or Basil Blackwood, in 1914, the motto which forms the title of this chapter had a different meaning to that given it by later poets disillusioned by the reality of the trenches.

There is a noticeable absence of hard evidence about the activities of the Irish upper classes during the war. This chapter attempts to resolve this lack of data by recourse to a survey of Irish nobles[1] as of August 1914, their sons and their brothers as listed in *Burke's Peerage* and *Thom's Directory*. This, by definition, leaves out uncles, nephews and in-laws, all of whom would make valid subjects for research, but whose inclusion would make the resulting database unwieldy and time-consuming. Describing any noble as 'Irish' may surprise some people; in this chapter it refers to nobles with an Irish residence – even if they also had other seats.[2] They were, despite some differences of wealth, religion and politics, an easily recognisable class with a great deal in common.

It has long been a commonplace assumption among military historians and students of the Irish élite that the Irish aristocracy was disproportionately represented in the British army compared with other classes and groups within the officer ranks.[3] In 1872, for example the ratio of Irish-born officers per capita to English-born officers per capita was 11:8.[4] Muenger has, however, raised a specific case study of the 5th Royal Irish Lancers in 1914 which seems to contradict this view. She found that of twenty-eight officers only five had Irish connections and only three of these were noble.[5] If we examine the data in Table 1, the solution may become clearer:

Table 1 Number of Irish peers, their sons and brothers, by regiment 1914–18

Regiment	Number	Regiment	Number
Bucks Imperial Yeomanry	2	Royal Air Force	2
Coldstream Guards	9	Royal Field Artillery	2
Dragoons	3	Royal Horse Artillery	2
Grenadier Guards	5	Rifle Brigade	6
Hussars	6	Royal Fusiliers	3
Irish Guards	10	Royal Horse Guards	3
King's Royal Rifle Corps	3	Royal Irish Regiment	2
Lancers	6	Royal Irish Rifles	2
Life Guards	4	Royal Scots Fusiliers	2
London	2	War office	2
Machine Gun Corps.	3	Others*	22
Navy	5		
Royal Artillary	2		

* *Others* refers to subjects who were the only members of that regiment in the sample or whose regiment was impossible to determine.
Source: Burke's Peerage and *Thom's Directory* 1918.

From this information we can see that, in many cases, Irish peers did not join Irish regiments. Therefore Muenger's data, while no doubt accurate, does not offer as useful a case study as might at first appear. The data does raise interesting questions about how peers chose their regiments, and, more importantly, why. It is possible that in choosing a British regiment over an Irish one, a noble was associating with his educational and social peers rather than with his tenants, many of whom did join their local regiments. This hypothesis is supported by the fact that most nobles were educated in Britain. The notable exception to this preference was the Irish Guards and this is consistent with the fact that thirty-two of those sampled were members of Guards regiments. This endorses Razzell's argument[6] that the advances made by the middle classes after 1870 pushed the aristocracy into particular regiments and ranks – notably the Guards.[7] Indeed the Grenadier Guards were referred to by Freddy Blackwood, the brother of Lord Dufferin

& Ava, as 'the Irish regiment of Guards'.[8] There are, however, some remarkable differences. A high proportion of Irish peers and their relatives joined the Coldstream Guards which Razzell found to have become less popular with the aristocracy in this period. This may indicate that many Irish-based noble families were no longer able to meet the financial demands of the élite regiments. Many Irish noble families had suffered a decline in rental incomes from 1881 which led many of them to sell land, particularly after 1903.[9] There were also a considerable number of Irish nobles in Artillery or Machine Gun regiments which usually showed a low level of aristocratic involvement.

The reasons behind Irish nobles' selection of regiments may be found in several places. The effect of personal choice and social pressure should not be ruled out – for example, Lady Fingall described how Killeen faced great pressure from family friends to join their favourites before joining the 17th Lancers on Douglas Haig's advice.[10] Lord Dunsany, on the other hand, joined the Royal Inniskilling Fusiliers because he had disliked his commanding officer in the Coldstream Guards during the South African war and did not relish serving under him again.[11] Financial considerations must also be given their proper importance. The life of an army officer was expensive (£600 per annum for a cavalry regiment in 1903),[12] but sometimes less so than living in the manner expected of a noble. The military offered a living appropriate to both the nobles' status and their means. This might explain the number of members of lower status (but relatively cheap) regiments in the survey.

Some idea of the atmosphere of the early days of the war can be found in a sermon, preached by the Archbishop of Armagh, John B. Crozier DD, and published in pamphlet form. He emphasised the self-sacrifice inherent in war and the absolute requirement that soldiers, in particular, act selflessly. This would be easier for them, he claimed, if others thought and prayed for them. In dealing with the horrors of war he argued that 'there are evils a thousand fold worse than a righteous war' which, to his thinking, extended from gambling, drink and impurity to a more general softness and sentimentality which he saw as afflicting the age and expressing itself in the pampering of children and prisoners.[13]

We can have little idea of how the average member of a noble family actually felt about the dangers of war. The overall impression is of a duty bound class rather than an enthusiastic race to the front. Lord Dunsany made no secret of his dislike for war but still joined up promptly and expected to fight.[14] He was greatly affected, it seems, by reports of German mistreatment of civilians, which were printed in the *Irish Times* and other newspapers.[15] Charles, the son of 5th Viscount Monck, was encouraged to join up by his huge debts and told his solicitor, 'If I die today my difficulties and those of my family would to a great extent disappear with me.'[16] A captain in the

Coldstream Guards, he was killed in action in 1914 leaving a wife and three children. Freddy Blackwood was also very aware of the risks he took and confided to his mother that, 'I only wish I were leaving Brenda [his wife] financially better off', but welcomed the war as a relief from the pressures of the home front. He reassured himself that, 'If I live through it I shall be happier in the future and if not anyhow you will all think well of me.'[17]

His brother, Basil, was also conscious of his class obligations. After he was wounded in France in 1914 he was made Private Secretary to Lord Wimbourne, the Lord Lieutenant. He found it 'mortifying to feel active and energetic and yet to be at the age when those qualities are supposed to evaporate. I *must* if I am prevented by something else but I will be very sad if I can find nothing to do in the Great War more useful than to act as an ADC to a general'.[18] Basil eventually got his wish but was killed on active service in 1917.

Many peers, whether soldiers or not, were involved in recruiting activities during 1914. These were often connected to their offices as His Majesty's Lieutenants (HMLs) for the counties. There was no legal obligation for the HML to raise recruits – a fact lamented by Lord Dunraven[19] – but this did not stop the Marquis of Ormonde from writing to the Deputy Lieutenants in each district.[20] They also used their position and celebrity to endorse various organisations; for example, the Earl of Meath was president of the Irish Association of Volunteer Training Corps,[21] while Lord Dunraven was involved in the Athletes' Volunteer Force.[22] A flavour of their rhetoric can be found in Lord Dunraven's appeal to readers of the *Irish Times*, which referred to alleged German war crimes in Belgium and reminders of the history of Irish regiments and cavalry.[23] Unionist peers such as Lord Farnham also seem to have been involved in recruiting from the ranks of the Ulster Volunteers.[24]

There is little evidence that peers were particularly effective as recruiters. Lord Farnham was reported to have addressed a small meeting in September 1914 that produced only three recruits. A government report commented that 'the bulk of recruiting in the South and West has been from two classes, landlord and lowest'[25] which implies that while nobles' own families and their poorest tenants had joined up, the middle classes had remained unimpressed.

The recruiting situation was further complicated by the importance of the Volunteer movement and the ambivalent relationship which nobles enjoyed with it during the war. John Redmond's initial speeches offering the Volunteers as a defensive force to allow Britain to deploy Irish-based forces at the front sparked a remarkable correspondence from members of the peerage. For one week from 6 August 1914, fifteen letters from peers appeared in the *Irish Times* supporting Redmond and, usually, the Volunteers. These letters expressed the hope that Redmond's offer would unify nationalists and unionists in a common cause. Several peers, including Monteagle, Headfort and Fingall, announced that they had joined, or intended to join, the Volunteers. Others who were not represented in the letters columns, such as Dunsany, also joined. The letters frequently stressed the need to train and supply the force properly. These calls peaked with the enthusiasm of Lord Powerscourt who wanted the war office to pay and equip it,[26] but he also displayed a hint of dissatisfaction with the level of organisation apparent in the movement; Powerscourt argued that 'persons of influence' should organise local Volunteer groups.[27] Lord Oranmore & Browne thought that all the groups should work together 'with the sanction and under the direction of the War Office'.[28]

The question of who should control the force lay at the heart of the disagreement between the Volunteers and the War Office. That some peers were more aware of it than they expressed publicly is evident from a letter written by Lord Meath to John Redmond on 5 August 1914. He expressed his desire to help recruiting for the movement but sought assurances that doing so would not compromise 'my loyal duty to his majesty the King'.[29] This reflects a more sophisticated response than was common at the time. Meath seemed aware, as few of his counterparts were, that Redmond's speech had not suddenly turned the Volunteers into a branch of the Territorial Army. Those peers who acted in accordance with their public statements gave speeches and firing drill for local battalions,[30] but it is not clear how well they were received. The owner/editor of the Cavan weekly newspaper, the *Anglo-Celt,* speaking in late August 1914, quoted a letter from a Fr Osborne of Arva warning 'beware of brand-new friends who were former enemies'. The speaker then promised, in a reference to Powerscourt and Fingall, that the people of Cavan would have 'none of that class' running the Volunteers.[31]

It is also clear that the Irish Unionist Alliance, which contained a significant number of noble members from both north and south, was divided by the question of how to respond to the Volunteers. In August 1914, Donoughmore wrote to R. J. Shaw, the secretary of the Executive Committee, to warn that, 'I have already subscribed to them [the Volunteers]; I intend to assist them in every way in my power and to encourage others to do so too.'[32] Shaw responded, with some embarrassment, that, 'the great majority of our members share your view. The committee, however felt that they [sic] could not disregard Sir Edward's [Carson's] advice [to ignore the volunteers]'.[33]

As the Volunteers' dispute with the War Office worsened, peers showed signs of losing patience. They were sympathetic to the demand that Irish troops be kept in the same divisions under Irish officers, and a call to that effect was issued by Lord Meath,[34] but their sense of frustration with the Volunteer leadership was made plain by Lord Fingall, who resigned as

Inspector of the Meath National Volunteers and published his reasons. He described his position as 'a fifth wheel to the coach', and that despite having been well received he was restricted by the fact that he had no clear duties and felt that any initiatives he might have taken would have been frowned upon by the county board. He called for every man to join Kitchener's army, concluding that he felt he could do nothing in the Volunteers.[35] His resignation clearly stung the Volunteer leadership and Fingall was attacked in the *Longford Leader* as a man who would 'place the English Empire before his country'.[36] Lord Dunsany left the Volunteers on account of their desire to operate under their own leaders rather than the War Office, claiming that 'no sane man in power could accept a force under these conditions'.[37] Ormonde recommended to the Secretary of the Volunteers that local members enlist in the Kilkenny Corps.[38] The last attempt by a peer to work with or support the Volunteers seems to have been a letter from Lord Dunraven in October claiming that 'no scheme for Irish service in the war which fails to take account of the National Volunteer Force can do justice to what Ireland can give', and arguing that those left behind could take the place of the Royal Irish Constabulary (RIC), thus allowing fit members of that force to enlist.[39]

Without the aid of the Volunteers, peers were thrown back on their own resources and attempts to promote recruitment seem to have become less common as the government took over. Fingall continued to address meetings, including one in Navan on 17 January 1915,[40] and Lord Meath offered a £5 bounty to the family of every one of his employees who enlisted, and guaranteed to try to keep their positions open for them until after the war.[41] Donoughmore's similar offer to continue to pay the wages of men who enlisted was unsuccessful. Despite the influence of the Countess and the head gardener,[42] only two men tried to join up, and one of them was refused on medical grounds.[43] The reason was provided by Donoughmore's agent, R. B. Seigne. Referring to the Volunteers, he claimed that the men 'are in fact rather hurt that no further notice has been taken of them'. He also warned that recruiting would slow down 'unless something is decided soon about the Home Rule Bill satisfactory to those who influence public opinion in the South and West of Ireland'.[44]

References to peers speaking at recruiting meetings or letters from them to the newspapers became less frequent after 1914. They did express their dissatisfaction with the slow pace of recruiting, a fact attributed by Lord Desart to violently active forces of disloyalty. Both Lords Midleton and Mayo criticised government inaction on the matter in the House of Lords.[45] The *Galway Observer* responded strongly to this blaming a labour shortage for the low level of enlistment. The same issue of that newspaper reprinted a letter from William O'Malley MP to the *Daily Chronicle* in which he attacked peers who had praised the Volunteers 'when they thought of being their leaders' but now abused them.[46] Lord Oranmore & Browne, in a recruiting speech in Mayo, accepted the significance of a labour shortage, claiming that as Ireland had so many men in the army prior to the war and was an agricultural country, it had few young men available.[47]

The conscription issue likewise found many peers out of step with nationalist opinion. Disillusioned with the apparent failure of voluntary recruiting, many seem to have agreed with the *Irish Times*' statement that 'we can find neither logic nor loyalty' in nationalist opposition to conscription.[48] The example of Lord Dunraven shows how a peer who usually tried to give nationalists the benefit of the doubt became disillusioned. In September 1916 he wrote that, 'It is useless trying to disguise the truth, Ireland has not done and is not doing her duty.' He found this puzzling as her regiments had an honourable record and blamed not sedition, but a combination of apathy and the absence of conscription.[49] In October he proposed a system whereby different social groups such as farmers or labourers would form distinctive companies. He claimed that the system would eventually evolve into conscription proper. To oversee such an arrangement he recommended the Duke of Connaught, on account of his Irish peerage, popularity, connection with the army, and association with Canada.[50] By 1918, however, Dunraven's support for conscription had earned him the enmity of local politicians – to the extent that a motion was put forward in Limerick Corporation to delete him from the roll of freemen of the city by a councillor Griffin who 'never thought his lordship would turn on his fellow countrymen and try to enforce a blood tax'.[51] Midleton later argued that conscription should have been imposed after the 1916 Easter Rising,[52] but that by 1917 nationalism – he made no distinction as to what kind – had become too entrenched to either accept it or be overcome;[53] this view was endorsed by Edith, Lady Londonderry.[54]

Apart from recruiting, peers and their families involved themselves in a wide variety of civilian organisations and activities. Most of these were aimed at raising funds for good causes while others provided more direct relief. Some nobles were directly involved in war work: Lady Dunsany, for example, arranged transfers for soldiers at a hospital in Exeter to allow them to be near their families.[55] Most, however, concentrated either on helping the troops or prisoners of war – through the Red Cross or by sending comforts – or raised funds to assist families, businesses or industries which had been hurt by the war. Noblewomen played an important role in these activities; many of their men were away and relief work was considered appropriate for them. Lady Fingall described how they took over 'public work' by which she meant committees, meetings and public speaking.[56] She organised classes on how to speak in public and chair meetings for her friends and herself and later served as chairman of the Central Committee for Women's Employment.[57]

Much of this work was made possible by the efforts of Edith, Lady Castlereagh who became Lady Londonderry in 1915. A pioneer in matters of women's rights, she took a careful line balancing the demands of women who wanted an active role against the complaints of traditionalists. In an article written in January 1915 she explained her position in detail. She argued that the new mode of warfare had brought about new conditions for civilians as well as for soldiers and asked, 'are women merely to be a burden to others, which in this case means their menfolk, and helpless as regards themselves?' Instead she sought a role for women, either in an organisational capacity, or working in industries or agricultural areas suffering a labour shortage. Her own Women's Volunteer Regiment was an attempt to form a disciplined group to undertake such tasks. Two other, less happy, eventualities had to be prepared for, she claimed. The first was the risk of invasion, under which circumstances women, children, the aged and the sick should be assembled in armed camps where they could defend themselves against the sort of atrocities perpetrated in Belgium. The second need to be faced was the inevitable loss of many male lives, which would require women to be more self-reliant after the war.[58] These were obviously radical views which would not have had the support of, for example, her mother-in-law, Theresa. A more moderate – but still significant – role for women was supported by an *Irish Times* leader in August 1914 which recommended that 'work is the only remedy for heartsickness' and reminded well-to-do women of their obligations to help those who had lost a breadwinner to the war effort.[59]

From the earliest weeks of the war societies sprang up to cater to the needs of the country and the troops. Some were intentionally short lived, for example the Fund for Departing Troops set up by Ladies Powerscourt and Arnott which raised £600 by 12 August 1914 to give a small package of comforts to each soldier in Ireland reassigned to the front.[60] Some funds focused on a particular regiment, usually linked to a locality, for example the 4th Battalion Royal Irish Regiment Fund (Kilkenny).[61] Others, such as the Soldiers' and Sailors' Family Association Cavan Branch, were new branches of existing bodies. The latter was merged into the Prince of Wales National Relief Fund[62] which, as well as offering a glamorous name to the fund raising, united several of the smaller organisations. It is possible that the Volunteer dispute may have hindered some activities – as evidenced by a letter from Monteagle to John Redmond claiming that his daughter was having trouble setting up a Red Cross branch while the matter remained unsettled.[63]

Civilian work seems to have been conducted through letter writing, meetings and newspaper publicity. Most of the money came in through subscriptions from individuals, though there were some fund raising events. Usually a committee was established; sometimes more than one as in Cavan where men, including Lord Farnham, set up the County Cavan War Relief Fund and women, including Lady Farnham, established the County Cavan Women's Patriotic Committee which had the support of the Roman Catholic Bishop of Kilmore, Dr Finegan, and which collected £840 through church collections.[64] Frequently a strong individual was at the centre of the organisation which was often made up of smaller local committees. The Countess of Courtown undertook the reorganisation of the Red Cross in Wexford with herself as president.[65] Lady Clonbrock's abilities were demonstrated by her successful organisation of a flag day which raised £821 within three weeks to send a motor ambulance to the front 'For the Connaught Rangers and their comrades from the people of the county of Galway'.[66] In 1915 Lord Clonbrock and Lord Killanin intervened and reorganised the operation. Lord Killanin recognised that the ladies had done well but claimed that there had been much waste and overlapping of duties. A new body was established to co-ordinate aid to the troops. Lady Clonbrock, however, was retained as president.[67]

In addition to appeals for subscriptions and donations of clothes, several peers used their positions and property to assist the war effort. The Ormondes opened Kilkenny Castle and the picture gallery to the public[68] and the Clonbrocks entertained supporters with a concert by Percy French in 1915.[69] Lady Ardilaun, agreeing to a petition from Macroom UDC (Urban District Council), donated a sum equivalent to one year's rent of the tolls of fairs and markets payable to her, for the relief of distress, caused by the war, in the area. Advertisements for such activities were frequently placed in local and national newspapers (including some of a nationalist disposition) of whom special rates and even free space were often requested.

Other methods of fund raising were attempted, including a meeting at the Mansion House organised by the Earl of Meath (who was HML for Dublin). At that meeting he claimed that the work being done had united Ireland by distracting Irish people from the domestic quarrels with which they occupied themselves 'when things are dull'; indeed he suggested a monument to the Kaiser for having, despite himself, achieved Irish unity.[70] In fact his optimism was groundless, and war relief work became a political football in both the unionist–nationalist debate and the northern–southern split in unionism. The former was highlighted by a scandal in October 1914 when a private letter from Lady Aberdeen, the wife of the Lord Lieutenant, to the editor of the *Freeman's Journal*, was leaked. In it she was alleged to have warned that unionists within the Red Cross were trying to control the organisation from London and to exclude 'Irish Volunteer people'.[71] Her failure to disown or explain the letter led to much commentary, as did the association of the Red Cross with a political debate. A political issue was again highlighted, if only in passing, by Lady Fingall who, having raised money for colours for the 16th Division, felt forced to return it when it became clear that the Division was not to have colours.[72] The growing north–south divide was touched on by Lady Londonderry at a meeting of the Ulster Women's Unionist Council when she asked whether other provinces had done as much as Ulster in recruiting and warned that the Ulster Question was only in abeyance.[73] Even by 1915 Lord Iveagh and Sir John Simon were unable to get a good turnout in support of the government's war loan.[74] These indicate that the hopeful façade of goodwill and comradeship during wartime did no more than cover political fissures which predated the conflict.

To the contemporary observer, the war brought unprecedented intrusions into law, the economy, industry and the social order. Peers could not, however, claim to have suffered any more than most, or even as much as many ordinary people who had to change their patterns of work and living.

One of the earliest government actions to affect peers was the occupation of the Curragh from 1 August 1914 which disrupted racing.[75] Racing was eventually banned completely in 1917, though Lord Decies negotiated meets for 8 May and 10 May.[76] Also significant to peers was the purchase, often compulsory, of horses. This gave rise to some inconvenience such as that highlighted by Lord Ormonde who had to seek the return of an old horse which had been mistakenly taken.[77] Peers – and their horses – also faced the gradual introduction of rationing. According to the letter books of the Ormonde estate, the main problem items were grain, sugar, butter and meat, though newspapers confirm that petrol restrictions were also most inconvenient. Rationing had little direct effect on peers who owned farms, but created difficulties due to the itinerant existence of many of the nobility which required them to send goods from residence to residence or to supply gifts to friends.[78] Sugar was required to preserve fruit[79] and grain was needed to feed those horses left to them.[80] It is probably the case that for many peers rationing represented an unaccustomed curtailment of their usual lifestyle rather than any objective hardship. Government taxation policy and rises in the price of such vital commodities as coal were probably more significant. The *Irish Times* supported the increasing of taxes in 1914 but warned that it would require 'sweeping economies' of 'even the very rich'.[81] The September 1915 budget raised Super Tax on incomes over £8,000, the first of several increases.[82] Lord Ormonde, for example, experienced a rapid rise in his Super Tax bill from £1,311 in 1915/16 to £2,421 in 1918/19; an increase of eighty-four per cent at a time when costs of his estates were fixed or rising.[83] His economies included ending his £2 per year subscription to the Protestant Orphans' Society.[84]

The war also affected peers indirectly through their involvement with the people of the locality. This may have been an extension of their traditional role as landlords and patrons of charitable societies and it may also indicate a popular belief that they retained some political influence with the administration in London or Dublin. An example of an attempt to help out was the Kilkenny County Committee which was established by Lords Ormonde and

Desart among others in 1914 to deal with distress in the county caused by the war.[85] Ormonde himself made donations of beef to workhouses at Christmas and sent milk to those in need.[86] There were also cases where petitioners approached the peer directly. Lady Farnham (whose husband was away at war) was approached at least twice for assistance.[87] The correspondence of the Duke of Abercorn contains many similar cases.[88] In several cases the unionist credentials of the applicants were emphasised.

The *Irish Times* had warned early on that 'before the war is over many old and respected families will have come to an end so far as their male line is concerned'.[89] Official notification that a loved one had died could be haphazard; this was not due to inefficiency on the part of the War Office but because of the confusion which often surrounded events at the front. In November 1914 Robert Stuart, the son of Lord Castlestewart, was killed, 'leading his company in a bayonet charge at Ypres'.[90] His wife refused to accept his death without clear proof and spent over a year investigating the possibility that he had been taken prisoner. Neither captured German officers, prisoner of war camps in Germany nor the Red Cross offered any word of him. She was so persistent that, even after the British Red Cross had informed her that it had an eyewitness who confirmed her husband's death, it withdrew the claim and apologised that it should have been 'wary of [the] unsupported word of a private [the only witness]'.[91] Her brother-in-law who was in the army was still trying to reconcile his family to their loss as late as September 1915. He wrote to his father that, 'although there is always the chance of Rob being a prisoner my own feeling from what I have seen is that he is lying out on the ground where he fell. Even behind our lines ... it is not always safe nor possible to bury bodies.'[92]

Peers had to adapt to the discipline of war. In 1918 Lady Rossmore was charged with making false statements of enemy progress as she had written a telegram saying 'Germans marching on Calais, Dover to be cleared'. The fact that her son was fighting in the war and that she worked at a Red Cross depot lent credibility to her claim that she was merely ignorant of the law but she was fined £10 with £5 costs.[93] The social pressures to keep up a supportive façade as the war dragged on were immense. This was shown by the response to Lord Lansdowne's letter in December 1917 which argued for negotiation with Germany. There appears to be little mention of it in private correspondence – which may indicate that it was too embarrassing. The *Irish Times* attacked the letter ferociously arguing that it had destroyed his reputation as 'on the very day when his attitude was likely to do most mischief, Lord Lansdowne suddenly enrols himself among the "pacifists"' and claimed that 'it is the letter of a man who has lost his nerve'.[94] The letter produced little published correspondence to the paper but one man did ask how one could praise Wilson but not Lansdowne – which was exactly what the *Irish Times* did.[95] Even Lansdowne's son, Lord Kerry, felt obliged to state that his opinions 'do not coincide with the views expressed in Lord Lansdowne's letter to the *Daily Telegraph*'.[96] He later tried to argue that his father had not suggested anything which would not have found favour with President Wilson.[97]

If we look at the results of the survey of nobles at war we can produce a reasonable profile of the average noble soldier. There were 185 men of military age in this period of whom 109 were mobilised. Table 2 shows the ages of those mobilised. The high number aged between 30 and 34 is surprising. This may reflect the fact that many of those who fought were already career soldiers or veterans of the South African war.

Table 2 Ages of noble soldiers

Ages	Number
19–24	25
25–29	13
30–34	29
35–39	20
40–44	11
45–49	8
50+	4

Partially as a result of their ages, the proportion of married men was high (47 of 109 or 43 per cent). The number of children these men left behind is illustrated in Table 3.

Table 3 Numbers of children in families of nobles at war

Children	Nobles
0	4
1	14
2	10
3	10
4+	9

It is clear that, despite their ages, many of these men had small families and few had large ones by Irish standards. When we add to these facts the finding that 43 (39 per cent) of those surveyed were heirs to the title we can see that several noble families faced a real threat to their survival in the war and others risked losing a large part of their next generation without leaving many children to take over.

Table 4 gives the numbers killed in action. This shows that while 29 (27 per cent) were killed this does not represent a 'lost generation' or anything like one. It does, however, reinforce Cannadine's point that they were worse off than ordinary members of the forces whose rate of loss was one in eight.[98] If we consider the proportion of married men and heirs respectively killed in action we can see that married men were only slightly less likely to die (23 per cent of deaths), as were heirs (26 per cent). This shows that heirs and married men were not significantly safer.

Table 4 Men killed in action

Type	Total	Killed	%	% of total dead
All nobles	109	29	27	100
Married	47	11	23	40
Heirs	43	11	26	40
Lieutenants	24	13	54	45
Captains	35	10	29	34
Major	21	3	14	10
Lt-Colonel	7	2	28	1
Aged under 30	38	12	32	41
Aged 30–40	49	12	24	41
Aged over 40	23	5	17	17

The age profile of noble fatalities is somewhat unusual. Only 41 per cent of nobles killed in action were under thirty. There is no clear explanation for this phenomenon though it is possible that older nobles sought, and were granted, front line duty. As has already been mentioned men like Basil Blackwood, who was in his forties, were not happy with safe postings; though whether this was unusual is not clear.

Twenty nobles were listed as wounded. Of these five were wounded more than once. It is important to note that these figures exclude those who died from wounds (who are considered to have been killed in action). Therefore we can conclude that out of a sample of 109 people, 48 (44 per cent) were killed or wounded during the war. A proviso must be added here, however, that wounds sustained in military action were usually recorded under 'World War I' even if, as was the case with Lord Dunsany, that wound was sustained from a rebel in Dublin in 1916. It is also the case, given that *Burke's Peerage* depended on nobles to volunteer information for their own entries, that some of those who simply stated 'served in Great War' may have been wounded.

These statistics are more useful if put into a wider context. According to Liam Kennedy, 13 per cent of Irish soldiers mobilised for the Great War died during it.[99] Nobles had a very high enlistment ratio of 59 per cent which meant that nearly all of them had family or friends who served. The peerage thus seems to have suffered disproportionately and the closeness of the aristocratic community intensified the sense of loss. Dooley has attempted to take a less emotional approach. In his survey of thirty-two 'Great House' families, not all of which were noble, he found that 146 men went to war of whom 41 died. Ten heirs had been lost but in eight cases the succession was not endangered. He concluded that the myth of the lost generation was exaggerated because it served as an easier explanation of the decline of the aristocracy than economic or political reasons.[100] This may be true, but it does not express the depth of feeling which surrounded aristocratic losses in the war. This can be more readily explained by the suddenness and number of the deaths in what was the biggest war to involve the empire.

Nobles shared as wide a range of wartime experiences as did other upper class officers. Letters home revealed how they faced alternating periods of boredom and horror and were at different times inspired or frustrated by the war. These letters were not too heavily censored. The Dowager Duchess of Abercorn, for example, advised her son Jack to use the field post because 'as far as I can see the letters are never opened or looked at by the censor'.[101]

In certain circumstances, British officers enjoyed considerable luxuries. On the other hand they often found the inactivity stifling. Arthur Stuart, son of Lord Castlestewart, declared that he was 'fed up' with Malta in 1916[102] and would have preferred 'the front, the trenches anywhere that [sic] in this beastly spot'.[103] This lack of action was, in some cases, due to the nobles' own status. Basil Blackwood was 'one of his [the commanding officer's] gallopers and just carr[ied] orders for him'.[104] Londonderry was also frustrated with his role as a glorified secretary whose duties included hosting two and a half hour lunches with French officers.[105] Even when he did reach the trenches he admitted that, 'I cannot pretend I am very uncomfortable'[106] and that he 'quite enjoyed my four days in the trenches'.[107] Some peers were able to keep a servant, including Lord Dunsany whose valet turned batman, Hoffman, served J. E. Nelson later in the war. Nelson certainly appreciated his care and attention: 'My Sam Browne shone, my spare uniform, neatly pressed, was laid out for me to change into after my evening bath, and he had the delicacy of a Jeeves when waking me in the morning.'[108] On another occasion Dunsany was able to buy a piano in Amiens and bring it to the front.[109] Arthur Stuart was likewise able to send gifts of lace to his family.[110]

These stories should not blind us to the fact that conditions at the front were harsh. In the aftermath of Mons the huge numbers of German soldiers confronting the British forces began to be recognised.[111] Claud Hamilton gave his mother a detailed account of the hardships he faced between 20 October and November 1914. He was under such pressure that he lost track of time and began dating letters several days ahead.[112] Within five days, five of his company's six officers were casualties. Initially he found it 'most exciting' to fire back 'after one has been shelled and shot at for a week'. His unit was relieved on 24 October 1914 by the Scots Guards but 'I now hear that within a couple of hours they were all killed'.[113] In a letter dated '4 or 5 November' he was still optimistic but wrote of how 'my battalion has taken a terrible hammering. Out of 30 officers and 1,100 men there is now 6 officers and about 200 men'. The casualties had been incurred in just three days. He was by this time suffering nervous tension from the constant shelling.[114] By what he thought was 7 November 1914, Claud Hamilton was depressed from the effects of constant bombardment even though he was by then a mile behind the firing line. He expected his battalion to be sent home because of the extent of its losses.[115]

Around the same time, Freddy Blackwood also found the loss of 'a great many' of his comrades 'a very trying time'.[116] Basil Blackwood also noted how 'one's standard of comfort is completely altered';[117] he was even able to find in a French hut which housed six officers 'an elegance not found in similar shelters built by English hands'.[118] The mental effects of living in cramped conditions and rapidly alternating periods of intense boredom with the threat of death are obvious to the modern reader. These were not widely accepted in this period however and the nobility were particularly fearful of mental illness as their class was dependent on hereditary succession. When his brother was sent home to hospital, Basil Blackwood was very concerned that people 'know that F[reddy] was actually wounded and that he is not in hospital on account of what is in any sense a breakdown'. Freddy was, indeed, suffering from concussion but he had also spent time in a trench with 'dead bodies that had been there six weeks!!'. Even Basil admitted privately that 'Freddy suffers very much mentally' but insisted that it would not 'take the form of losing control of his nerves'.[119] Eventually, Freddy Blackwood recovered and, as Lord Dufferin & Ava, served as Speaker of the Northern Ireland senate. He was a career soldier who had served in the South African War of 1899–1900. By contrast, his brother Basil, who had been so desperate to return to the front, was a barrister and an illustrator of children's books. Arthur Stuart also found himself depressed by his experiences. He confessed to his mother that 'the deaths of all the fellows one knew starts one off inspecting oneself and seeing how utterly worthless one is & what chances one has thrown away'. He felt guilty that he had survived and concluded that God had spared 'the inferior to give them a chance of retrieving themselves'.[120]

The hardships they endured and witnessed led many nobles to question their commanders and the whole conduct of the war. Basil Blackwood began the campaign with such naïve optimism that he discarded his maps of France thinking they would be unnecessary.[121] By 27 August he was unhappy that his unit 'wandered about the country in what seemed a very aimless and inconsequent fashion, starting in one direction under orders that were countermanded'.[122] Londonderry was even less happy and complained that the soldiers 'have been asked to do impossible things and perhaps the highest command take a long time to realise what is impossible'.[123] In August he fumed 'I really believe half the Authorities are clean off their heads ... you cannot imagine how irritating it is to listen to all the exploits they suppose the cavalry are going to perform. One wonders where they have lived and what they were learning for the last two years.'[124] For a class accustomed to authority, criticism of others came naturally so it is no surprise that one of the most senior political peers, Lord Granard, was among the most scathing in his comments. Writing to his wife from Suvla in July 1915 he declared 'the way this campaign is being run is an absolute disgrace'.[125] After his men suffered heavy losses he complained about the lack of artillery,[126] and he was so enraged by the circumstances leading to General Mahon's resignation that he wrote, 'I cannot tell you what I think of the way he has been treated and I hope that you will let ... others know of it as well'.[127]

A measure of peers' martial spirit was the importance they accorded to being mentioned in despatches and the receipt of awards. Of the subjects surveyed, 28 (26 per cent) were mentioned in despatches; most were mentioned only once but multiple mentions occurred occasionally. An example of the importance of this is a letter to Lady Farnham from her son, Somerset, which shows little fear for his father's safety but comments 'is it not splendid about Dad being mentioned in despatches'.[128] Some higher achievements were recognised by awards and medals; 24 (22 per cent) of those sampled received at least one, with the Distinguished Service Order (DSO) being the most common (it was received by ten men). These awards, along with the casualty rates discussed above, suggest that the peers had much to be proud of in their contribution to the war effort.

Unfortunately for the nobility, the war they were fighting was rapidly losing support in Ireland. As has already been shown, peers sympathetic to nationalism such as Dunraven were alienated by the anti-conscription campaign. Midleton wrote to Asquith in January 1916 to warn him that the Volunteers were stockpiling arms[129] and in March he advised Birrell that Sinn Féin were fund raising in America and 'they must do something to justify it [the money], and if they have explosives ... they will use them'.[130] The 1916 Rising was, however, a shock to most nobles when it came. They were also unclear as to what had really happened due to press censorship and the variety of wild rumours which swept the country. Most nobles, for example Midleton, blamed the government for being too soft on separatist nationalism from 1914 on,[131] while Basil Blackwood had such a low opinion of the rebels that he did not blame the administration for not believing them capable of a rising.[132]

The overwhelming attitude to the war seems to have been that it was a dirty business but that it was Germany, and the Kaiser in particular, who was to blame. This was certainly the view nobles put forward in public and in correspondence.[133] As a result their response to the victory (and they certainly saw it as victory) in 1918 was weary rather than joyful. Lady Fingall commented that 'we seemed drained of all feeling';[134] Lord Dunsany entitled his victory poem the 'Dirge of Victory'.[135] Lady Dunsany, however, saw a brighter future and noted that 'Randal [her son] and his generation will be muffs if they can't make something of it'.[136] The sad truth was that the Great War was to be their last chance to play their traditional role of defenders of the empire and leaders in their local communities. Apart from some insightful figures such as Midleton, Dunraven and Ashbourne, few nobles seemed aware of this. Some peers, such as Lord Iveagh even welcomed Sinn Féin's victory in the 1918 election, believing it would give unionism a new chance to 'make the best possible terms'.[137] The forces unleashed in Ireland by the rise of separatist nationalism would ensure that such hopes would be dashed.

Notes

1 A note on terminology: a *peer* is a titled person holding the rank of Baron or higher. They need not actually have a seat in the House of Lords. A *noble* is a member of a family in the peerage. The term *aristocrat* is a more general description of a member of the landed upper class. All peers are nobles, not all nobles are peers. When I refer to 'nobles' I mean peers and their families, whereas references to peers are to title holders alone.

2 For a more detailed discussion of nobles and Irish identity see my MA thesis, 'Irish Peers 1909–24: the decline of an aristocratic class' (National University of Ireland, University College, Dublin, 1998), chapters 3–6. The definitions used in that work were broader to allow for discussion of politics, economics and historical links which are not relevant to this article.

3 See for example: T. A. M. Dooley, 'The decline of the big house in Ireland 1879–1950' (PhD Thesis, National University of Ireland, St Patrick's College Maynooth, 2 Vols.), vol. 1, pp. 59–60; K. Jeffery, 'The Irish military tradition and the British Empire', in K. Jeffery (ed), *An Irish Empire? Aspects of Ireland and the British Empire* (Manchester, Manchester University Press, 1996), p. 108; D. Fitzpatrick, 'Militarism in Ireland 1900–22', in T. Bartlett and K. Jeffery (eds), *A Military History of Ireland* (Cambridge, Cambridge University Press, 1996), p. 499.

4 P. Karsten, 'Irish soldiers in the British army, 1792–1922: suborned or subordinated?', *Journal of Social History,* vol. 17 (1983), p. 36.

5 E. A. Muenger, *The British Military Dilemma in Ireland: Occupation Politics 1864–1914* (Dublin, Gill & Macmillan, 1991), p. 18.

6 P. E. Razzell, 'Social origins of officers in the Indian and British Home Army 1758–1962', *British Journal of Sociology,* vol. 14 (1963), pp. 248–60.

7 *Ibid.,* p. 255.

8 PRONI, D/1231/G/4/83, Freddy Blackwood to his mother, 19 September 1915, Blackwood Papers.

9 Martin, 'Irish Peers 1909–24', pp. 124–6.

10 Elizabeth, Countess of Fingall, *Seventy Years Young, Memories of Elizabeth, Countess of Fingall as told to Pamela Hinkson* (Dublin, Lilliput Press, [1937] 1991), p. 364.

11 M. Amory, *A Biography of Lord Dunsany* (London, Collins, 1972), p. 113.

12 Muenger, *The British Military Dilemma in Ireland,* p. 13.

13 NLI, Ms. 18616 (1), *Sermon of the Archbishop of Armagh, John B. Crozier, 16 August*

1914 *for the Prince of Wales National Relief Fund*, Farnham Papers.

14 Amory, *Biography of Lord Dunsany*, p. 26.

15 *Ibid.*, p. 116.

16 Dooley, 'The decline of the big house in Ireland', vol. 2, p. 538.

17 PRONI, D/1231/G/4/87, Freddy Blackwood to his mother, n.d. [1916?], Blackwood Papers.

18 PRONI, D/1231/G/5/289, Basil Blackwood to his mother, 16 August 1915, Blackwood Papers.

19 Letter from Lord Dunraven, *Irish Times*, 5 October 1914.

20 NLI, Ms. 23618, J. T. Seigne to H. A. Aston, 22 June 1914, Ormonde Papers.

21 *Notes from Ireland*, February 1915.

22 *Irish Times*, 7 November 1914.

23 *Ibid.*, 5 October 1914.

24 E. Reilly, 'Cavan in the era of the Great War', in R. Gillespie (ed.), *Cavan: Essays on the History of an Irish County* (Dublin, Irish Academic Press, 1995), p. 183.

25 Karsten, 'Irish soldiers in the British Army', p. 34.

26 *Irish Times*, 12 August 1914.

27 *Ibid.*, 8 August 1914.

28 *Ibid.*, 12 August 1914.

29 NLI, Ms. 22187, Meath to John Redmond, 5 August 1914, Redmond Papers.

30 Amory, *Biography of Lord Dunsany*, p. 114.

31 Reilly, 'Cavan in the era of the Great War', p. 184.

32 TCD, K/27/36, Donoughmore to Shaw, 11 August 1914, Donoughmore Papers.

33 *Ibid.*, K/27/37, Shaw to Donoughmore, 13 August 1914.

34 *Irish Times*, 26 September 1914.

35 *Ibid.*, 1 September 1914.

36 *Notes from Ireland*, November 1914, quotes *Longford Leader*, 5 September 1914.

37 Amory, *Biography of Lord Dunsany*, p. 115.

38 NLI, Ms. 23616, J. T. Seigne to the Secretary of the Irish National Volunteers, 17 September 1914, Ormonde Papers.

39 *Irish Times*, 5 October 1914.

40 *Notes from Ireland*, February 1915.

41 *Irish Times*, 4 September 1914.

42 TCD, K/27/54, J. Wadding to Countess Donoughmore, 4 September [1914], Donoughmore Papers.

43 *Ibid.*, K/27/57, Ellis to Countess Donoughmore, 8 September 1914.

44 *Ibid.*, K/27/55, R. B. Seigne to Countess Donoughmore, 7 September 1914.

45 *Notes from Ireland*, February 1915.

46 *Galway Observer*, 16 January 1915.

47 *Irish Times*, 12 January 1915.

48 *Ibid.*, 9 June 1915.

49 *Ibid.*, 20 September 1916.

50 *Ibid.*, 17 October 1916.

51 *Ibid.*, 27 April 1918.

52 Earl of Midleton, *Records and Reactions 1856–1939* (London, John Murray, 1939), p. 232.

53 *Ibid.*, p. 248.

54 Edith, Marchioness of Londonderry, *Retrospect* (London, Frederick Miller, 1938), p. 167.

55 Amory, *Biography of Lord Dunsany*, p. 142.

56 Fingall, *Seventy Years Young*, p. 262.

57 *Ibid.*, p. 263.

58 PRONI, D/3099/3/1/5B, Edith, Marchioness of Londonderry, 'Women and war', draft copy, Londonderry Papers.
59 *Irish Times*, 11 August 1914.
60 *Ibid.*, 12 August 1914.
61 NLI, Ms. 23997, Account book of the Prince of Wales National Relief Fund and the 4th Battalion Royal Irish Regiment Comforts Fund, Ormonde Papers.
62 NLI, Ms. 18616 (1), T. Lough to T. C. Burrowes, 17 August 1914, Farnham Papers.
63 NLI, Ms. 22187, Monteagle to J. Redmond, 26 August [1914], Redmond Papers.
64 Reilly, 'Cavan in the era of the Great War', pp. 183–4.
65 *Irish Times*, 16 July 1915.
66 NLI, Ms. 19671, Clonbrock Papers.
67 *Ibid.*.
68 NLI, Ms. 23620–1, Ormonde Papers.
69 NLI, Ms. 19671, Clonbrock Papers,
70 *Irish Times*, 14 August 1914.
71 *Ibid.*, 31 October 1914.
72 *Ibid.*, 2 November 1914.
73 *Ibid.*, 20 January 1915.
74 *Ibid.*, 6 July 1915.
75 F. D'Arcy, *Horses, Lords and Racing Men, the Turf Club 1790–1990* (The Curragh, Co. Kildare, Turf Club, 1991), p. 243.
76 *Ibid.*, p. 252.
77 NLI, Ms. 23616, J. T. Seigne to CO, The Barracks, Kilkenny, 12 August 1914, Ormonde Papers.
78 *Ibid.*, Ms. 23622, Letter to Lord Arthur Butler, 22 May 1918; Letter to Mrs F. Douglas Jones, 16 January 1918.
79 *Ibid.*, J. T. Seigne to C. S. Redeastle, 22 September 1917; to the Secretary, Ministry of Food, 26 September 1917; to E. Booth, Ministry of Food, 26 March 1918.
80 *Ibid.*, J. T. Seigne to the District Inspector, RIC, Kilkenny, 24 May 1917.
81 *Irish Times*, 18 November 1914.
82 Sir L. Woodward, *Great Britain and the War of 1914–18* (London, Methuen, 1967), p. 516.
83 NLI, Ms. 23945, Personal bank book, Ormonde Papers.
84 *Ibid.*, Ms. 23619, A. G. Davies to Mrs Poe, 30 May 1916.
85 *Ibid.*, Ms. 23617, J. T. Seigne to the Secretary of the Local Government Board, Dublin, 24 October 1914.
86 *Ibid.*, Ms. 23886, Establishment and Personal expenditure account of the Marquis of Ormonde.
87 NLI, Ms. 18616 (2), Cyril Malcomson to Lady Farnham, 20 July 1917, Farnham Papers; *Ibid.*, (4), Henry Byers to Lady Farnham, 6 September 1917.
88 PRONI, D/623/A/348/8–19, [MIC 18/11], Abercorn Papers.
89 *Irish Times*, 1 October 1914.
90 PRONI, D/1618/15/15, Sergeant F. Edlin to B. W. Young, 11 August 1915, Castlestewart Papers.
91 *Ibid.*, Louis Mallet to Mrs Stuart, n.d.
92 *Ibid.*, Andrew Stuart to his father, 1 September 1915.
93 *Irish Times*, 22 April 1918.
94 *Ibid.*, 1 December 1917.
95 J. Mackie, Dublin, in *Irish Times*, 8 December 1917.
96 *Irish Times*, 11 December 1917.
97 *Ibid.*, 17 December 1917.

98 D. Cannadine *The Decline and Fall of the British Aristocracy* (London, Picador, 1992), p. 83.
99 L. Kennedy, *Colonialism, Religion & Nationalism in Ireland* (Belfast, Institute of Irish Studies, 1996), p. 191.
100 Dooley, 'The decline of the big house in Ireland', vol. 2, p. 541.
101 PRONI, D/623/A/344/7, Dowager Duchess of Abercorn to Jack, 26 September 1914, Abercorn Papers.
102 PRONI, D/1618/15/15, A[rthur] to Lady Castlestewart, 5 November 1916, Castlestewart Papers.
103 *Ibid.*, 14 November 1916.
104 PRONI, D/1231/G/15/275, Basil Blackwood to Marchioness Dufferin and Ava, 23 October 1914, Blackwood Papers.
105 PRONI, D/3099/3/2/133, Londonderry to Lady Londonderry, 16 January [1916?], Londonderry Papers.
106 *Ibid.*, Londonderry to [?], 20 January [1916].
107 *Ibid.*, D/3099/3/2/132, Londonderry to Colonel Hanley, 24 January [1916].
108 J. E. Nelson, 'Irish soldiers in the Great War, some personal experiences', *Irish Sword*, vol. 11 (1973–4), p. 170.
109 Amory, *Biography of Lord Dunsany*, p. 143.
110 PRONI, D/1618/15/15, Arthur Stuart to Lady Castlestewart, 14 November 1916, Castlestewart Papers.
111 PRONI, D/623/A/344/5, Jack to Dowager Duchess Abercorn, 31 August 1914, Abercorn Papers.
112 *Ibid.*, D/623/A/344/13, Claud Hamilton to Dowager Duchess Abercorn, 7 November 1914.
113 *Ibid.*, 24 October 1914.
114 *Ibid.*
115 *Ibid.*, 7 November 1914.
116 PRONI, D/1231/G/4/74, Freddy Blackwood to Marchioness Dufferin and Ava, 26 October 1914, Blackwood Papers.
117 *Ibid.*, D/1231/G/5/300, Basil Blackwood to his mother, 26 November 1916.
118 *Ibid.*, D/1231/G/5/302, 7 December 1916.
119 *Ibid.*, D/1231/G/5/288, Basil Blackwood to his mother, [1915?].
120 PRONI, D/1618/15/15, Arthur Stuart to Lady Castlestewart, [Feb. 1917?], Castlestewart Papers.
121 PRONI, D/1071/KE/9/8/1, Basil Blackwood, 'Account of BEF', n.d., Dufferin and Ava Papers.
122 *Ibid.*.
123 PRONI, D/3099/2/4/7, Londonderry to Lady Londonderry, 16 July 1916, Londonderry Papers.
124 *Ibid.*, D/3099/3/2/133, 15 August 1916.
125 PRONI, T/3765/K/12/2, Granard to Lady Granard, 28 July 1915, Granard Papers, photocopy collection.
126 *Ibid.*, 28 July 1915.
127 *Ibid.*, 16 August 1915.
128 NLI, Ms. 18616 (6), Somerset to Lady Farnham, 16 December 1917, Farnham Papers.
129 PRO, 30/67 31/1561, Midleton to Asquith, 26 January 1916, Midleton Papers.
130 *Ibid.*, 31/1568, Midleton to Birrell, 13 March 1916.
131 *Ibid.*, 31/1577–84, Midleton, 'Diary of events connected with the Irish Rebellion, April 1916'.
132 PRONI, D/1231/G/5/290, Basil Blackwood to his mother, 1 May 1916, Blackwood Papers.

133 See for example, Lord Dunsany, *Tales of War* (Dublin, Talbot Press, 1918), p. 84.
134 Fingall, *Seventy Years Young*, p. 386.
135 Amory, *Biography of Lord Dunsany*, p. 154.
136 *Ibid.*, p. 153.
137 *Galway Observer*, 7 December 1918.

3

Women and voluntary war work

EILEEN REILLY

Responding to the outbreak of war, many Irishwomen quickly mobilised themselves to 'succour the brave men now fighting for our rights and liberties'.[1] Women all over the country responded to the appeal articulated by Lady Aberdeen on behalf of Queen Alexandra and the British Red Cross Society, in which she called for the organisation of instruction in first aid and emergency nursing under the auspices of the Department of Agriculture and Technical Training. A request was also issued for volunteers to produce necessary garments and bandages, and to provide comforts for soldiers.

The initial gathering of those interested in establishing Red Cross work in Ireland took place in Leinster House, Dublin, on 10 August 1914. Lady Aberdeen described the occasion in her subsequent press release, stating that 'the hall was packed from roof to floor, hundreds of people being unable to gain admittance'.[2] It was a singularly representative assembly given the political differences of those in attendance. In addition to Red Cross spokespersons, there were representatives from the St John's Ambulance Association, the Women's National Health Association (WNHA), the United Irishwomen, the Irish Volunteers Aid Association, the Dublin Branch of the Ulster Volunteers and Cumann na mBan.[3] Leading members of the medical and nursing professions were also present, promising their practical co-operation in effecting the success of the work.

The British Red Cross Society was formally constituted at a meeting of the International Society at Geneva in 1905 as a direct result of Queen Alexandra's belief in the need for such an association following the Boer War. It received the Royal Charter in 1908. In addition to organising education in first aid, the society established Voluntary Aid Detachments (VADs) of men and women who were trained to be of civil and auxiliary military service in the event of war. Queen Alexandra became the first president of the society. In turn, the wives of county lord lieutenants acted as regional presidents and were responsible for organising local committees which undertook to provide classes in first aid and to train the VADs. As such, Lady Aberdeen had formed a Red Cross Ladies Committee in Aberdeenshire during the Boer War that, given its then unofficial status, had operated under the patronage of St Andrew's Ambulance Association. Her committee had served twin wartime purposes, collecting funds and providing garments and comforts for the troops. In 1909 an autonomous Scottish branch of the society was established with emphasis on improving public health and engaging in emergency relief work.

Lord Aberdeen was appointed Viceroy to Ireland for the second time in 1906, having served very briefly in the same position in 1886. Lady Aberdeen's energy was legendary. Reminiscences of those who knew her noted that she appeared not to need sleep, but rather could work through the night until dawn when her maid would often find her at her desk in the clothes she had worn the previous evening.[4] They were a controversial couple, and had been so since the early days of their marriage when wild rumours on the subject of their relationship with their servants captured even Queen Victoria's attention. Characteristically, the young Ishbel Marjoribanks Gordon, the recently married Countess of Aberdeen, had set about reforming her new home, Haddo House, with zeal and imagination. With the support of her husband, she formed a 'Household Club' which their servants were invited to join. The emphasis of this club was on education and self-improvement, subjects which were significant to the Countess throughout her life and informed her activities in both Canada and Ireland.[5] The personal interaction of the couple with their servants gave rise to opinion among some of their peers that they were dangerous social radicals, given that the gossipmongers passed along such titbits as the fictitious story that the Aberdeens played hide and seek with their staff. Even the monarch sought denial from the Prime Minister, Lord Rosebery, of the report that the couple dined with their servants once a week.[6] Undeterred by negative attention, Lady Aberdeen also organised the Haddo House Association, which established education by correspondence for female servants who lived and worked on local farms, and the 'Onward and Upward Association', which set out to improve the lives of young female workers. The organisation spread throughout Scotland with Lady Aberdeen serving as its president and as the editor of its monthly magazine. In 1885, then a mother of four, she co-founded with her friend, Lady Tavistock, the very successful Associated Workers' League to 'co-ordinate the charitable work of the London ladies of fashion'.[7]

In the short time of her first experience in Ireland in 1886 she had involved herself in the Mansion House Ladies' Committee for the Relief of Distress and in the foundation of the Irish Home Industries Association. Despite the brevity of her husband's first Irish viceroyalty – seven months due to the fall of Gladstone's government over the Home Rule Bill – Lady Aberdeen retained her interest in Ireland and continued her work on behalf of the Irish Industries Association, as it was renamed, by establishing and supervising a London branch, by purchasing herself the building which housed the Irish Lace Depot in Dublin and by producing the very successful Irish village exhibit at the World's Fair held in Chicago in 1893. She approached her renewed role as Vicereine of Ireland in 1906 with the same impatience of the convention which dictated almost absolute inactivity for the lady lieutenant and the burning energy that made it possible for her to be active in so many organisations.

While she continued her support of the Irish Industries Association and was instrumental in the very successful International Exhibition held in Dublin in 1907 that showcased Irish craft industries, her position as President of the International Council of Women had facilitated her education on the subject of tuberculosis. By the first decade of the twentieth century it was accepted that the disease was caused by airborne bacillus. Mortality rates had been slowly decreasing in England and Scotland over the previous decades but in Ireland, where tuberculosis was the most common cause of death, there was little sign of improvement.

Lady Aberdeen adopted the fight against the disease specifically, and the campaign to educate and improve public health in general, as her personal mission. She founded the Women's National Health Association to these ends in 1907.[8] The association had three central aims which comprised: education on matters of public health; the fight against disease; and the promotion of a healthy and vigorous race. As the sovereign of the home and mother of the next generation, this was a woman's mission as far as Lady Aberdeen was concerned, and she sought to attract support from all Irish women irrespective of political or religious differences. A success in many ways, this organisation and its originator found it almost impossible to negotiate the political schisms in Ireland. Lady Aberdeen was dedicated to her cause but often lacked delicacy, and in pursuing support without due diplomacy, antagonised many. Sir Horace Plunkett disliked her thoroughly, while the administrative power behind the Local Government Board, Sir Henry Robinson, battled with her over applications for funding. *Sinn Féin* accused her of inventing the tuberculosis crisis while nationalists such as Alice Milligan characterised her health campaign as modern souperism.[9] Unionists, hostile to a viceroyalty which they viewed as sympathetic to nationalist goals, regarded Lady Aberdeen and her association as politically partisan and intrusive. Undaunted 'Lady Microbe', as detractors christened her, established and edited a magazine for the WNHA with the title *Sláinte* (Health) in 1909, while one of the chief achievements of the association was the extensive *Uí Breasail* (the utopia of Irish mythology) Exhibition which opened in Dublin in May 1911 and included displays on health, education and town planning.[10] A second successful Civic Exhibition opened in the summer of 1914; it even earned reluctant approval from that caustic organ of nativism, the *Leader*.[11]

War provided a new platform for Lady Aberdeen and the WNHA. Patron

of the British Red Cross in Ireland, she initiated the organisation of instruction in nursing skills and ambulance driving for the VADs, with the financial
and administrative support of the Department of Agriculture and Technical
Training. Classes were organised through County Council Technical
Committees and qualified for departmental grants which covered the
expenses involved.[12] A bureau of information about voluntary work and a
clothing and comforts depot was opened at Ely House in Dublin which
shortly after was experiencing a 'steady demand' for garment patterns and
information. Support was 'legion' reported Lady Aberdeen.[13] It seemed an
auspicious moment for the foundation of an Irish Red Cross Society in the
same manner as in Scotland, which would recognise and encourage such
work undertaken in support of the war effort. Lady Aberdeen believed that
this was essential in order to attract and retain the support of nationalist
women in particular. She confided this in a hand-written note to the editor
of the mainstream nationalist newspaper, the *Freeman's Journal*:

> I'm afraid there is a bit of a plot among the Unionists to capture the Red Cross
> Society in Ireland and run it in such a way from London and through County
> Lieutenants and Deputy Lieutenants that it will be unacceptable to the Irish
> Volunteer people, etc. You will understand, I am sure. I believe that ultimately we
> may be able to have an Irish Red Cross Society directly under the War Office
> without the intermediary of the British Red Cross.[14]

This private communication found its way to Arthur Griffith who promptly
reproduced it in *Sinn Féin*.[15] It also appeared in the *Irish Worker*. Both
newspapers seized the opportunity to sully the *Freeman's Journal* and by
association, the Irish Parliamentary Party, with accusations of collusion with
British rule in Ireland. The County Dublin branch of the Red Cross
expressed its disapproval of the episode and through its Honorary Secretary,
Denis Pack-Beresford, initiated a correspondence which requested that Lady
Aberdeen disavow the authenticity of the letter which charged 'a body of
Irish men and Irish women with seizing the occasion of a great public
calamity to use the Red Cross for political purposes'.[16] Lady Aberdeen
replied that she could not do so and refused to discuss the episode further. A
leading article in the *Irish Times* sympathised with the passionate resentment
of those accused of 'an offence which at any time would be inconceivably
base'.[17] This controversy coincided with a letter from Prime Minister
Asquith making clear his plan to replace Lord Aberdeen as Viceroy although
this change was delayed until February 1915.[18]

Despite her deep disappointment at this news and the furore over the
publication of her private note, Lady Aberdeen continued her efforts on
behalf of the Red Cross. Evading the issue of the letter in her memoir she
suggests that the proposal to form an Irish Red Cross Society had been
impossible as only sovereign nations could affiliate with the International

Society. While factually based, this explanation avoids discussing the placement of the Red Cross in Ireland on the same footing as in Scotland, where it operated as an autonomous regional branch. This had been proposed at the initial meeting of 10 August 1914, but most likely with the political situation in mind, Lady Aberdeen had suspended consideration of the issue by prioritising the organisation of the society in each county – whose representatives could meet at a future date to discuss a national branch. In the meantime individual counties could affiliate with the British society.

County Dublin was one of the first to do so under the patronage of the Countess of Meath, Isabel, Lady Talbot de Malahide, while Lady Aberdeen herself undertook the presidency of the City of Dublin branch.[19] Responding to the October appeal from Queen Mary's Needlework Guild for the manufacture of 300,000 pairs of socks and 300,000 belts, the WNHA employed seamstresses to fill War Office contracts and raised funds for the purchase of necessary materials.[20] A request for volunteers to augment this work was made, offering free patterns and instructions available from Mrs Hill Tickell, Workroom Secretary, at the information bureau in Ely Place. This work was co-ordinated by the Central Committee for Women's Employment in Ireland, chaired by Elizabeth, Countess of Fingall. Fellow committee members included Lady Talbot de Malahide and Lady Arnott.[21] An editorial in the *Church of Ireland Gazette* declared that 'no worthier appeal has been addressed to Irishwomen' and noted the cumulative value of women undertaking the cost and effort of producing clothing for 'our gallant Irish soldiers' or of simply subscribing to the WNHA's fund. Of particular satisfaction to the editor was the fact that the work was suitably domestic and charitable; 'our mothers, sisters, wives and daughters, each in her own unobtrusive sphere, may thus contribute to the glory that awaits our arms'.[22]

Lady Aberdeen recalled with pride the achievements of the Dublin City branch of the Red Cross. Noting it was 'only one out of many' she stated:

14,146 garments were made and sent forward to headquarters; 3,038 students took First Aid and Home Nursing courses.

Christmas gifts were supplied to every soldier and sailor in the hospitals of the City and County of Dublin by the Comforts Depot, and the same department collected and distributed newspapers and magazines for the men. After 1917 they also distributed 891 lbs. of tobacco and 78,578 cigarettes. This latter duty had, previous to 1917 been undertaken by the City of Dublin V.A.D.s, of which there were ten detachments, which were passed on to the central headquarters of the County Director, Mr. W. Geoghan, M.B.E.

These same detachments were most helpful in connection with the six Social Clubs we started for the wives, mothers, and other relatives of soldiers and sailors in Dublin, of whom there were a great number, Dublin having always been largely represented in the British Army. These Clubs proved to be a great comfort to the women, who were thus able to get information about their menfolk and send them parcels easily.

Mr. Edward Lee placed premises at the disposal of the Branch; enabling it to carry on a Depot for the collection and distribution of fruit, vegetables, and game for the use of wounded soldiers in Dublin hospitals. The railway companies carried these goods free of cost, but the hampers had to be fetched from the station, and sorted before delivery, and this involved no little labour and exertion to the V.A.D.s. 3411 hampers were thus delivered to seventeen hospitals between May, 1915 and May, 1917, in addition to honey, jam, cake, flowers, etc., taken by hand.[23]

The work of the social clubs was deemed constructive for morale and morality. Editorials in *Sláinte* stressed that they were 'of the utmost importance in providing centres where these women can gather for mutual comfort and help'.[24] Information, communication and education were the principal aims of the centres which encouraged the female relatives of men at the front to support each other, to engage in voluntary work and to avoid intemperance. At the Special Council meeting of the WNHA held early in December, a Special Committee was formed to co-ordinate the clubs throughout the country and to organise gifts of reading material and toys for children. As with all activities of the association, strong and generally successful efforts were made to attract support from both religious communities. The local Catholic curate, Fr McCarthy, and the Methodist minister, Rev Mr Abbott, both served on the committee of the Aberdeen Club in Kilmainham.[25] The WNHA encouraged organisation of similar centres in

all districts where there are a number of these women, so that they may have a place of their own, where they can go to meet friends, and get reliable information about the war, and where also they can be given help in regard to their letters and parcels to their friends at the front, and where, if they so desire it, they can obtain instruction regarding cooking, sewing, or anything else which will help them in the brightening of their homes. Music and various forms of recreation, together with light refreshments, should form part of the programme of the Clubs.[26]

Unease regarding women's immorality and intemperance led to a public meeting in Dublin to establish an Irishwomen's League of Honour in November 1914. Reports in British newspapers concerning the increase in drinking and inappropriate behaviour among soldiers' wives and other women had led to the foundation of the League in London to combat the moral dangers which war posed. Women's irresponsible misuse of their husbands' service payments was viewed as the chief reason for an increase in drunkenness. Of equal concern was the potential breakdown of appropriate behaviour between the sexes during the stress of wartime. The Church of Ireland Primate, Archbishop Crozier, addressed the Dublin meeting and outlined the purpose of the League:

> It is proposed to band together women and girls with the object of upholding the standard of women's duty and honour during the time of the war, to raise a strong force of public opinion and support amongst women and girls with which to combat some of the social and moral dangers emphasised by the war; to deepen amongst women and girls the sense of their responsibility for the honour of the nation, and by their influence to uplift manhood, and to provide opportunities for mutual help, encouragement and spiritual influence.[27]

Women were viewed as both moral agents and immoral actors although the dangers posed to Irish womanhood by the war were intimated rather than detailed. The Archbishop referred to the spiritual necessity of sending men to the front with 'clean hands and pure hearts' despite the natural inclination of women to cheer and comfort them. The Dean of St Patrick's Cathedral also proposed that Irishwomen shun those who would not volunteer for service: 'Visit them with the severest disapproval, and when they expect a smile just look them straight in the face and turn away.'[28] Lady Aberdeen took the opportunity of explaining the purpose of the WNHA social clubs which provided women with 'homely influences' as a shield against the 'many dangers which beset them now'.[29] Rachel Mahaffy, daughter of the Trinity College Provost, undertook to call a second meeting to organise the League in due course and called on women of all classes and creeds to join it. Despite the large attendance reported at the initial meeting, the activities of the League appear to have been rather limited. No further details concerning its development appeared in the press and the following autumn Lady Fingall publicly complained that Dublin streets at night were a disgrace to Christianity. A letter to the *Irish Times* followed this by one who described her own 'woman patrol' of Sackville Street, which she characterised as 'one great low saloon where young girls, soldiers, sailors and civilians loiter about'.[30]

Recognising the need for auxiliary hospital accommodation for wounded soldiers, the Dublin Red Cross proposed to build hospital pavilions in the Phoenix Park. The cost of the scheme was estimated at £10,000. Lady Aberdeen proposed an alternative and received royal approval of her idea to turn the State apartments at Dublin Castle into a hospital. King George V and his mother Queen Alexandra each donated £100 to begin the subscription campaign. The Presidents of the Royal Colleges of Physicians and Surgeons, Dr McDowel Cosgrave and Sir F. Conway Dwyer together with the Castle physician, Sir John Lentaigne, inspected and approved the apartments. The Board of Works agreed to meet the cost of structural changes and the War Office undertook to provide a maintenance capitation grant. An estimated 480 beds would be made available at a cost of £10 each with the Dublin Red Cross undertaking general management and the provision of equipment and personnel. The *Irish Times* and the *Freeman's Journal* heartily approved of the efficiency, economy and suitability of the scheme. The latter particularly welcomed the conversion of the Castle 'to a purpose more humane and useful than it has ever known in its long grim history'.[31]

Under the chairmanship of the Lord Mayor, 'who personally advocated and commended the Red Cross hospital to the support of the public', a meeting was held at the Mansion House on 30 November and £1,000 was immediately subscribed. Lady Aberdeen 'with customary lucidity of expression' addressed the meeting and outlined the genesis of the scheme.[32] Sir Conway Dwyer followed, observing that the numbers of wounded soldiers returning from the war had seriously encroached upon space in city hospitals to the detriment of other patients, and that upon detailed inspection the Castle had been found quite suitable. Nationalist MPs J. G. Swift MacNeill and P. J. Brady attended, each speaking in support of the hospital.[33] Given the positive reception of the scheme, Lady Aberdeen later recollected her initial optimism: 'Donations from all parts of Ireland, and from all classes, poured in, and it appeared that, for the first time in its life, the Castle was actually going to be popular.'[34]

Yet despite general approval, notes of dissension appeared. Sir Thomas Myles, in a letter to the *Irish Times* on the same day, discussed the strengths of the proposal but noted three important objections. The first questioned the suitability of the Castle on hygienic grounds, stating that, 'the Castle is insanitary; that its drainage is defective; and that people whose duty compels them to live there are constantly complaining of ill-health'. The succeeding point stated that the 'large and lofty' rooms were unsuitable for a hospital but the third objection addressed the control of funds and intimated that the involvement of Lady Aberdeen in particular was unwelcome. Having disposed of the first objection by stating that drainage and sanitation in the Castle had been recently overhauled and that the chief medical authorities were satisfied with its suitability, Sir Thomas dealt with the third criticism, which he saw as the most important obstacle in attracting public support:

> For reasons which need not be discussed now, the class of people in Dublin and throughout Ireland which in the past has subscribed most generously to charitable objects is completely out of sympathy with the principal promoters of the scheme under discussion, and will not join in any movement in the control of which it is not guaranteed its due share.[35]

He suggested that this difficulty could be overcome by electing a temporary Executive Committee to oversee the collection of subscriptions and the subsequent election of a Board of Administration which would be responsible for expenditure. He called for self-sacrifice and self-effacement and reminded the reader that 'our brave soldiers, heroes, nameless too often, lying in the frozen sludge of the trenches, giving their lives without a

murmur, enduring with stoical fortitude atrocious suffering' were the priority.[36] The editorial in the *Irish Times* agreed pointedly, stating that it 'is not
a question of personal influence or *prestige*'.[37]

Following the close of the subscription meeting at the Mansion House, the
City of Dublin Red Cross met and appointed a Committee of Management. It
had been previously agreed at the general meeting that the presidents of the
Royal Colleges of Physicians and Surgeons, and the president and honorary
treasurers of the city branch of the Red Cross should be *ex officio* members.
Six men and four women joined them with provision for ten others from the
medical profession to be nominated by the ten clinical hospitals in Dublin.
Miss M. A. MacDonnell, RRC, was appointed as Matron.[38] In its report of the
meeting the *Freeman's Journal* noted with satisfaction the success of the
meeting 'representing all parties and creeds'.[39] Myles' misgivings about Lady
Aberdeen's unpopularity and the control of finances as obstacles to the success
of the hospital proved unfounded. Within a week half of the targeted £5,000
had been subscribed and tenders were invited for hospital supplies and laundry
services. Rather, it was the suspicion that the Castle was unsanitary which
threatened to destroy the campaign.

Lady Aberdeen characterised the succeeding controversy as 'an extraordinary and inexplicable campaign against the whole scheme'.[40] A lively
correspondence ensued in the columns of the *Irish Times* with many attesting to their ill health as a result of staying in the Castle. Lady Fingall wrote
that she had suffered from 'Castle throat', concluding that there 'is something in the air which seems to induce headache and minor maladies of a
lowering nature'.[41] Sir John Lentaigne refuted this stating that the few
cases of illness during his time as Castle physician were common cases of
colds brought on by late hours and overheated rooms during the social
season.[42] He emphatically refuted charges that the Castle was unsanitary,
as did Alice Ann Bellingham, wife of Captain Roger Bellingham ADC, who
had lived in the Castle for over two years – but it took an official declaration from the Board of Works that the Castle met all sanitary requirements to end the debate.[43]

Worried about the impact of the controversy upon subscriptions, the
Management Committee wrote to urban and county councils requesting
donations, while the Dublin Red Cross organised a special matinee in the
Tivoli Theatre in aid of the hospital fund. Subscription lists published in the
Irish Times recorded all amounts in addition to gifts such as beds, bed linen,
nightshirts, slippers, books and bandages. Branches of the WNHA in
Mullingar and Tralee collected consignments of clothes which they subse-
quently forwarded by rail.[44]

A further difficulty arose when it was reported that the War Office had
vetoed the hospital scheme. Some claimed that the difficulties the proposal
was experiencing were due to personal and political prejudice, especially

against Lady Aberdeen, but it was discovered when a deputation travelled to London to demand an explanation that the War Office did indeed have serious misgivings based on the plans which it was studying.[45] When it was realised that the plans in question were out of date and did not reflect the structural changes undertaken in recent years the misgivings vanished and work went ahead. A variety entertainment organised by the Working Girls of Dublin at the Abbey Theatre realised enough to equip four beds while the Georgian Society donated £41. By the official opening of the hospital on 27 January 1915, less than a month before the Aberdeens left Ireland, £4,813 had been raised although expenditure was over £6,000.[46] The Dublin VADs organised whist drives while the proceeds from sales of Katharine Tynan Hinkson's collection of war poems, *Flower of Youth*, were donated to the hospital fund.[47] Organised by C. J. Jones of the Tivoli Theatre, entertainment for the patients was provided every Thursday evening. Sustained fundraising efforts involving subscriptions, jumble sales, concerts and flag days throughout the war years ensured sufficient finances.[48]

Alice Brunton Henry joined the Royal College of Science Women's VAD upon its establishment in 1914 and was appointed as Quartermaster of the Irish War Hospital Supply Depot (IWHSD) in 1915.[49] Under the presidency of the Marchioness of Waterford, the central depot at 40 Merrion Square was established to co-ordinate the 'steadily increasing number of "Hospital Supply Depots", for the supply of surgical dressings, which are being formed in the country districts of Ireland'.[50] Irish bogs became vital to war work. Seventeen species and twenty-five varieties of sphagnum moss were found in Ireland. Used in Germany for over three decades as a surgical dressing, sphagnum moss when dried was found to act as a superior absorbent and natural deodorant. Mrs M. C. Wright, a botanist at the Royal College of Science, and Alice Brunton Henry obtained permission from the Department of Agriculture and Technical Instruction to set up a national sphagnum centre as part of the IWHSD.[51] Mrs Wright initially utilised the services of the Geological Survey of Ireland in collecting samples, but only a sustained national volunteer program could meet the increasing demand for dressings. Appeals were issued to Irish women and children to collect, dry, pack and send the moss to Dublin. Mrs Ralph Coote of Ballyfin, Queen's County, organised her children to do so while Mary Pakenham recalled how she and her siblings did likewise:[52]

> Easily the most picturesque of our war activities was the gathering of sphagnum moss from the bog ... We had a special sort of two-ended sack which we hung round our necks like a stole and we went barefoot over the bog fishing the clumps of moss out of the pools. There were three sorts, brown-and-thick, green-and-straggly and the commonest and much despised third class stuff which was red-

and-measly. After the stuff was got home it had to be dried and picked over, and by the time the war ended we had evolved a most elegant paraphernalia for doing it. The boxes in which it was dispatched to the hospitals were miracles of fair device, divided into graded compartments and lined with lily white paper. I became quite snobbish over the whole question and my head was turned when I heard that our lot had been put on exhibition at the hospital.[53]

The moss was made up into standardised dressings of different sizes by members of the VADs and then sent to the British Red Cross and the *Croix Rouge Française* for distribution in allied hospitals. Fifteen regional depots were established by February 1916 but with the addition of sphagnum moss to the War Office's list of surgical dressings, demand surged. In March 1916 Alice Brunton Henry noted in her diary that the War Office 'sent us word requisitioning 5,000 moss dressings per month', a fifty per cent increase of average monthly production.[54] Mrs Wright, in a letter to the press, emphasised the 'urgent need' for more sphagnum moss and appealed for collectors.[55] Production increased dramatically. 160 women were occupied full time making dressings at the central depot while male volunteers made the wooden packing cases and were responsible for dispatching the finished product. The Easter Rising severely disrupted production during April, but by May 1916 the demand had been met and exceeded.[56] Forty-five regional depots located throughout the country were active in moss production by the end of 1917 when the total output of dressings was over 300,000.

Modelled on the pioneering Queen's College in London, Dublin's Alexandra College was established in 1866 with the aim of providing for the higher education of Irish women.[57] Quickly proving itself an influential force in women's education, the college prided itself on preparing its students for university study, on providing specialised training courses to enable its graduates to successfully enter the employment market and on its social work. The College Guild was founded in 1897 to undertake 'useful work', to 'form a bond of union among present students' and to 'keep past students in touch with the College'.[58] The first project undertaken by the Guild was the purchase and management of five tenement houses.[59] A Social Service Union was established in 1901 to provide bursaries for 'ladies of gentle birth and education, who, either from age or ill-health are unable to support themselves' and a Working Girls' Hostel was founded in 1913.[60]

In 1914 the Guild was composed of almost 1,000 members and it responded immediately to the war with three projects: a house for Belgian refugees, a workroom for unemployed women and a club for soldiers' wives.[61] Principal of the College, Miss White, led each of the organising committees. The hostel for the refugees was at first located at 16 Northbrook Road in a house belonging to the Adelaide Road Presbyterian Church.

Assisted in minor part by the Local Government Board, the expenses of running the hostel were met almost completely by subscription while members of the Guild also donated furniture, clothes and foodstuffs. Eight women were initially employed as knitters in the Guild Workroom located in Westland Row while the social club was opened in D'Olier Street.[62]

Membership of the club was limited to those wives, mothers and sisters of men on active service and, as with the WNHA clubs and the League of Honour, the Guild was highly conscious of its role in providing an alternative to intemperance and other temptations. Made as 'attractive as possible' with a 'piano, gramophone, illustrated papers, comfortable chairs and brightly burning fires', the club was open from 5pm to 10pm each weekday evening.[63] Responding to the wishes of the seventy members, a programme of education and recreation was designed by the organising committee and managed by the students. The programme scheduled music and singing on Monday, sewing on Tuesday, health education on Wednesday, cooking on Thursday and children's drill on Friday. Reports in the college magazine indicate that while cooking and sewing were very popular, regrettably 'the same anxiety is not shown as regards the learning of health culture'. In her 1915 report, Dorothy Bewley, the Honorary Secretary of the War Club Committee, thanked those who had provided pleasant entertainments, judged that the club 'rivalled very successfully the enticements of undesirable places of entertainment' and concluded that

> on the whole we have reason to be satisfied with our work. The women have often spoken to the helpers of what a comfort the Club has been to them, and if we have indeed lightened in some measure the burden of these, our sisters, we feel our work has not been in vain.[64]

The Guild Workroom, which produced socks, opened in November 1914 with eight employees, but six months later had added four more staff. Between twenty and thirty outworkers were also employed. The Guild initially received some help towards the cost of the project with grants from the Mansion House and from the Rathmines Relief Committee but in addition to financial support from Guild subscribers, the survival of the workroom depended on the sale of its goods. Helen M. Hutton, Honorary Secretary of the Workroom Committee, recorded that the workers 'assured Miss Stoney, who manages this department, that the work we have provided them with has practically saved some of them from starvation'.[65] Despite rapidly increasing stock which threatened 'to stifle us' employment was stable and appeals to the public in the *Irish Times* produced sufficient sales.[66]

Fourteen Belgian refugees were accommodated at the Guild hostel in Northbrook Road. Two of the men gained immediate employment, making glass at the Royal College of Science. Another made 'most ingenious toys' whose sale aided the running costs of the hostel.[67] The group also included a language teacher and an organist. While the Guild contributed a weekly allowance and paid for a servant to do rough work, the inhabitants managed the household and cultivated the garden themselves. When the Presbyterian Church found a paying tenant for the house in March 1915, the Guild was obliged to rent a house, which proved a heavy strain on their financial resources, but the Local Government Board provided a rent-free house in September 1916 and the hostel continued to operate until 1920. Mrs R. H. Murray, who acted as the hostel's supervisor from 1917, was later awarded the *Medaille de la Reine Elizabeth* by the Belgian government for her individual work and in recognition of the contribution made by the Guild.[68]

In addition to these projects, Alexandra pupils, past and present, contributed to the war effort at home and abroad. Students organised 'patriotic entertainments' to raise funds for the Guild and diligently attended a special series of lectures on modern European history in order to deepen their understanding of the war. A knitting association was formed; during its time it produced over 2,000 articles of clothing for soldiers at the front, particularly for those of the Leinster Regiment in which many of the members' brothers and other male relatives served. Another popular activity was filling sandbags in response to the appeal by the Irish Sandbag Committee which had been organised specifically to send sandbags to Irish regiments on active service. Fifty-three girls participated in the college nursing division formed by Edith McComas as part of the St John's Ambulance Brigade and were responsible for cleaning and maintaining the Irish War Hospital Supply Depot in Merrion Square.[69]

Great pride was taken in recording the doings of old girls, 'the goodly list of our war workers', many of whom served in VADs at home and in England and France. F. S. Bushe opened the first social club for soldiers' and sailors' wives in Belfast. Aileen Preston drove a motor ambulance at the front. Bertha McComas worked in the Sandes Soldiers' Home in the Curragh, Co. Kildare. Elsie Eldred and Eleanor Corgin travelled to Serbia with the Red Cross. Drina Onslow drove an ambulance at Dunkirk. Mary St. Clair Swanzy acted as recruiting officer in Ireland for the recently established Queen Mary's Auxiliary Army Corps which provided catering, administrative and clerical services for the army. Other graduates held clerical positions in the Press Censor's Office, the War Office, the Ministry of Munitions, the Royal Air Force and the Coal Controller's Office. Elsie Reeves, Hazel Irwin and Louie Brownrigg joined the nursing staff of King George's Hospital in London while Louie Despard and Violet Poole worked as masseuses to the wounded. By 1917 ten alumni were serving as nursing sisters at the front while twenty others in domestic hospitals were listed.[70] Norah Fitzpatrick established the Soldiers' Recreation Room at St Stephen's Green:

[It] owes its success not only to the skill but the untiring devotion of Miss Fitzpatrick, who attends there every day in the week including Sunday. It is this certainty of finding in the Recreation Room a friend who takes real interest in them that gives its real popularity to the room among the soldiers, even more than what is provided for them. The attendance constantly runs to 200, often to 280.

The men can get a large cup of tea and bread and butter and cake for 1d. They read, play games, talk, write letters, or – unfailing pleasure – pick out airs on the piano. The same men come regularly, and some have come back after one or more visits to the 'front', to what they say is 'like home'.[71]

Mrs M. Lorimer first worked for the Red Cross in London, 'dealing with German correspondence related to the wounded and missing', and then took on the position of Director of the Inquiry Department at Alexandria with responsibility for organising and recording all information furnished by Egyptian hospitals regarding allied troops.[72]

Alice Bernard and Aileen Dougherty worked in the Foreign Office while Gabrielle Webb and Althea Hannay both served in Young Men's Christian Association canteens in France. Daughter of the writer James Owen Hannay, better known as George A. Birmingham, Althea had worked in an English military hospital before joining Rosamund Leather in her work at a camp in Boulogne in 1917. Her father had served as a chaplain there for two years and admired the difficult work undertaken by Rosamund Leather with whom he remained very friendly after the war. Their correspondence reveals the extraordinary efforts that these workers went to in order to provide hot drinks, entertainments and cheery encouragement to weary and wounded soldiers during the depths of winter. Prior to Althea's arrival, Rosamund wrote to Hannay that she had established a new canteen hut and confided her hopes of providing hot suppers if she could get enough helpers. While the weather was so cold that 'the coffee froze in the oven the other night – I love iced coffee but that was a little too much for me', she wrote of her 'longing for more hands so that I can do a thousand and one other things'.[73] Whist drives and draughts tournaments were typical activities in cold weather but the irrepressible Miss Leather wrote that she planned 'heaps more amusements' when the weather improved, including making a cricket pitch. Althea arrived in March just as the canteen was re-opening after an epidemic of measles.

Althea keeps us all alive – her efforts to wake up the other two girls who are most frightfully quiet – are quite amusing. I wish you could see her dealing out fruit and (what we call) custard perched on a box – talking hard with a large and very cheery crowd of men around her. I don't know what she says to them but they all have broad grins on their faces! She has fallen into the work awfully well and has a tremendous admiration for the men which, of course, is the proper spirit.[74]

Despite the long duration of the war and the other work of the Guild, war work remained a priority at Alexandra College. Following the example of the Girls' Friendly Society and encouraged by Sir Algernon Coote, a College War Savings Association was formed early in 1918 and over £3,000 was invested within the year. A fête for the college's war charities was held realising £906 in June 1918. The celebration of the college's golden jubilee was finally held in 1919, having been postponed for nearly three years due to the war. As patroness of the school, Queen Alexandra wrote a letter, read by the Archbishop of Dublin, congratulating the college on its many achievements, noting particularly the sterling record of its war work. The Lord Lieutenant, Lord French, and Field Marshal Sir Henry Wilson also acknowledged the beneficial war work carried out by Alexandra women.[75]

The Ulster Women's Unionist Council (UWUC) was also active in war work, establishing a Gift Fund for Soldiers, organising comforts and bandages for troops and prisoners of war and financing an Ulster Volunteer Force hospital in Pau, France until 1916.[76] In a letter to the Lord Mayor of Belfast 'practical citizenship' was offered throughout the province of Ulster.[77] Presided over by Theresa, Marchioness of Londonderry, Rosalind, Duchess of Abercorn and Harriet, Countess of Dufferin and Ava, in most respects the war work undertaken by the UWUC was similar to that of other women's organisations but it was singular in its separatist political stance. Reminding Ulsterwomen of their imperial duty, the UWUC organised its own nursing and ambulance corps, its own sphagnum moss depots and in some cases women's rifle corps. Yet political partiality did not inform every war work organisation in the province.

The County Cavan Women's Patriotic Committee (CCWPC) was formed to 'assist in alleviating the distress that must inevitably follow the outbreak of war' and serves as a vigorous example of the voluntary work undertaken at the local level in Ireland by women from both political and religious traditions.[78] The objects of the organisation were to assist in the work of the Soldiers' and Sailors' Families Association, which provided help to distressed families of those on active service, to make and provide garments and comforts for the troops and to organise first aid classes. From its inception it aimed to be representative 'of all sections of the community' and counted among its members women from unionist and nationalist backgrounds. Mrs E. H. Lough, married to county lord lieutenant Thomas Lough MP, served as committee president.[79] Also prominent was Cecilia Beatrice Kennedy whose husband, Vincent Kennedy, was a nationalist MP. Aileen, Lady Farnham, served as patron of the county Red Cross branch and as president of the county Soldiers' and Sailors' Families Association in addition to her fundraising and organisational work on behalf of the committee. The wives and daughters of unionist county deputy lieutenants, T. J. Burrowes and Fane Vernon, also played an active role, while the rest of the membership was made up of mostly middle-class women from the towns and rural areas throughout the county.

In a letter to the local press the Roman Catholic bishop of Kilmore, Dr Finegan, recorded his support for the organisation and 'appealed to each woman and girl' in the county to become involved.[80] At one local meeting held in the Catholic Young Men's Recreation Rooms in Newbliss, Fr J. P. McKenna spoke of his audience's duty to support the Irish soldiers.[81] Local committees formed throughout the county and quickly organised working parties, nursing classes and fundraising entertainments. Relief of Belgian refugees was a priority with collections organised by the Church of Ireland and the Catholic Church with the support of the CCWPC. Cross-community collaboration in this endeavour was warmly expressed and the first collections netted £840.[82] Belgian refugees were welcomed to the county with the arrival of the first family in January 1915, while 'ladies from the town and neighbourhood of Cootehill' recognised 'Ireland's debt to Belgium in resisting the German invasion' and undertook to financially support two Belgian families in the area who arrived in March 1915.[83]

Concerts proved to be the most popular and successful method of fundraising for the committee and detailed accounts of the musical programmes were printed in the local press. As a rule young ladies performed on pianoforte, sang or recited with the choice of material incorporating both imperial ('The British Empire') and national themes ('There's No Land Like Ireland'). The anthems of the allied nations were always sung and the evening's entertainment often included short sketches and tableaux.[84] Patriotic dances which were organised in the homes of CCWPC members attracted the county élite. Mrs Stuart and Mrs Simms organised such a gathering in Belturbet with 'lots of flags and bunting, and hothouse flowers from Mrs Vernon's Erne Hill House. Fifty to sixty couples responded to the invitations and danced the night away to the music of Mr J. H. Read's Select Orchestra, Belfast'.[85] An entertainment in Redhills opened with 'some splendid phonograph selections' followed by a 'magic lantern exhibition on the war' organised by the Ballyhaise rector, Rev A. R. Burris, and finished with a variety concert.[86] Other fundraising activities included jumble sales, badminton tournaments, bridge drives and shooting, knitting and cake competitions.[87]

Six months after its formation the CCWPC reported that 3,500 garments had been sent to the troops and £450 collected. 'In addition to these, tobacco, cigarettes, matches, foot-powder, bandages, bootlaces, soap, candles, pencils, towels, notepaper etc. have also been sent.'[88] Almost 200 women were thanked by name for their work and contributions by committee secretary, Mrs L. Ida Blackley.[89] One of the CCWPC's most energetic campaigns was the collection of eggs for wounded soldiers, a drive initiated by the Dublin Red Cross. In a letter to the *Irish Post* in May 1915, Mrs Blackley appealed particularly to local teachers to organise donations from their pupils and recorded the contributions already received from schools: 'Convent School, Cavan, 14 dozen; Farnham School, 12 dozen; Stradone School, 9 dozen'.[90] Other schools in the county had supported the war effort in different ways. The pupils of the national school at Ballymachugh had raised money which was forwarded to buy 'tobacco and cigarettes for the soldiers in France', while their second collection of £7 6s was sent to the YMCA's fund for canteen huts.[91] Killeshandra and Aghakee national schools formed knitting groups which produced mittens and mufflers which were sent to the 2nd Battalion of the county regiment, the Royal Irish Fusiliers, at Salonika. At its first annual general meeting fundraising and egg collections for the year were noted with Cavan town leading the latter campaign with donations of 7,000 eggs in four months. The committee decided to add to its agenda the provision of comforts for Irish prisoners of war through the recently formed Irish Women's Association in London and planned a concert in aid of this work, which was held in December in the new Catholic Hall in Templeport.[92] Active throughout the county for the duration of the war, the CCWPC illustrates the commitment of rural women to war work and the variety of activities that were undertaken. Its emphasis on women working together despite confessional or political differences provides an instance of the national pattern.[93]

The Irish Women's Association formed in London in the spring of 1915 for the purpose of providing food and comforts for prisoners of war belonging to Irish regiments. Its members were largely drawn from the titled and upper ranks of Irish society and it announced itself to be non-political and non-sectarian, 'its only object being the bodily comfort and well-being of all Irish Regiments without distinction'.[94] Mrs John Redmond, Rachel Mahaffy and the Gaelic scholar Eleanor Hull were listed as active members. Led by Lady MacDonnell of Swinford, for the first months of its existence the association depended exclusively on private subscriptions and regimental support but by the summer had to appeal for public assistance. Accommodated initially by the Free Trade Union in Victoria Street, the association organised fortnightly parcels which were packed and sent by volunteer workers to some 1,600 prisoners of war whose names had been supplied by the various Irish regiments. A further 300 men had been 'godmothered'; for twelve shillings a month one could ensure the dispatch of two parcels to a specific individual. Each parcel, made up of two boxes, contained food, tobacco, and comforts and cost six shillings to pack and send to the prisoner.[95]

Lady Edith Gordon judged that of all the organisations connected with the war 'none is more likely to appeal to the hearts and to the imagination of the Irish people' and commended the 'most business-like principles' of its work.[96] In 1916 the association moved into rooms in Kensington Palace at the invitation of Queen Alexandra. Adopting the shamrock as its emblem, the association published appeals at regular intervals in the Irish press which included excerpts from letters received by grateful prisoners attesting to the necessity of the parcels in maintaining their health and in some cases, their lives. A private in the Royal Munster Fusiliers wrote that the association was 'a glorious organisation' while a private in the Royal Irish Rifles wrote that 'the boys here call the ladies their Irish Angels'.[97] An effective and energetic publicist, Lady Gordon declared that it 'is the paramount duty of every Irishman and Irishwoman whose heart has ever thrilled with pride at the immortal glory won by Ireland's sons in every battle in every land to which they have gone "to do or die"' to support the association's work. [98] Special Christmas parcels were available for purchase at three shillings and sixpence and consignments of comforts were also sent to all the Irish regiments at the front throughout the duration of the war.

Class, religion and politics were influential factors in the adoption of war work. As voluntary service required the investment of time with no remuneration, women active in such work necessarily had leisure time and stable financial circumstances which permitted them to pursue these activities. Many of those involved in the organisations detailed above were from the upper echelons of Irish society: the titled ladies of the landed gentry, and the wives and daughters of senior officials, politicians, businessmen, clergymen and professionals. These women were not required to earn their own living and thus had the opportunity to engage in voluntary pursuits. As recent work demonstrates, a robust and ambitious Catholic middle class, conscious of the tantalising immediacy of Home Rule and anticipating imperial accomplishment, responded positively to the summons to arms.[99] The majority of Irish nationalists were in accord with John Redmond's commitment to the war effort, but the evidence to date suggests that the majority of those involved in war work were Protestant women. Certainly those of the Irish gentry classes, with very few exceptions, were Protestant, yet there was a more equitable division of religion among the women of the upper middle and middle classes and, with the exception of the UWUC, the organisations discussed in this article accentuated their appeal to Irishwomen of all religious affiliations.

One explanation for this timidity may be that lay charity work had long been considered an exclusively Protestant endeavour and was still suspected by some as serving as a cover for proselytism. Katharine Tynan Hinkson, taking up the theme of recent articles in the *Irish Monthly* on the failure of Irish Catholic women to engage in social work, wrote that she recognised in rural Ireland particularly 'there is usually a singular lack of any effort, single or concerted, on the part of Catholic women to lend a hand in work for the general good'.[100] Advocating a pluralist approach to voluntary work, she also supported the creation in Ireland of a Catholic Women's League to encourage women into social work. Without doubt, Catholic women such as Cecilia Beatrice Kennedy in Cavan participated, and those who took first aid classes, fundraised or knitted articles for the troops around the country were not exclusively Protestant. An investigation of the impact of the Catholic Church's attitude to the war effort may prove illuminating. Evidence of the clergy's approval of war work exists, but this must be balanced with the view articulated in the *Catholic Bulletin* which urged its youthful readers to 'pray that Irishmen may not be tempted to offer foreign service; that they may see that their first duty is to Ireland'.[101] This periodical's monthly section 'For Mothers and Daughters' by 'Bean a' Tighe' (woman of the house) advised economy of foodstuffs and increased production of vegetables in 'war-time gardens' but made no mention of any type of war work.[102]

Many other themes await further work. The shift in nationalist political priorities in the aftermath of the 1916 rebellion and the rise of Sinn Féin in 1917 certainly impacted upon women's support of the war effort and an investigation into how this change registered itself on a local and national scale needs to be carried out. The role of Irish working-class women in the munitions factories in Dublin and in England has yet to be explored in depth. The general activities and war work of Anglican societies in Ireland such as the Mothers' Union and the Girl's Friendly Society have received no attention. The roles of female Irish doctors, nurses, ambulance drivers, canteen workers and numerous other war occupations have not been examined at all. The relatively recent historiography of Irish women in this period strongly favours discussions of radical nationalists in the thick of revolutionary activities yet accounts of what other women valued and achieved can only enrich the historical record. While this article offers a concise examination of some aspects of Irish women and war work it does so as an inquiry commenced rather than completed. The research conducted to date on women and the war has been negligible and the subject requires much clarification before a thorough understanding is achieved.[103]

Notes

1 *Church of Ireland Gazette*, 21 August 1914.
2 *Ibid.*, 25 September 1914.
3 Lord and Lady Aberdeen, '*We Twa': Reminiscences of Lord and Lady Aberdeen*, vol. 2 (London, W. Collins & Sons, 1925), p. 230; Lady Aberdeen notes here that although there were members of Cumann na mBan (a nationalist women's organisation) present they did not act as representatives of the organisation. The presence of members at this meeting preceded the split in the Irish Volunteers over supporting the war effort and Cumann na mBan's decision to back the minority anti-war faction which then emerged. It is likely that the members who expressed this early and short-lived interest in Red Cross work did so

conscious of an opportunity to learn skills that they believed would be employed in the nationalist cause. The United Irishwomen (renamed as the Irish Countrywomen's Association in 1935) was founded in 1911 by Anita Lett as a female auxiliary to Horace Plunkett's Irish Agriculture Organisation Society with similar aims to those of Lady Aberdeen's Women's National Health Association although it focused upon improving rural life in all respects.

4 M. Keane, *Ishbel, Lady Aberdeen in Ireland* (Newtownards, Northern Ireland, Colourpoint Books, 1999), pp. 210–11.

5 Lord Aberdeen served as Governor-General of Canada from 1893–98. During this time Ishbel founded the Canadian National Council of Women and the Victorian Order of Nurses for Canada. She also served as President of the International Council of Women.

6 Keane, *Ishbel*, pp. 19–20.

7 *Ibid.*, pp. 21–2 and 27.

8 Ishbel, Marchioness of Aberdeen & Temair, *Musings of a Scottish Granny* (London, Heath Cranton, 1936), pp. 146–63; Keane, *Ishbel*, pp. 123–44; J. Bourke, 'The health caravan: domestic education and female labour in rural Ireland 1890–1914', *Éire-Ireland*, vol. 22 (1989), pp. 21–38.

9 Keane, *Ishbel*, pp. 155–60.

10 By 1909 the association had 150 branches throughout the country and while the fight against the 'White Demon' of tuberculosis was paramount, it also launched campaigns on a variety of other issues. Of particular concern was the education of new mothers, improving sanitation and children's nutrition. The 1911 exhibition led to the foundation of an Irish Town Planning Association at the end of the year over which the indefatigable Ishbel presided.

11 Keane, *Ishbel*, p. 206.

12 Five weeks after the initial meeting Lady Aberdeen reported that 170 first aid and ambulance classes with an average membership of twenty to thirty had been established under this scheme and that students were preparing for certificate examinations to be given by the Department. The British Red Cross and the War Office recognised these certificates. These classes were in addition to those organised by the St John and St Patrick Ambulance Associations. The majority of students were female. Individual Dublin hospitals also participated in the education of Red Cross workers. Lady Aberdeen later claimed that during 'the ensuing six months some ten thousand persons in various parts of Ireland qualified for Red Cross service by joining these classes and obtaining certificates'; Lord and Lady Aberdeen, *'We Twa'*, vol. 2, p. 231.

13 *Church of Ireland Gazette*, 25 September 1914.

14 Keane, *Ishbel*, p. 220; M. Bence-Jones, *Twilight of the Ascendancy* (London, Constable, 1987), pp. 165–6.

15 *Sinn Féin*, 17 October 1914.

16 *Irish Times*, 31 October 1914.

17 *Ibid.*

18 Some interpreted this action as a direct response to 'a gaucherie which the Government could not overlook in the wife of the King's Representative'. R. F. Brooke, *The Brimming River* (Dublin, Allen, Figgis & Co., 1961), p. 99. The Aberdeens and the Asquiths had a friendly relationship and had almost been connected by marriage. Archie Gordon, the Aberdeens' youngest son, and Violet Asquith, daughter of the Prime Minister, had been expected to marry. They became engaged in 1909, as Archie was dying from injuries he received in an automobile accident.

19 The Cork branch was very active under the leadership of Lady Cotter and Mrs Sharman Crawford. Dr Lucy Smith taught first aid and nursing classes with an average attendance of thirty members. Several working parties were organised throughout the county to

produce required garments and the society was successful in fundraising for the Cork Motor Ambulance Association. Seventeen Red Cross branches were active In Ireland by the beginning of 1915.

20 Another productive Dublin needlework guild was that of the Soldiers' and Sailors' Help Society located in Lower Mount Street.

21 Elizabeth, Countess of Fingall, *Seventy Years Young* (London, Collins, 1937), pp. 361–3. The Central Committee for Women's Employment was formed by Cabinet Committee and was intended to act in an advisory capacity regarding all schemes for Women's Employment. Recognising the need for proficiency in public speaking as an essential aspect of such work, Daisy Fingall organised an elocution class taught by Mademoiselle D'Esterre, well known in London for her tutelage of inexperienced Members of Parliament. Declaring that the teacher was more terrifying than any audience could be, Daisy also noted that Lady Talbot de Malahide was the best pupil.

22 *Church of Ireland Gazette*, 9 October 1914.

23 Lord and Lady Aberdeen, *'We Twa'*, vol. 2, pp. 231–3. The City of Dublin detachments were predominantly female with a full strength of twenty-three members in each excluding officers.

24 *Sláinte*, vol. 5 (December 1914).

25 'The club premises are neatly appointed and commodious, and provide a reading and writing room, tea room, meeting room, and babies' club.' *Sláinte*, vol. 6 (January 1915).

26 *Ibid*. The clubs operating in Dublin were the Sibail Club in Lower Gardiner Street, the Shamrock Club in Ringsend, the Aberdeen Club in Kilmainham, the Collogue Club in the Coombe and the Sláinte Club in Ormond Market. Three more unnamed centres were being organised at this time, one in the Convent in Henrietta Street, another on Arran Quay and a third at Golden Lane.

27 *Church of Ireland Gazette*, 27 November 1914.

28 *Irish Times*, 20 November 1914.

29 *Church of Ireland Gazette*, 27 November 1914.

30 *Irish Times*, 21 October 1915.

31 *Ibid*., 28 November 1914; *Freeman's Journal*, 28 November 1914. The *Yorkshire Observer* agreed with the *Freeman's Journal* and expressed the still lively expectation that Home Rule was imminent. 'To Irishmen, at all events, Dublin Castle has carried with it hitherto rather sinister associations, and this picturesque metamorphosis will be no unhappy transition to the future change which they hope for when the new Irish administration will take the building over for Government offices.' *Yorkshire Observer*, 2 December 1914.

32 *Evening Telegraph*, 1 December 1914.

33 Swift McNeill subscribed £5 5 s; other subscriptions included ten pounds each from Dublin businesses such as Brown, Thomas & Co., Findlater and Co., and Switzer and Co. James Talbot Power of Power's Distillery gave £25. Lord Pirrie of Harland & Wolff gave the highest amount, £250, while the most unusual subscription was ten pounds from the Hindu students at King's Inns. *Irish Times*, 3 December 1914.

34 Lord and Lady Aberdeen, *'We Twa'*, vol. 2, p. 236.

35 *Irish Times*, 30 November 1914.

36 *Ibid*.

37 *Ibid*. Alice Brunton Henry noted the scheme in her diary commenting that 'Lady Aberdeen [was] bossing it all'; NLI, Ms. 7982, Diaries of Mrs Augustine Henry.

38 Miss MacDonnell had been in charge of the Irish Hospital in South Africa during the Boer War for which she received the Royal Red Cross from King Edward VII.

39 *Freeman's Journal*, 1 December 1914.

40 Lord and Lady Aberdeen, *'We Twa'*, vol. 2, p. 236.

41 *Irish Times*, 14 December 1914. 'Castle throat' referred to the condition of a sore throat, which many correspondents claimed was rife throughout the Castle season of February and March.

42 *Ibid.*, 15 December 1914.

43 Captain Bellingham was killed in action in 1915.

44 The Mullingar branch of the WNHA was particularly active; at its annual meeting for 1914 the activities of the sewing class organised by Mrs Hyde had resulted in 'bales, consisting of shirts, socks, body belts, mufflers, helmets, gloves, mittens, etc. sent to the Front for the comforts of the troops'. *Westmeath Examiner*, 19 December 1914.

45 *Irish Times*, 17 December 1914.

46 *Freeman's Journal*, 28 January 1915.

47 K. Tynan Hinkson warmly admired Lady Aberdeen. She contributed articles to *Sláinte* and composed an ode of tribute (whose style imitates the Catholic Marian litany) upon her departure from Ireland: 'Lady of the Shining Heart, /Love and prayer your praises tell, /Now 'tis time for us to part, /Hail, beloved, and farewell! /Lady of the Giving Hand –/You who spent yourself so free/For this green and pleasant land/God, go with you oversea' etc., *Irish Independent*, 13 February 1915.

48 The hospital treated 6,496 patients in total. 176 patients were admitted as a result of the Easter rebellion including James Connolly.

49 Married to Dr Augustine Henry, she was the niece of nationalist historian Alice Stopford Green.

50 NLI, Ms. 7984, Diaries of Mrs Augustine Henry.

51 The depot opened in November 1915.

52 Bence-Jones, *Twilight of the Ascendancy*, p. 166.

53 M. Pakenham, *Brought Up and Brought Out* (London, Cobden-Sanderson, 1938), pp. 44–5.

54 NLI, Ms. 7984, Diaries of Mrs Augustine Henry.

55 *Irish Independent*, 25 March 1916.

56 Alice Henry Brunton provides detailed descriptions of her attempts to move around Dublin during the rebellion on IWHSD business, NLI, Ms. 7984. The Annual Report of the Central Sphagnum Depot for 1915–16 gives the following production figures for moss dressings during one of the bloodiest summers of the war – June 1916: 8,951; July 16: 15,200; August 1916: 11,444. The total number of dressings produced from November 1915 to October 1916 was 66,549. In listing some of the new production centres outside Dublin, the formation of the Ulster Sphagnum Moss Association, June 1916, is noted.

57 The majority of the students belonged to the Church of Ireland but religious toleration was a cherished aim of the institution and Catholics, Jews, Presbyterians and Methodists also attended.

58 A. V. O'Connor and S. M. Parkes, *Gladly Learn and Gladly Teach: Alexandra College and School 1866–1966* (Dublin, Blackwater Press, 1984), p. 69.

59 This scheme was inspired by social reformer Octavia Hill's work in London. The houses were renovated and moderate rents charged as the scheme was to be run on commercial lines. The tenants were responsible for the cleanliness of the properties while the Guild members provided and supervised a children's playroom, subsidised the price of coal, held sewing and singing classes, and established a Savings Bank and a tenants' library. Shakespeare, Scott and Dickens were the most popular authors.

60 O'Connor and Parkes, *Gladly Learn and Gladly Teach*, p. 73. Other projects included a club for factory girls in Harold's Cross with classes, a Penny Bank and a library; the Alexandra Children's Holiday Fund which provided a fortnight in the country for children from the tenement project and the factory girls; and the Pembroke Garden Village, twelve model cottages built by the Earl of Pembroke as a memorial to his father.

61 Lady Aberdeen served as President of the Guild until her departure in 1915 when her successor as Vicereine, Lady Wimborne, took over the role.

62 Merchant Thomas McCormick, whose two daughters were graduates of the College and members of the Guild, lent the premises for the workroom and the club.

63 *Alexandra College Magazine*, no. 46 (June 1915).

64 *Ibid.*. Enid Starkie, herself a past pupil of Alexandra College, recollected her mother's war work. May Starkie had also attended Alexandra College and was very active in Guild work. 'My mother followed my father in his devotion to the Allied cause. During the whole war she worked daily at a Red Cross depot rolling bandages and making sphagnum moss dressings for dispatch to the front. She helped also to organise a club for soldiers' wives, to keep them occupied in an innocent and innocuous manner, to prevent them from squandering on mere frivolity, their separation allowances. She sat on a committee of the Alexandra College Guild, which opened what Lizzie used to call a "hostile" for working girls, for young girls who had come up to town from the country to work in munitions factories.' E. Starkie, *A Lady's Child* (London, Faber & Faber, 1942), p. 200.

65 *Alexandra College Magazine*, no. 46 (June 1915).

66 *Ibid.* The workroom operated until 1916 when most of its employees found work in the munitions factory in Parkgate Street.

67 *Ibid.*

68 The cost of maintaining the hostel was estimated at £1,800. Alexandra College, *Alexandra College, Dublin: its History and its Work 1866–1916* (Dublin, Maunsel, 1919), p. 49.

69 Assisted by members of the nursing division, Dr Ella Webb, a former student of the college, transformed the depot into an improvised hospital during the Easter rebellion.

70 O'Connor and Parkes, *Gladly Learn and Gladly Teach*, pp. 100–2. Louisa Despard 'who was one of the pioneers of massage and physiotherapy, had written a standard textbook in 1910 and she supervised the massage department for wounded soldiers at the Ministry of Pensions Hospital at Blackrock.'

71 *Alexandra College Magazine*, no. 46 (June 1915).

72 *Ibid.*

73 NLI, Ms. 8271 (141), Hannay Papers, 24 January 1917.

74 *Ibid.*, Ms. 8271 (148), 29 May 1917.

75 Alexandra College, *Alexandra College*, p. 58. O'Connor and Parkes, *Gladly Learn and Gladly Teach*, pp. 118–19.

76 For a cursory consideration of this work see D. Urquhart, '"The female of the species is more deadlier than the male"? The Ulster Women's Unionist Council, 1911–40', in J. Holmes and D. Urquhart (eds), *Coming into the Light: The Work, Politics and Religion of Women in Ulster 1840–1940* (Belfast, Institute of Irish Studies, 1994), pp. 93–123.

77 *Belfast Telegraph*, 15 August 1914.

78 *Irish Post and Weekly Telegraph for Cavan and the Midlands*, 5 September 1914.

79 Mrs Lough also served as president of the Cavan branch of the WNHA and as Honorary Treasurer of the Irish Women's Association.

80 *Irish Post*, 3 October 1914; *Anglo-Celt*, 3 October 1914.

81 *Irish Post*, 21 November 1914.

82 *Anglo-Celt*, 17 October 1914.

83 *Irish Post*, 20 February 1915.

84 *Ibid.* At a fundraising concert CCWPC members formed a tableau depicting the allied nations and Lady Farnham sang 'with much sweetness of voice "When Irish Eyes Are Smiling", and in reply to an encore gave "Mother Machree".'

85 *Irish Post*, 12 December 1914.

86 *Ibid.*, 13 March 1915.

87 *Ibid.*, 6 March 1915.

88 *Ibid.*, 13 February 1915.

89 *Ibid.*, 27 March 1915.

90 *Ibid.*, 5 June 1915.

91 *Ibid.* This edition also noted that the Bawnboy branch of the CCWPC 'have sent 22 pounds of tobacco, 7,500 cigarettes, 24 briar pipes, and a large quantity of matches' to the 1st Battalion of the Royal Irish Rifles.

92 *Ibid.*, 4 September 1915, 4 December 1915. Cavan women also actively supported Julia, Lady Dartrey's Ambulance Fund for the Royal Irish Fusiliers. Enough money was raised to purchase three motor ambulances.

93 Research of individual counties during this period must be systematically undertaken in order to establish the complete picture of women's war work in Ireland but the evidence suggests that Cavan was typical in its activities and in its rejection of political and sectarian division within relevant women's associations. The exception to this is the work engaged in by women supporting the Ulster Volunteer Force who focused on the 36th Ulster Division as the sole beneficiary of their efforts, and, through the UWUC, emphasised their political partiality. No thorough research has been carried out on the war work of the UWUC.

94 *Church of Ireland Gazette*, 5 November 1915. Among the long list of titled patronesses were the Marchioness of Sligo, the Marchioness of Ormonde, the Dowager Marchioness of Dufferin and Ava, the Countess of Granard, the Countess of Antrim, the Countess of Mayo, the Countess of Bandon, the Countess of Kenmare, the Countess of Kerry, the Viscountess Gormanston, the Viscountess Powerscourt, the Lady Gwendolen Guinness, the Lady Clonbrock, the Lady Russell of Killowen and the Lady Fitzgerald of Valentia.

95 The association purchased all of its supplies at wholesale prices and established a bonded warehouse to avoid paying duty on items such as tea, sugar and cigarettes. Each parcel contained tins of biscuits, beef, vegetables, milk, soup, fish, Worcester sauce, jam or syrup, tea, sugar, fruit, cocoa, coffee or cheese, mustard, salt, cigarettes or tobacco, soap and a pair of socks or a towel.

96 *Church of Ireland Gazette*, 10 December 1915.

97 *Ibid.*, 10 December 1915 and 8 June 1917. Another prisoner sent his thanks in rhyming couplet – 'Many thanks for your kindness done/For your Parcels keep us going strong;/Prisoners all, with best respects,/Remember the Women, who did not forget.'

98 *Ibid.*, 11 February 1916.

99 S. Pašeta, *Before the Revolution: Nationalism, Social Change and Ireland's Catholic Elite, 1879–1922* (Cork, Cork University Press, 1999).

100 *Irish Monthly*, December 1917.

101 *Catholic Bulletin*, September 1914.

102 *Ibid.*, July 1915.

103 The solitary and deeply unsatisfactory example of such research is C. A. Culleton's 'Irish working-class women and World War I', in S. Shaw Sailer, (ed.) *Representing Ireland: Gender, Class, Nationality* (Florida, University Press of Florida, 1997), pp. 156–80.

4

Work, warfare and wages: industrial controls and Irish trade unionism in the First World War

THERESA MORIARTY

At the end of the First World War the increased political power of working-class men, whose lives were spent on the killing fields of Europe and beyond, was affirmed in political systems from manhood suffrage to Bolshevism. The radical promise of pre-war labour battles was realised by strong trade union membership and a more cohesive labour movement in all the industrialised countries that had been at war. This chapter will look at part of that process as it unfolded in Ireland. This is not a study of Irish trade unions' response to war, though it will touch on that question. It deliberately avoids traditional narratives and moves the spotlight from well-known dramatic events in order to accommodate the background picture against which these took place.

In 1914 Irish trade unionism was retrenching after a period of militancy which lasted from 1911–13. Its movement was structured around craftsmen's organisations, both Irish and British, with Irish branches of British amalgamated unions, and newer general unions for unskilled workers. Foremost among these was the relatively new Irish Transport and General Workers' Union (ITGWU) formed in 1909. Trade unionism was strongest in Belfast and Dublin, and in those cities or towns where trades councils organised around local priorities. Its most public presence was the national forum of the Irish Trade Union Congress (ITUC), held every year since 1894, for affiliated trade unions and trades councils to air their grievances and determine policy.

In 1914 the ITUC comprised a more class conscious, socialist leadership – a consequence of the years of militancy – which was represented by its president that year, James Larkin, general secretary of the ITGWU, the first leader of an unskilled union to hold that position. Congress demonstrated its keener political interest by redrafting its title as the ITUC and Labour Party between 1912 and 1914. Its affiliated membership in 1914 was 110,000.[1] Much of the Irish workforce existed beyond the structures of this official movement, in unions that remained aloof from local or national structures or at workplaces beyond the remit of trade unionism altogether.

Dublin trade unionism was drained after the six months' long city and county lockout of 1913. It was the largest and longest industrial struggle in a year noted for the highest number of recorded strikes in the United Kingdom. It had engaged the city's entire trade union movement, and taken an enormous toll on finances, stamina and members. Many workers had lost their jobs, and were refused reinstatement after the formal end of the dispute in February 1914. An exhausted Jim Larkin left Ireland for the United States in November 1914.

Irish trade unions organised workers in a hostile climate. Employers, whether paternalistic dynasties like Guinness, or strong employers' associations that governed the linen industry, opposed trade unions. Although some had reached accommodation with skilled workers' unions, they were unanimously hostile to general labourers' unions. Dublin's employers had demonstrated their unity dramatically during 1913 when over 400 combined against their workers in the lockout.[2]

A third party had ventured onto the contested ground between workers and employers as the British state increasingly mediated between them through a number of new agencies, frequently modelled on developments in other countries, which admitted workers' representation. A conciliation process had been in place for nearly twenty years through the Conciliation Act of 1896, which acknowledged trade union principles of collective bargaining and negotiation. State initiatives with most impact were more recent. Trade boards, set up in 1909, included employers' and workers' representatives, to address questions of long hours, poor conditions and low wages in the sweated industries where women worked. Established in the same year, labour exchanges had made little impact on high Irish unemployment figures. The most onerous burden of state intervention on trade unions was the National Insurance Act, 1911. Approved trade unions collected subscriptions from their members to supplement unemployment and sickness benefit paid in by employers and state contributions. Insured workers could claim unemployment benefit at the new exchanges.

Such measures had made little impact in Ireland. In 1914 the single Irish trade board was for paper box making, with Delia Larkin, secretary of the Irish Women Workers' Union (IWWU) as a workers' representative. The report of the 1912–13 linen trade inquiry promised a trade board, but it had not been set up. National Insurance was difficult to collect, and many unions' financial dealings did not measure up to the strict scrutiny that state administration required. Few Irish labour exchanges were opened. Unemployed workers were not required to register while employers were not compelled to advertise vacancies. Workers were allowed to turn down employment at non-union rates. Traditional routes of employment, through craft unions' 'idle books' of unemployed members, or nomination by family members 'speaking for' a relative, remained more effective. These state agencies underwent significant modification in war, as wartime controls multiplied.

War had a mixed effect on Ireland's industrial fortunes. The immediate impact of war was disruption of industry. Belfast shipbuilding, which was to flourish in wartime conditions, suffered initial dislocation as reserve soldiers were called up in August on the declaration of war, and workers left for other industrial districts in Britain.[3] Employment in that city's engineering industry was badly affected by the loss of continental demand for textile machinery. Linen workers were put on short time in Belfast, Lurgan, Antrim and Drogheda. For two weeks after war was declared Belfast weavers worked a twenty-eight hour week while spinners dropped to forty hours per week. Derry shirtworkers' hours were cut to thirty five hours per week for about a month. Short time, which protected workers from dismissal, had a devastating impact on low wages, especially for women textile workers. In the linen industry wages fell by ten per cent.[4]

Workers in 'non-essential' trades felt the greatest impact of wartime disturbance. Luxury trades suffered most. Bespoke tailors in Belfast were on a two-day week. The shirt collar industry collapsed, putting shirt laundries on short time. There was unemployment in 'certain classes of handkerchief makers in Belfast'. Printing was slack. In Dublin unemployment was high among cabinetmakers, and seamstresses were dismissed. Clerical workers, too, were laid off. Engineering was virtually at a standstill in the city. In some respects wartime dislocation reinforced the unsettled pattern of pre-war industry with high unemployment and poor trade. The war's impact on industry was to affect the course of Irish trade unionism over the next four years.

The call-up of army reservists had an immediate effect on wartime industry. Enlisted men who had completed military service were on twelve years' reserve in August 1914. Their mobilisation began immediately war was declared, and overrode any essential industrial skills they possessed. The customary preference of some industries to employ ex-soldiers added to immediate shortages in male occupations. An enthusiastic recruitment campaign added to this scarcity. Shortages of skilled workers, generally trade union members to a man, led to extended short time in many industries. The competing demands for men and supplies continued throughout the war. Elsewhere in Ireland, in unskilled occupations the call-up and recruitment sometimes benefited workers' employment. There was 'a scarcity of men, owing to the numbers who had been called to the colours' among Cork and Limerick dockworkers.[5]

By the first spring of the war, when industry had settled down to wartime conditions, and the 'butchers bill'[6] began to be reckoned, 2,700 ITWGU members, mostly unskilled, were in the trenches, 'equivalent to over half the union's membership on the eve of the Easter Rising'.[7] A frequent complaint arose that employers forced men into the army. The *Workers' Republic*, edited by James Connolly, reporting the Dublin trades council's unanimous resolution to oppose conscription suggests the practice was widespread:

> Dismissing men of military age from their employment, both married and single, and endeavouring to starve themselves and their families, is a very obnoxious form of Conscription, as it enables the well-to-do and upper classes to evade their duties. Nearly all the employers are doing it.[8]

Murray's study of Dublin's Power's distillery recounts how one Dublin employer co-operated with Department of Recruitment initiatives to encourage their workmen of military age to join up.[9] In 1914 domestic politics was more concerned with the 'apparent approach of Home Rule [which] most powerfully stimulated Labour's interest in political questions'.[10] The outbreak of war in August 1914 sent tremors through Ireland, which was already wracked by political divisions about its contested future.

The cost of living rose sharply on the outbreak of war, as food prices quickly increased. In Belfast and Dublin the cost of a 4lb loaf of bread increased by a halfpenny between August and October 1914.[11] An early public response to war by the Irish trade union movement was the ITUC manifesto, 'Why should Ireland starve?'. Its author rehearsed a classic socialist critique of war, as 'the aggrandisement of the capitalistic class' and called for the more efficient use of land.[12] Congress called on local authorities to take immediate control of Ireland's food supply. It evoked memories of the Famine, in direct challenge to any government policy to use Ireland as a food supply and exhorted Irish workers to prevent food exports:

> To the men of our class who are armed we say, keep your arms and use them if necessary ... Do not allow our crops to be gleaned for any other country ... Keep them at home by the strength of your right arm![13]

This demonstrated in militant language that Irish labour would not comply with government wartime measures that put British needs above Irish necessity. Irish trade unionism stated its aloofness from any dealing with government, whilst it was almost certainly not consulted.

The official trade union response in Britain was quite different from Ireland's. The day after war with Germany was declared an Emergency Workers' National Committee was called, representing 'virtually every section of the labour movement'.[14] Before the first month of war was over the British Labour Party appealed for an industrial truce and an immediate end to all existing trade disputes. This was negotiated between the government and trade unions in the Treasury agreement on 17 March 1915, signed by the TUC, to stop all 'trade practices' for the duration of the hostilities.

Government wartime policy towards industry was built on this compliance and shaped itself around four persistent issues on the home front: the need to maintain essential war supplies; the need to address labour shortages arising from military mobilisation, the rising cost of living; and the necessity of keeping the peace in industry. Wartime production needed unions' support. Asquith's Liberal government, already committed to state intervention in industry, signalled its readiness for fuller intervention by taking over the railways in Britain, and some time later in Ireland in 1917. The state adopted apparently labour-friendly policies, which included workers' representatives on a series of wartime committees. Government control of industry was distributed through a network of committees and state agencies. The committees increased regulation of industry as government contracted wartime supplies. Expensive and urgent government contracts required co-operation and control over employers, which eventually spread to the takeover of necessary industries.

Industrial co-operation required concessions as well as coercion. In an attempt to meet complaints about wartime profits, concessions were made to collective bargaining. Ship builders and engineers won national wage agreements at a uniform rate. The state, led by government policies, asserted its role as national arbiter through the crisis of war. This approach intensified as the war stretched out and the government went into coalition, first under Asquith in 1915, and especially in 1916, when British Labour Party leaders joined the Lloyd George coalition.

Sir George Askwith, who led the inquiry into the Dublin lockout in 1913, headed the first and most powerful Committee on Production in February 1915 to regulate shipbuilding and engineering. This body, on which employers sat, but not trade unionists, set the wartime industrial agenda: a ban on strikes and lockouts, compulsory arbitration and suspension of restrictive practices, based on traditional working customs.

The Munitions of War Act in July 1915 broadened these terms to include all wartime industry. It outlawed all strikes and lockouts in munitions work; enacted powers to extend this ban to any other stoppages, and enforced binding arbitration, by demanding 21 days' notice of disputes to allow referral to arbitration. It classified private companies on munitions contracts as 'controlled establishments' where profits were limited, and practices or customs that restricted production or employment were suspended for the duration of the war. Companies were forbidden to employ anyone without leaving certificates from their previous employers, before six weeks had elapsed. Munitions tribunals consisted of a lawyer, sitting with an employer and trade unionist. Further modifications of this law were made in 1916 and 1917.

Though the munitions acts were intended to ward off damaging strikes, their impact was far wider. Compulsory and binding arbitration applied to disputes across industry and were not limited to munitions factories. Lloyd George's plan to control drink was less successful. Nationalisation of the liquor industry was ruled out, in favour of licensing hours – a legacy which

Irish and British governments still grapple with. (A striking exception was the nationalisation of pubs and the brewery in Carlisle, a centre of munitions production, until privatisation by Heath's conservative government in the 1970s.)

The expanding army, conscripted in Britain from May 1916, had to be supplied. A slow build-up of War Office contracts arrived for Irish firms, principally textile and clothing companies, overwhelmingly staffed by women. Irish firms produced a wide range of military supplies, from leather accoutrements to water supplies for military camps. By 1917 Irish woollen mills were turning out blankets throughout the country. Woollen mills in Midleton, Glenties, Foxford, Tralee, Ballygawley, Dripsey, Galway, Beaufort, Lisbellaw, Castlederg, Kilmeaden and Crumlin, Co. Antrim were working on War Office contracts. In Derry and Belfast twenty-three companies supplied shirts and flannel. Uniforms were manufactured in Belfast, Dublin and Limerick. Boilers were supplied from the Sirrocco Works in Belfast. Irish companies supplied bedding and brushes. Others maintained war department buildings. There was a little haberdashery, and some public works, frequently building national schools.[15] Virtually all such work came under munitions legislation in 1915.

War Department orders modified employment cutbacks in a number of industries. The hours of Derry shirtworkers on short time lengthened again, towards the end of August 1914, 'owing to the receipt of government orders'.[16] 'One large firm in [the] South on short time', resumed full time production towards the end of December.[17] Linen fabrics, including tablecloths and towels, were ordered from all the prominent linen manufacturers in Belfast. Flannel bands were ordered from Welch and Margetson in Derry, hosiery from the Templecrone Co-op in Dungloe, saddlery from the Enniscorthy Agricultural Co-operative, roof felting from R. McCalmont in Belfast and even panniers from J. H. Hewitt's Workshops for the Industrious Blind in Belfast. Irish printing firms received orders for Irish recruitment posters[18] though apparently little of the massive print runs, amounting to tens of thousands, for army pay books and the reams of official documentation required in the mass military mobilisation.

Awards of government contracts to Irish firms did not compare with the scale of war work done by British companies, and much of it was concentrated in the north. It was a constant complaint throughout the war that Ireland had not benefited from the award of such contracts. Procuring war contracts by Irish firms became a contested political issue, especially by the Irish Parliamentary Party. It centred on calls for munitions, and local committees formed to urge the opening of munitions works. In Galway a local pressure group was formed in April 1916 to urge the Ministry of Munitions to establish a shell factory in Galway. The Harbour Board, County Council, and the UDC supported the campaign. The committee included local worthies including the Lord Lieutenant of the county, and Martin McDonagh, chairman of the UDC. After months of lobbying with support from John Redmond, the shell factory was opened. On 17 February the first shell was manufactured under the supervision of Captain Downie, chief expert of the munitions ministry in Ireland. It was inscribed and dedicated to Martin McDonagh. [19]

Wartime needs, the urgency of production, and labour shortages, combined to provide unprecedented bargaining strength to workers' claims. It was no longer necessary to depend on mass strikes backed by community support to win recognition for collective bargaining from unwilling employers – an approach which had characterised pre-war trade union strategies. Procedures were in place that recognised collective bargaining, constructed on recognised points of negotiation.

An immediate domestic impact of war was hardship. In addition to the call up of male breadwinners, short time, dismissals and lost wages, prices began an inexorable rise as the war economy took hold, demanding high production, long hours and fewer goods in an inflationary spiral. The swift and remorseless rise in the cost of living forced a war time bonus in industry. The war bonus, 'recognised as due and dependent on the existence of abnormal conditions now prevailing in consequence of the war',[20] was paid directly from government or employers' profits from government contracts or price rises, on which the war bonus rate was based. The war bonus built in a negotiating standard to pay claims, and was a frequent element of union claims. Irish employers, who were consistently accused of paying lower rates, now answered to the arbitration of state appointed lawyers, who frequently had to assess awards on agreements elsewhere.

An Industrial Commissioner or the Committee on Production conducted compulsory arbitration. In munitions cases after 1915 a Special Arbitration Tribunal sat. Claims for arbitration were inevitably brought by trade unions, against named employers or their association. This conciliation and arbitration process rarely dismissed claims, though it sometimes reduced them, and enforced their awards against reluctant employers. Refusal to comply by either side was punishable by fines, which if not paid, might lead to imprisonment.

Compulsory arbitration, which trade unions feared as industrial conscription, conversely encouraged trade unionism. It established consistently successful representation and negotiation by unions, which attracted members. It encouraged group claims by unions, and comparative claims, both of which encouraged the influence of British-based unions in Ireland.

Ireland's key wartime industries were shipbuilding and engineering. In this they most closely mirrored the British wartime industrial profile. North of Ireland workers in both industries staked claim after claim in the war years, which were referred to the Committee on Production. This committee

awarded time workers at both Harland & Wolff and Workman, Clark shipyards three shillings a week in a claim made by twenty unions in 1916. There
were similar group claims by unions in the engineering and foundry trades.

Success in one place encouraged workers elsewhere. An engineers' claim,
followed by labourers, at one of the Irish 'National Projectile Factories' in
1917 was based on a Committee on Production award to unskilled and semi-
skilled workers in the London engineering trade. The British-based labourers' unions, the Workers' Union and National Union of General Workers,
failed to make their case. Skilled men would be paid a war bonus on output.
Many strikes involved large numbers of the workforce. A dispute in Belfast
and Lurgan begun on 10 September 1917 by 370 tenters ultimately involved
12,000 workers, for a wage increase of £1 a week.[21]

Not only were British-based unions engaged in this process, but Irish
unions too took advantage of the opportunity offered by compulsory arbitration to attempt a range of wage-bargaining strategies. For example, high
bread prices led to disputes with the master bakers. A drawn-out process of
arbitration in the Dublin bakery trade began in November 1916. In March
1917 the Irish Bakers National Amalgamated Union won 'supplemental
terms of agreement'. In November the bakery workers' union and the
ITGWU, made a bold and comprehensive claim for across the board wage
increases of fifteen shillings a week for bakers, twelve shilling a week for
breadvan drivers, and six shillings for apprentices. They also demanded an
eight-hour day, the abolition of Sunday work, increased overtime rates, and
trade union labour. The claim was, however, only partially successful. Time
workers' wages were increased by three shillings a week, and piece workers
won a ten per cent rise as war bonus. Carters were awarded a further shilling
for travelling costs. In 1917 an IWWU claim for an advance on wages
against Tighe & Sons, Dublin led to an award of double their war bonus.
Workers at the Blackrock Hosiery Company in Dublin, organised by the
IWWU, were paid the same war bonus as hosiery workers in Leicester,
England's primary hosiery district.[22]

Arbitration encouraged organisation. In August 1917 engineers and
bricklayers represented by the Amalgamated Society of Engineers (ASE) and
the Ancient Guild of Incorporated Brick and Stone Layers, with company
engine drivers and boilermen, brought separate claims for increases against
Kynoch's, which produced cordite explosives on War Department contracts
in Arklow. A counter-claim by the company not to pay the boilermen was
turned down.[23] Within weeks of the awards being issued a massive explosion
at the factory on 21 September killed twenty-seven men working in the
explosives factory.[24] An ITGWU branch was formed there shortly afterwards.[25]

The government's determination to head off strikes through arbitration
led to the converse result. A consequence of its policy was to encourage

strikes. The conciliation process, demanding three weeks' notification, did not allow for short eruptions of protest. But a strike could settle a dispute within a few days. Strikes and the threat of strikes could also guarantee arbitration, bringing reluctant sides to the negotiating table. A strike call by Irish railwaymen, at the end of November 1916, forced the government to take control of the Irish railway companies, as they had done in Britain at the start of the war, and workers received a seven shilling bonus.

In the only study of wartime strikes in Ireland, David Fitzpatrick argues that before the war, with the exception of the Dublin lockout, Irish trade unionism 'was abnormally docile in every sector analysed'.[26] Heavy unemployment, 'nearly twice the average rates for the United Kingdom', in the major industries of building, engineering, shipbuilding and printing, hampered trade union organisation. Military necessity eclipsed such obstacles. The first Irish dispute of the war recorded by the Board of Trade was in October 1914, when carpenters constructing huts at Ballykinlar Camp, Co. Down went on strike for a week for higher wages. Army hut building supplied necessary work for branches of the building trade, where men had been thrown out of work at the outset of war.

'In each successive year between 1915 and 1918 Irish strike activity became more intense, whether measured according to the number of strikes, strikers or workdays lost.'[27] In 1915 there was a drawn-out dispute on Dublin docks. The following year there were large-scale strikes among printers, builders, transport workers, male linen workers, shipyard workers, engineers and labourers throughout the country. One dispute that has received little attention from historians was a building strike called on 1 April 1916 involving 1,500 bricklayers, carpenters, joiners, plasterers, and building labourers in Dublin.[28] It lasted thirty-three working days, including the week of the Easter Rising, and led to a 'modified advance' in wages.

Strikes could guarantee arbitration. 250 Dublin gas workers, striking for wage increases resumed work after five days, pending arbitration. Some disputes involved large groups of workers. An unsuccessful flax spinners' strike in October 1917 involved over a thousand linen workers in Belfast. A month later a strike in Belfast's shipyards, which lasted ten days and involved 3,000 piece workers in many grades of work, led to negotiations. In the last year of the war strike activity increased dramatically. The strike record of 1918 was higher than any previous year, with the exception of 1913. In April 1918 four of the fourteen principal disputes in Britain and Ireland, reported in the *Labour Gazette*, took place in Ireland.

A measure of unions' increasing confidence in strike action is seen in non-waged issues in some 1918 disputes. A strike in June 1918 at the Dublin shell factory protested against the dismissal of trade unionists when male dilutees (unskilled workers taken on in skilled trades) were retained. An engineering workers' strike in July and August won the reinstatement of two workmen.

Cork linen workers struck against bonus deductions because of machinery breakdown. Dublin building workers struck against the 'alleged dismissal of work people without due notice'.[29] Belfast printers combined a wages claim with a demand for trade union recognition. Newry linen workers went on strike at the end of January, refusing to work with non trade unionists. The April anti-conscription general strike was not counted by the Board of Trade, but a follow-up two-day strike by Drogheda building workers, who 'refused to work with certain men who had not observed the "play day" on 23rd April against the application of conscription to Ireland', was.

As wartime measures regulated industry, labour exchanges became a more coercive control for managing labour shortages. Their function now harmonised with National Insurance, which paid unemployment benefit, and Munitions of War legislation, which prohibited workers leaving employment without a permit. A more specific purpose of Irish labour exchanges was to recruit Irish workers to fill labour shortages in Britain. 'Refusal of reasonable offers would result in the cessation of dole payments. Those accepting work were guaranteed exemption from conscription.'[30] Official exemption did not guarantee a welcome to such essential labour. In November 1916 a thousand metal workers in the English midlands struck for one day, refusing to work with Irishmen of military age. The *Labour Gazette* dryly records that the result was that the Irishmen returned to Ireland.[31] The Irish trade union movement complained that unemployed, insured workers were offered work that took no account of their skills. The 1917 report of the ITUC detailed a number of cases.[32]

One of the more public examples of this form of industrial coercion was the case of John Swift, later general secretary of the bakers' union. He was offered building work in Scotland. When this damaged the young bakery worker's health he returned to Dublin and was offered a job in a London leadworks. There he led a strike against working conditions and was brought before a tribunal. He was charged under the Defence of the Realm Act, court-martialled, and imprisoned in Wormwood Scrubbs. He was conscripted, despite the intervention of his parents, and questions raised in parliament. He fought in France during the German spring offensive of 1918, and was not demobilised until November 1919.[33]

The greatest impact of wartime measures on Irish trade unionism was to encourage organisation among workers previously outside the trade union movement. Before the outbreak of war, trade unionism's urban and male character had not extended its organisation in any significant way to either agricultural workers or women. Agricultural labourers' circumstances were transformed by wartime conditions. Many joined up; others went to Britain to work. For the first time there was a perceptible shortage of agricultural labour. High food prices benefiting the farmers provided a national grievance about wages and conditions.[34]

A rural organisation campaign led by the ITGWU came in the wake of two government measures. The Corn Production Act of 1917 enforced the transfer of pasture to tillage, a more intensive form of agriculture which required more labour. The act established a National Agricultural Wages Board for Ireland to include workers' representatives. It made its first award in September for implementation in November, of minimum weekly rates of twenty-five shillings for men over twenty-one, and fifteen shillings for women over eighteen years. Rates for younger men were fixed in January. Wages were fixed on a summer and winter rate, for eight-, nine- and ten-hour days. 'Settlements above the minimum could be won where organisation was strong.'[35] J. J. Mallon, the Irishman who had headed the Anti-Sweating League in Britain which led to the Trades Board Act in 1906, and secretary to workers' representatives on the Irish trade boards, carried a detailed report of the award in the trade union paper, Irish Opinion, in January 1918. The act legislated the trade union demand of the 1914 ITUC, for grazing land to be cultivated. The 1917 ITUC delegates heard a call for a minimum wage for all agricultural workers, and were informed of protests in Kenmare where the following was allegedly observed: 'smashing the farmers and letting the potatoes run about the streets for the people'.[36]

The first workers' representatives were drawn from the Irish Land and Labour Associations.[37] By January 1918 the ITGWU represented agricultural labourers on the National Wages Board and many local boards.[38] The lesson, as Irish Opinion stated, was that they should join a union. Agricultural workers quickly responded to the ITGWU recruitment drive, joining up in unprecedented numbers, which accounted for the spectacular growth of that union. The new confidence among agricultural labour was highlighted by the organisation of west of Ireland potato harvesters by Peadar O'Donnell, linking up with the Scottish Farm Servant Workers' Union, in a boycott of the 1918 harvest in Scotland. Young men and women refused to travel, though the Irish Railway Executive, now running the state-controlled railways, sent a train hired by the farmers and their agents.[39]

Another important change, which has received little attention, was the growth and spread of trade unionism among women workers during these years. The substitution of male workers with women was not as widespread in Irish industry as it was in Britain: most Irish women continued to work in traditional industries. Women industrial workers, like agricultural workers, were outside the official trade union movement in 1914. Few women attended the ITUC as delegates, and the only female representation at the annual conferences came from the few existing women's unions: the Textile Operatives Society of Ireland (TOSI), affiliated to the ITUC since 1901, the Lurgan Hemmers and Veiners, affiliated briefly in 1911,[40] and the IWWU from 1912.

The majority of craft unions, Irish and British, excluded women. Many

viewed women's labour as a threat, undermining traditional working practices. Women were employed in mechanised sectors within printing, tailor-
ing, food processing, or in domestic manufacturing, where trade unions did
not reach. Women were still viewed as a relatively new industrial workforce
and as a source of cheap labour. Non-industrial trade unions, like the
Drapers' Assistants' Association and the Irish National Teachers'
Organisation – which eschewed the term trade union in their titles – had
women members. The Drapers' Assistants had formed a women's section in
1912, though no women represented them at Congress, and the National
Teachers' Organisation, with reserved seats for women on their national
executive, were not affiliated to the ITUC until 1918, when they sent two
women delegates. Other unions such as the Flax Roughers and Yarn
Spinners admitted women members, but they had no full-time women officials.

The largest group of trade unionised women were linen workers. In 1914
just over 3,000 women linen workers were trade union members, in TOSI or
the Flax Roughers and Yarn Spinners, both Belfast unions. The insured
workforce of Irish linen workers totalled 30,000, almost two-thirds of them
in Belfast. The linen industry, Ireland's largest, employed a huge workforce
outside the factory system. Short time remained a problem within this industry throughout the war. The secretary of TOSI, Mary Galway, complained
that wages had been cut rather than allowing the 'older hands to work a full
week, and release three or four thousand of the younger for munition work'.
Even the wages on war department contracts making aeroplane linen had
dropped: in one case she cited, from nine shillings to just over six.[41]

Most linen workplaces were on War Department contracts, making everything from uniforms to tea towels. There were a number of strikes by linen
workers for wage increases, mainly in Belfast, where the linen unions
frequently went into arbitration together. Linen may have been one of the
industries where the wartime volunteer workforce made an impact on
employment. It was reported that 'bitter complaints against voluntary
workers come from the textile workers'.[42]

But the need for linen did not enhance the status of the unions with the
authorities. When the Flax (Restriction of Consumption) Order 1917 came
into force in January 1918, prohibiting linen processing without a permit,
the Irish Flax Control Board was composed only of linen manufacturers. 'A
labour advisory committee was to be established when questions involving
the interest of labour are under consideration.'[43] Despite this, women's trade
unionism increased. By 1915 TOSI had branches across the north, and in
Drogheda and Kilkenny. The long promised trade board for the linen industry was finally set up. At the end of the war 20,000 women were trade union
members. These were divided equally between TOSI, 'entirely officered by
women', and the Flax Roughers and Yarn Spinners.[44]

The clothing industry, among the most disrupted by the outbreak of war, was working to a steady supply of war contracts, especially in the shirt factories of the north west, with a mainly female workforce. Derry shirt factories were on short time for much of the war. The Amalgamated Society of Tailors and Tailoresses (ASTT), with a British headquarters, organised the Irish clothing trade. It was a craft society, with a largely male membership, many in the bespoke trade, which had suffered badly in the war. It had strong centres in Cork and Dublin, but its most prominent figure was James McCarron, a Derry tailor. He had been President of the ITUC on three occasions. A 'Londonderry Factory Workers' branch appears in the ASTT reports from 1913. Its first secretary was Kathy Young. The wartime growth of a rival British union, the United Garment Workers, after 1915 forced the ASTT, against its inclinations, to recruit factory workers, mainly women. A further impetus to unionise came from the formation of a shirtmaking trade board for Ireland at the end of 1915. Three women and one man joined as workers' representatives, including Miss K. Young, suggesting they were nominated by the ASTT.[45] Membership of the branch grew to more than 3,000 in 1917.[46] At the end of the war ASTT membership in Britain and Ireland had increased from 12,000 to 27,000, two-thirds of them women.[47] At the 1918 ITUC the eight ASTT delegates included two Dublin women from the 'Female Section', the first ASTT women members to attend.

A Confectionery and Jam Making Wages Board had been established for the Irish food processing industry in September 1915. The British National Federation of Women Workers (NFWW) nominated three women and J. J. Mallon as workers' representatives. This Irish trade board fixed a minimum wage of 10s 10d a week. One firm was found to be paying its women 4s 6d.[48]

The IWWU had not matched this steady pattern of organisation in the early years of the war. This Dublin-based organisation, led by Delia Larkin as an adjunct of the ITGWU, organised a variety of different workers. In 1914 half of its members were still unemployed after the Dublin lockout. Its activities centred on co-operative workshops in Liberty Hall, where it, and its secretary in particular, were the focus of acrimonious in-fighting. Delia Larkin, isolated after her charismatic brother, James, went to America in November 1914, left the union and Ireland in the summer of 1915.[49] James Connolly appointed Helena Molony to reorganise the union. The preparations for and the aftermath of the Easter Rising, in which Helena Molony and many IWWU members participated as members of the Citizen Army, brought further disruption to its trade union organisation.[50]

In October 1916 the *Woman Worker*, the monthly journal of the NFWW, paid tribute to the IWWU. It stated: 'Ireland has been in everyone's thoughts since the events of last Easter week', acknowledging that the effect of the rising on the Irish labour movement, 'and on women workers in particular', had not had the 'attention it deserves':

The rising has left the ranks of Irish Trade Unionism sadly depleted, and the Irish Women Workers' Union has had to bear its share of the losses ... We wish the Irish Union of Women Workers the very best of luck.[51]

Women were also active in the manufacturing of munitions. The increasing demand for munitions on the war front required women to enter this industry. By 1917 National Shell Factories were established in Cork, Dublin, Galway and Waterford. There were other women munitions workers in Ireland at company-owned works such as Pierces in Wexford or Mackies in Belfast. The workforce in the new shell factories was overwhelmingly female. Only five per cent of this industrial workforce could be male under government munitions regulations. The women recruited to work in these factories were unionised by the NFWW. It had never organised in Ireland before. Its pre-war association in Ireland was with TOSI and its secretary, Mary Galway, through their joint origins in the Women's Trade Union League (WTUL).[52] Mary Macarthur, NFWW secretary, and a trade unionist of some experience in the WTUL,[53] formed the national federation from scattered local women's unions, mostly in traditional female industries, in 1906. That year she had worked with Mary Galway in the Belfast linen strike. By 1918 the NFWW maintained offices in London, Glasgow and the Black Country.

The NFWW arrived in Ireland with a decade of industrial experience organising women workers and a record of successful challenges on their behalf. In 1915 it won negotiating rights for women in wartime engineering with the agreement of the ASE, who were anxious to limit other unions organising semi-skilled and unskilled engineering workers. The growth of women's munition work supplied the NFWW with new strength and bargaining power. Its monthly journal, the *Woman Worker*, relaunched in 1916, kept an occasional watching brief on developments within women's trade unionism in Ireland. In 1916 it reported on women's low wages at an Irish wire hosemaking manufacturers', 'the one factory of the kind in Ireland', complaining that, 'The machinery of the Munitions Act has not been applied systematically to Ireland'.[54]

The Federation opened branches in Ireland in 1918, almost as part of the machinery of wartime regulation, giving it a distinct advantage over any other women's union in Ireland. The Federation worked to its strengths. Its aim, as its earlier report had signalled, was to enforce munitions regulations, standardising Irish practice for women workers, including a compulsory minimum wage of £1 per week to all women in government controlled employment, where it had most leverage. It organised on a far wider geographical spread than any Irish women's union, with branches in Cork, Dublin, Galway, Londonderry, Waterford and Wexford, all districts with numerically significant women's employment outside munitions work. Irish branches retained one-sixth of their funds for expenses. The rest went 'to England'. Contributions of between 3d and 8d a week included sickness benefit and unemployment benefit.[55] It appointed Irish organisers, first Helen Flowers, and later Margaret Buckley, NFWW Irish president. From May 1918 until August 1919 the *Woman Worker* carried regular branch reports as 'Irish Notes', signed by 'our Irish correspondent'.

During its short term in Ireland between 1918 and 1919 the NFWW contributed much to Irish trade unionism. It reinforced the increasing visibility of women in the trade union movement, and built a structure for a national women's union. Its main wartime achievement was its successful claim for women munition workers. In April 1918 a Special Arbitration Tribunal for Women Employed on Munitions Work hearing at Dublin's Shelbourne Hotel raised Irish rates and war bonus. Increases and back pay were not only paid to the shell workers, but also to messengers, canteen attendants, charwomen and cloakroom women. The NFWW saw the charwomen's case being 'useful all over the country'.[56] The award put Irish women's pay on an equal footing with women workers doing similar work in Britain. It had been a frequent complaint by trade unionists that Irish women worked at a consistently lower wage than British women.

The NFWW provided many women with their first experience of national trade unionism. In Cork it organised women in the shell factory and a later second branch in the Douglas woollen mills. The Cork branch held its 'First real branch meeting' in June 1918.[57] The Derry branch, 'Silence is their golden rule', was affiliated to the city trade council by May 1918. In Dublin a successful compensation claim in May 1918 abolished the overlapping half hour (an unpaid half hour to cover shift changes) in all the national shell factories. In September 1918, at the Dublin shell factory, 29 men went on strike and 595 women were locked out, and another NFWW ambition was realised: 'We have got that Shop-Stewards Committee so long sought for by us.'[58]

In Galway, probably its most successful centre, there were three branches of the NFWW: the first in the shell factory; the second in the Galway Woollen Mills, and the third in the Corrib hosiery factory. Free rooms were provided to the women's union branches at the dockers' union hall. Shell production in Waterford began in 1917, at a converted railway terminus with a local workforce that had been trained in Britain.[59] The NFWW anticipated setting up more branches in the city. In Wexford the core of the NFWW was the munitions workers in Pierces, but it included knitting workers organised in 1918, and a printing section. Both appear to be the remaining branch members after the war. There may have been members in other districts – an NFWW badge has been dug up in a garden in Bennetstown, Co Kilkenny.

Branch members not only joined trade union structures, but they engaged with its culture as organised workers. On May Day 1918 in Waterford 'The Federation took the place of honour in the procession', and Helen Flowers spoke at the rally, encouraging women from another company in the city to join up.[60] In 1919 the NFWW was represented at May Day parades in Dublin, Cork, Galway, Waterford and Wexford, with Margaret Buckley on the Cork platform and Helen Flowers on the Galway one.[61]

The NFWW branches did not long survive the war. They lost members immediately the work of the shell factories ended. In February 1919 Waterford members held their first meeting since the closing of the factory, planning to hold monthly meetings 'so as to keep in touch with one another'. The secretary reported, 'this the first meeting was very poorly attended and I am feeling very disheartened. But Waterford is not the only place where the members have in the last few weeks forgotten they ever had a Union and what the Union had done for them. The same happened in Cork and Galway and even in Dublin.' [62]

After the armistice, on 20 November 300 women in the Dublin shell factory were dismissed. Three days' holidays for munition workers began the following day. One of the last cases taken by the NFWW was for a full week's notice or pay. The directors refused and the London office appealed to the Ministry of Labour. The NFWW was also busy dealing with appeals from women whose unemployment benefit was suspended because they had turned down work (which they were entitled to do if it paid less than 25 shillings a week). Women in Cork, Galway and Waterford were left for months without benefit.[63]

By the summer of 1919 Irish NFWW members were scattered, and branches had disbanded. Few women found new jobs. There were no training centres similar to the ones established in Britain. Those on benefit received seven shillings a week.[64] By August the National Shell factories were sold off. Pre-war employment patterns for women began to reassert themselves. At the labour exchange, 'The members have been pushed into domestic service'.[65] A woman who had been a Dublin National Shell factory machinist from 1916 to 1918 was offered work as an ironer in England, and a shell worker was offered work as a general cook, also in England. Federation officials took both cases to the Labour Exchange umpires, arguing that the women had dependent relatives at home, one a mother of 72 years old, the other a disabled husband.

Strike action by the IWWU in 1917 marked its reorganisation.[66] The Irish branches of the Federation decided early in 1919, 'that in view of the political situation in Ireland, it would be better for them to transfer to a purely Irish union'. The Federation executive agreed 'in the circumstances', and the Irish branches of the Federation transferred to the IWWU, under the direction of Louie Bennett, 'our very good friend and colleague'. The NFWW Irish organiser, Margaret Buckley, was appointed an IWWU official.[67] In

Britain the NFWW joined the National Union of General Workers in January 1921.

Irish trade unionism had been reshaped by the war years. New unions such as the Irish Bank Officials' Association (established in 1918) had been formed. Others had been revived. The National Union of Dock Labourers, eclipsed by its breakaway, the ITGWU, from 1909, re-established itself in many Irish ports, and became part of the foundation of the Amalgamated Transport and General Workers' Union presence in Ireland from 1922. The National Amalgamated Union of Labour, which organised labourers in engineering, was one of three largest British general unions. During the war it extended its membership to the north of Ireland, benefiting from Committee on Production awards in shipbuilding and engineering industries. It became a foundation union of the General Municipal Workers' Union in 1924.

The ITUC had more than doubled its strength to 250,000 from its pre-war membership. Its first wartime congress was held in 1916, in the aftermath of the Easter Rising. It had not held a 1915 Congress, 'with the minds of the people for the most part engrossed in the progress of the European War'.[68] The *Workers' Republic*, edited by James Connolly, reported on its editorial page the following Easter:

> The Congress of last year was not held as it was felt that the intense political feelings engendered by the war would probably inject themselves into the proceedings of Congress with the possible result that in the heat of passion things might be said and done that would cause irreparable breaches in the ranks of Labour. Notably it was apprehended that the position of many of the delegates from Unions in the North would be seriously compromised, and the adhesion of their Unions to the Congress endangered.

In addition it was feared,

> that no amount of caution could prevent delegates from perhaps inadvertently raising some point connected with the administration and regulation of Labour under wartime conditions ... For these reasons it was agreed to abandon the holding of the Congress in 1915.[69]

In 1916 Thomas Johnson won a 'token of respect' from the delegates for lives lost, 'whatever their views may be in regard to the war or rebellion'.[70] The ITUC had remained united by avoiding a discussion of the war aims. The only time it approached the topic was a debate on a mandate for Irish delegates to attend the Stockholm peace conference. Unity at the ITUC was further maintained by the virtual withdrawal by delegates from many of the British unions, such as the ASE, who did not return in numbers until 1918. By then some of its member unions had grown and new unions had affiliated. In November 1918 a special conference of the ILP and TUC launched a new political constitution and discussed a labour policy for the coming general election. Irish trade unionism was developing a political foundation to challenge the old home rule consensus of divided loyalties, from which, like the 1915 Congress, it was later to withdraw.

By 1919 trade unionism in Ireland emerged, as elsewhere, a stronger movement than it had ever been. The chief beneficiary of these years was the ITGWU, which had acquired an unprecedented dominance in the Irish trade union movement. Along with its large agricultural labourers' membership, the ITGWU absorbed a number of smaller Irish unions in 1918, such as the Irish Asylum Workers' Union and the Irish Glass Bottle Makers' Union, following the 1917 Trade Union Amalgamation Act which relaxed the process of trade union mergers.

Irish trade unionism had also been extended beyond its male, urban and manual boundaries. Unions in industries where women worked admitted them as equal members: some, like the ITGWU, recruiting women for the first time, increasingly in competition with the IWWU. But the war did not dramatically alter women's working conditions. Barbara Drake concluded, 'war neither raised new, nor solved old problems for female labour, but brought matters to a head'.[71] However, in Ireland, where old employment patterns were quickly reasserted it had led most visibly to the admission of women into the general trade union movement, and ended the strategy of women only unions for women.

Irish unions were now closely bound into a state system of arbitration and industrial representation unimaginable before the First World War. The Irish trade boards had been expanded, with trade union representation, setting minimum wages, and women took their place as official trade union representatives. Whitely Councils, joint industrial councils of employers and trade unionists, including the potential of shop steward representation, were set up towards the end of the war. By end of the war Ireland had vestiges of independent administration and representation in the Food Control Committee, wages and trade boards and in February 1919 an Irish Department of the Ministry of Labour opened. [72]

None of this development was unique to Ireland. But the Irish unions' experience of war has been rarely examined. The importance of James Connolly's legacy, and the outcome of post-war events, understandably led labour history inquiry towards the engagement of the Irish trade union participation in Easter Week and the nationalist movement of these years. Studies have concentrated on labour's leadership of the anti-conscription campaign and its decision not to contest the 1918 election. Other factors than the narrative outlined in this article contributed to the changes in Irish trade unionism. The emphasis on the background pattern of industrial controls, suggests ways these contributed to the new and extended forms of trade union organisation in Ireland, neglected in most studies of the war years.

Compulsory arbitration, cost of living bonus awards, and national bargaining played a more important part than most accounts indicate. If Irish wartime disputes were predominantly concerned with wage questions, as Fitzpatrick's study states, it was because this was the surest means of success in the wartime industrial climate. This was an aspect of wartime trade unionism that the most successful organisers recognised. In 1918 William O'Brien, Chairman of the ITUC that year, stressed the importance of wage increases that had been achieved:

> To meet the tremendous rise in the cost of living we have, all of us, been clamouring for more wages, and some of us have even been winning for our members increases nominally equivalent to the increase in the cost of living.[73]

His union, the ITGWU, went even further in its annual report two years later, directly linking trade union advances with wartime struggle: 'In the early days of the Union's "rebirth" (1916–1918) war necessities naturally gave a tremendous fillip to labour organisation.'

Notes

1 This figure (and subsequent years') includes double counting of membership of affiliated trades council as well as unions. See D. Nevin, *Trade Union Century* (Cork, Mercier Press, 1994), p. 434.
2 P. Yeates, *Lockout Dublin 1913* (Dublin, Gill & Macmillan, 2000).
3 Board of Trade, *Labour Gazette*, vol. 22 (September 1914), p. 331.
4 *Ibid.*, p. 334.
5 *Ibid.*, p. 412.
6 A phrase from Shelby Foote's momentous history of the American civil war.
7 D. Fitzpatrick, 'Strikes in Ireland, 1914–21', *Saothar* 6 (1980), p. 28.
8 *Workers' Republic*, 13 November 1915.
9 P. Murray, 'The first world war and a Dublin distillery workforce: recruiting and redundancy at John Power & Son, 1915–1917' *Saothar* 15 (1990), pp. 48–56.
10 J. Dunsmore Clarkson, *Labour and Nationalism in Ireland* (New York, AMS Press, [1925] 1970), p. 289.
11 *Labour Gazette*, vol. 22 (December 1914), p. 452.
12 P. T. Daly , secretary of the ITUC drafted the manifesto; S. Cody, J. O'Dowd, P. Rigney, *The Parliament of Labour: 100 Years of the Dublin Council of Trade Unions* (Dublin, Dublin Council of Trade Unions, 1986), p. 107.
13 National Executive Irish Trades Union Congress and Labour Party, *The Present Situation. Why Should Ireland Starve: Manifesto to the Workers of Ireland*. ILHS, WUI/7/4/1.
14 H. A. Clegg, *A History of British Trade Unions since 1889, Volume II, 1911–1933* (Oxford, Oxford University Press, 1985), p. 118.
15 *Labour Gazette*, vol. 22 (September 1914), p. 337.
16 Ibid., p. 441.
17 *Ibid.*, vol. 25 (January–December 1917).
18 M. Tierney, P. Bowen and D. Fitzpatrick, 'Recruitment posters', in D. Fitzpatrick, (ed.), *Ireland and the First World War* (Mullingar, 1988), pp. 47–58.
19 Information on Galway campaign from Mary Clancy, unpublished paper to 'Working for

Progress', 21st annual conference of the Irish Labour History Society in association with the Irish Congress of Trade Unions Centenary, Dublin, 1994.

20 Award IC 7051; Dispute between Dublin Master Bakers' Committee, ITGWU and Bakers' National Amalgamated Union, 21 November 1917. ILHS, 19/ITGWU

21 *Labour Gazette*, vol. 25 (December 1917), p. 255.

22 WA 9528 Award, 25 February 1919, ILHS, 19/ITG

23 *Labour Gazette*, vol. 25 (October 1917), p. 379.

24 H. Murphy, *The Kynoch Era in Arklow, 1895–1918* (Arklow, 1977), pp. 48–52.

25 C. Desmond Greaves, *The Irish Transport and General Workers' Union: The Formative Years, 1910–1923* (Dublin, Gill and Macmillan, 1982), p. 193.

26 Fitzpatrick, 'Strikes in Ireland', p. 26.

27 *Ibid.*, p. 28.

28 My thanks to Charles Callan for drawing my notice to this concurrence.

29 *Labour Gazette*, vol. 26 (September 1918), p. 365.

30 J. P. Swift, *John Swift: An Irish Dissident* (Dublin, Gill and Macmillan, 1991), p. 28.

31 *Labour Gazette*, vol. 24 (December 1916), p. 467.

32 See ITUC, Report of the 23rd annual meeting, 1917, pp. 33–7.

33 Swift, *John Swift*, pp. 29–48.

34 See E. O'Connor, 'Agrarian unrest and the labour movement in County Waterford 1917–1923', *Saothar* 6 (1980), pp. 40–58; T. N. Crean, 'Labour and politics in Kerry during the First World War', *Saothar* 19 (1994), pp. 27–39.

35 E. O'Connor, *Syndicalism in Ireland, 1971–1923* (Cork, Cork University Press, 1988), p. 37.

36 In a debate on grazing lands, Mr [Patrick] Lynch of the Amalgamated Society of Tailors and Tailoresses and the Cork Trades Council; ITUC, Annual Report, 1917, p. 18.

37 D. Bradley, *Farm Labourers: Irish Struggle 1900–1976* (Belfast, Athol, 1988), pp. 32–3.

38 *Irish Opinion*, vol. 1 (January 1918).

39 D. Ó Drisceoil, *Peadar O'Donnell* (Cork, Cork University Press, 2001), pp. 9–10.

40 The Lurgan Hemmers and Veiners Trade Union, formed in 1885 had 'faded away' by 1889, and was re-launched in 1901–2. Membership grew after 1907: M. Greiff, '"Marching through the streets singing and shouting": industrial struggles and trade unions among female linen workers in Belfast and Lurgan, 1872–1910', *Saothar* 22 (1997), pp. 29–44.

41 'Munition work in Ireland', *Woman Worker*, July 1916. This was the first report on Ireland carried by the relaunched *Woman Worker*, monthly journal of the National Federation of Women Workers. From May 1918 such reports were carried on 'Our Irish Page'.

42 *Ibid.* Soldon suggests women with university degrees and motor cars were particularly resented in Belfast, but the original text states this was at Beardmore's in Glasgow; Soldon, *Women in British Trade Unions*, p. 80.

43 The Irish sub-committee was composed of five representatives from the Belfast Flax Spinners' Association, five from the Irish Power Loom Manufacturers' Association, and two from the Council of the Linen Merchants' Association, with government department representatives. *Labour Gazette*, vol. 26 (January 1918), p. 7.

44 B. Drake, *Women in Trade Unions* (London, Virago, [1920] 1984), pp. 131–2.

45 'Trade Boards Act 1909, Shirt Making Trade, Ireland', reported that Miss B. Canny, Miss L. Duffy, Mr T McGerrigal and Miss K. Young were selected as workers' representatives; *Labour Gazette*, vol. 24 (May 1916), p. 193.

46 Information on the Londonderry Factory Workers' branch from Andrew Finlay.

47 Clegg, *History of British Trade Unions since 1889*, p. 200.

48 *Woman Worker*, December 1916.

49 T. Moriarty, 'Delia Larkin: relative obscurity', in D. Nevin (ed), *James Larkin: Lion of the Fold* (Dublin, Gill and Macmillan in association with RTE and SIPTU, 1998), pp. 434–5.

50 N. Regan, 'Helena Molony (1883–1967)', in M. Cullen and M. Luddy (eds), *Female Activists: Irish Women and Change 1900–1960* (Dublin, Woodfield Press, 2001), pp. 141–68.

51 'Dear old Ireland', *Woman Worker*, October 1916.

52 T. Moriarty, 'Mary Galway (1864–1928)', in Cullen and Luddy, *Female Activists*, pp. 9–36.

53 Mary Macarthur, general secretary of the NFWW, served on a number of wartime committees. She was the only woman on the War Emergency Workers' National Committee, and the Central Munitions Labour Supply Committee. She was also a member of the Central Committee for Women's Training and Employment; chairperson of the Standing Joint Committee of Working Women's Organisations, and a panel member of Joint Industrial Courts. (See Lewenhak, *Women and Trade Unions: An Outline History of Women in the British Trade Union Movement* (London, Benn, 1977).) In the early months of the war she was recovering from a stillbirth and had her first child in July 1915. She died in 1920; Soldon, *Women in British Trade Unions*, p. 79.

54 So far this factory has not been identified among the war contracts.

55 ILHS, 19/IWWU, Minutes, 18 December 1919.

56 'The tribunal, Irish National Shell Factories', *Woman Worker*, May 1918.

57 *Ibid.*, July.

58 'In Erin's isle', *ibid.*, September.

59 E. O'Connor, *A Labour History of Waterford* (Waterford, Waterford Council of Trade Unions, 1989), p. 135.

60 'Our Irish Page', *Woman Worker*, July 1918.

61 'Irish notes', *ibid.*, June 1919.

62 *Ibid.*, May.

63 *Ibid.*, February.

64 *Ibid.*, June.

65 *Ibid.*, August.

66 M. Jones, *These Obstreperous Lassies: A History of the Irish Women Workers Union* (Dublin, Gill and Macmillan, 1988).

67 NFWW, Tenth Annual Report, 1919.

68 ITUC Annual Report, 1916, p. 5.

69 *Workers' Republic*, vol. 1, 15 April 1916.

70 ITUC Annual Report, 1916, p. 23.

71 Drake, *Women in Trade Unions*, p. 105.

72 The Irish Department was to correspond to departments of the ministry in London, responsible for all labour matters in Ireland, including national insurance, conciliation, wages regulation and trade boards; *Labour Gazette*, vol. 27 (March 1919), p. 84.

73 ITUC Annual Report, 1918, p. 18.

5

The arming of Ireland: gun-running and the Great War, 1914–16

BEN NOVICK

The Rifle is the Keystone of Liberty. (Irish Volunteers' Motto, October 1914)[1]

Firearms are our worst enemies. (Augustine Birrell to Sir Matthew Nathan, 6 December 1914)[2]

Ranging from antiquated rifles to modern machine guns, firearms had been brought into Ireland in ever-increasing numbers since the Home Rule crisis of 1912. Beginning with the UVF, and quickly followed by the National Volunteers and the Irish Volunteers, paramilitary groups around the island began to arm for possible battle. Ironically, given the later history of armed struggle in Ireland, rifles were initially seen by nationalists of all stripes as a unifying symbol of resistance to British rule. While members of the UVF might have been reluctant to characterise their activities as necessarily opposed to British rule, nationalists such as Eoin MacNeill saw the organisation of Ulster as a first demonstration of the possibility of Irish might. Writing in 1914 shortly after the *Irish Volunteer* paper was censored for the first time by British authorities, MacNeill declared:

> Ireland needs armed Irishmen, not disarmed Irishmen. When the present confusion passes away, as it is rapidly passing, the more armed Irishmen we have, no matter what shade of national politics may be theirs, the better for Ireland.[3]

Were these weapons brought in for the conscious purpose of armed insurrection? Or was the value of a rifle as much symbolic as real? For the UVF, the answer must certainly be the former.[4] By March 1915, the British government estimated that 55,000 rifles and a brigade's complement of machine guns had been brought in by the UVF. In contrast, the National Volunteers under Redmond held only 9,000 antiquated rifles, and the more radical Irish Volunteers fewer than 2,000.[5] The realistic value of the 11,000 rifles held by nationalist paramilitary forces was very low. Advanced nationalist newspapers delighted in autumn 1914 in instructing their readers how to acquire the 'gas-pipe' rifles popular among Redmondites, claiming that they could be found only at military curio dealers.[6] Furthermore, they claimed that the same rifles were circulated around the country, showing up at every review attended by Redmond.[7] Although these newspapers encouraged radical nationalists to join local volunteer organisations and to learn to drill with whatever weaponry available, promising that grants would be available from the central volunteer committee to purchase rifles,[8] there was a begrudging acceptance in the advanced nationalist community that more rifles were needed before anything practical could be done with them. Rifles featured in stories throughout the early months of the war, mentioned whenever members of the Irish Volunteers or Irish Citizen Army attended reviews, but journalists admitted that the situation was dire. A letter in an August 1914 *Sinn Féin* even confessed that only 10 per cent of the Irish Volunteers had rifles, and that members should be trained in the use of pikes.[9]

In controlling the flow of arms into Ireland during the war, the British government was faced with an especially delicate task. The UVF and the National Volunteers were nominally loyal, and thus would require special treatment to keep them co-operative. In turn, the intelligence community also had to determine how significant the importation of arms by advanced nationalist groups actually was. Were these arms being brought in for purely propagandist purposes, or was this a first instance in which the actions suggested in textual and graphic propaganda could be made real, converting the war of words which already raged in Ireland into a war of bullets and blood?

The question of the 'use' intended for these weapons is secondary. The simple facts are these: the British government, both military and civilian, attempted to discourage the importation of arms during the Great War. Nevertheless, more than 66,000 rifles were in Ireland, in the hands of paramilitary organisations, by March 1915. This chapter will explore how this situation came to pass, how the British government allowed into Ireland the agent that created the realistic possibility (and then actual reality) of armed insurrection at Easter 1916. Examining the legal means by which the British attempted to control the import of arms, and the different sort of problems the British faced when dealing with Redmondite and advanced nationalist arms smuggling, this chapter will demonstrate how the struggle to control the importation of arms by different nationalist and unionist groups during the First World War characterised the constant dilemma between coercion and conciliation which so crippled British governmental policy in Ireland in the years before the Easter Rising of 1916.

As with many other areas covered by the new Defence of the Realm Act (DORA) in August 1914, arms smuggling and importation had been a nagging problem for the British government before the First World War broke out. Unlike censorship of the radical press, or the interception of political suspects' post – both of which legally occurred to a limited extent before DORA consolidated these powers[10] – legal methods for controlling the flow of arms into Ireland hardly existed before December 1913. As Charles Townshend astutely points out, the Ulster and Irish Volunteer Forces were able to exploit the 1881 Peace Preservation Act, which prohibited the import of arms or ammunition into Ireland except at the ports of Dublin, Belfast, Cork, Limerick, Londonderry, Waterford, Galway, Sligo, Drogheda, Dundalk, Greenore, Newry, Wexford, Larne, Carrickfergus, Glenarm, and Westport.[11] In other words, so long as volunteers chose to legally purchase their weapons with a licence which was easily obtainable, and import their arms at a major port, they were doing nothing illegal. This situation was somewhat rectified in December 1913 when the British, realising that the two bodies were reaching army strength,[12] issued a Royal Proclamation under the Customs Control Act of 1877, banning the importation of arms or ammunition into Ireland without a permit. This proclamation was extremely unpopular in Ireland, sparking legal challenges from gun manufacturers and protests from nationalists. Arthur Lynch, Irish Parliamentary Party MP and veteran of the Irish Brigade in the Boer War, confronted Augustine Birrell at Westminster, claiming that the date of the Royal Proclamation (4 December 1913), clearly demonstrated a governmental bias against the Irish Volunteers. The Irish Volunteers had been founded on 25 November 1913, giving them only ten days to amass arms before the Proclamation came into force, while the UVF had had since early January 1913.[13] Lynch was mistaken, at least about the avowed intent of the government's actions, since the cabinet paper suggesting the Royal Proclamation was aimed at disrupting arms supplies to both forces, and had been promulgated once the threat of two armed groups in Ireland had come to the fore.[14]

Following the demonstration of the British Army's implicit sympathy to them during the Curragh Incident, in April 1914 the Ulster Volunteer Force smuggled 25,000 rifles – along with ammunition and some machine guns, all of which had been purchased in Germany – into County Antrim's Larne Harbour under the noses of the British. Very little effort was made by the UVF to hide what it was doing: many UVF members, from all over Ulster, loaded automobiles with the weapons in broad daylight and drove calmly back into Belfast.

Although there was sympathy for the UVF among British officials in Ireland,[15] detailed attention was still paid to the activities of the organisation by the members of the Judicial Division and Crime Special Branch of the Chief Secretary's Office. Throughout the winter and spring of 1914, the confidential monthly intelligence notes compiled by Crime Special Branch for the Chief Secretary's Office focus almost completely on extremist Protestant activities in Ulster. In January 1914, to cite but one example, Special Branch officers in Belfast reported that 'all principal football clubs in the city have voted to suspend practice until the end of the season to give the men time to drill with the UVF'.[16] In contrast, the men watching nationalist

activity around the island could report only that P. S. O'Hegarty gave a
lecture at the Sinn Féin Rooms in Harcourt Street in Dublin to an audience
that included John (Sean) MacDermott, M. J. O'Rahilly, T. J. Cuffe, and
Arthur Griffith, and that an anti-recruiting leaflet had been found lying on a
muddy footpath in Schull, Co. Cork.[17] Customs officials in Ireland were far
more concerned with the gun-running undertaken by the UVF than by the
activities of the Irish Volunteers. Immediately following the King's
Proclamation in December 1913, 40,000 rounds of ·303 calibre ammunition
intended for the UVF were seized by the Royal Irish Constabulary in
Limerick. Once war broke out in August 1914, the ammunition was given to
the Army for military use.[18] Nine tonnes of ammunition was seized early in
1914 *en route* from Yorkshire to Belfast. Sealed in cement trucks, it was
being carried across the Irish Sea declared as 'pure cement ballast'. Tipped
off by an informer, customs and Special Branch Officers were waiting for the
ship when it arrived in Belfast Harbour.[19]

The perception of British favouritism towards the unionists, however,
remained strong. This was greatly reinforced following the Howth gun-
running by the Irish Volunteers in July 1914. Partly in response to the
arming of the Ulster Volunteer Force, and partly in an attempt to challenge
the British in Dublin, the Irish Volunteers had dispatched Erskine Childers,
the brilliant sailor and author of the best-selling 1903 thriller *The Riddle of
the Sands*, to a secret rendezvous off the coast of Germany, where he picked
up a consignment of arms and ammunition. He returned to Ireland on 26
July, landing at Howth, about ten miles north of Dublin. Over 900 rifles and
29,000 rounds of ammunition were put ashore, and Irish Volunteers and
Fianna boys from Dublin marched back towards the city. A large party was
stopped by Dublin Metropolitan Police Assistant Commissioner, W. V.
Harrel, backed up by a body of armed police and army troops. Led by
Thomas MacDonagh, Bulmer Hobson, and Darrell Figgis, the Volunteers
forced the police to back down. Harrel sent his troops back to Dublin.
There, along Bachelor's Walk, tempers frayed, and troops of the King's Own
Scottish Borderers opened fire on a crowd that had been taunting them and
hurling stones. Within a short time, three civilians were killed and thirty-
eight wounded. Small riots erupted around the city, and the British troops
had to be confined to their barracks. Though Augustine Birrell responded
immediately and suspended Harrel from duty,[20] waves of anger still carried
throughout the nationalist community. At Westminster, Redmond
denounced the British, crying:

Let the House clearly understand that four-fifths of the Irish people will not
submit any longer to be bullied, or punished, or shot, for conduct which is permitted to go scot-free in the open light of day in every county in Ulster by other
sections of their fellow countrymen.[21]

Maeve Cavanagh, who had just published in the *Evening Telegraph* her poem 'The White Swan', which she had composed to celebrate the landing of the guns at Howth, rushed to compose a 'Requiem' for the victims of the King's Own Scottish Borderers. The new poem was published in the *Irish Worker* of 1 August 1914:

> Whence Ireland forges with bruised feet,
> Thro' tenebrous years the dawn to greet,
> To her crown and throne;
> Nor gallows, nor sword, her way could bar,
> Ever she worshipped the one fair star,
> From fields death strown.[22]

Whether marked by Redmond's angry words, Cavanagh's dreadful poetry, or by the men and women who rioted following the incident at Bachelor's Walk, it was certain to the British that the gun running and its aftermath had certainly heightened tensions.[23] The over-reaction of the British in Dublin, coupled with their virtual failure to act in Ulster, created a situation in which there were now two groups, both freshly armed, and both with grievances against the government.

Given the level of tension in nationalist Ireland, it is surprising to consider the support received by John Redmond on 4 August 1914 when, in the House of Commons, he pledged the assistance of the Irish Volunteers for the home defence of Ireland during the First World War. Nevertheless, his unexpected speech received great support around Ireland, and the first two months of the war were characterised by high levels of voluntary recruiting, and a marked decline in inter-party and inter-religious rivalry all around the island. Redmond and his followers vied with Carson and his Unionist supporters to demonstrate their loyalty to the war effort.[24] In the midst of these displays of loyalty, and the quick passage of the Defence of the Realm Act to ensure domestic security, the King's Proclamation of December 1913 was abolished. Strangely, not only was the only legal method of controlling arms smuggling removed one day after the outbreak of the war,[25] but to top that, no section of DORA initially covered arms importation or exportation. Initially, with the island seemingly united behind the war effort and UVF and Irish Volunteers flocking to join the colours, this lapse of judgement may have seemed harmless. All this changed, however, on 20 September 1914. At Woodenbridge, Redmond dropped another bombshell, pledging his volunteers to service abroad – stating that 'the Volunteers will go wherever the firing line extends, in defence of right, of freedom, and of religion in this war'.[26] A small group of the Irish Volunteers, already antagonised by Redmond's *coup-d'état* in the previous summer,[27] reacted furiously, and split from the ranks. These men, led by Eoin MacNeill, numbered only

6,000, but included in their ranks most of the advanced nationalists in Ireland, and the majority of the future leaders of the 1916 Rising. In Dublin, over 2,000 men broke away to follow the new movement. Suddenly, the British were faced with a dilemma of their own making. Both the Irish Volunteers and the National Volunteers[28] well knew the advantages, both psychologically and physically, of arming themselves, and at the moment, no law existed to stop them importing arms from an allied country.

Germany, the major source for arms imported into Ireland before the First World War, was mostly out of the picture after the outbreak of war. The UVF gave most of its arms and ammunition to the British army, while the Irish Volunteers' main arms buyer, the erstwhile MP Tom Kettle, was so horrified by the German atrocities he witnessed in Belgium in August 1914 while attempting to purchase arms for the Volunteers that he immediately volunteered for the British army. This left the German market open to the Irish Volunteers and their more extreme supporters in New York, the Clanna-Gael, who sent Joseph Plunkett, Robert Monteith and Roger Casement to Berlin between 1914 and 1916 to negotiate for German support for a future Rising. Originally, the Germans planned not only to send the armed force of Casement's Irish Brigade, but also a shipment of 20,000 modern rifles, 10 machine guns and 5,000,000 rounds of ammunition.[29] In the end, the Germans reneged on their initial promises, and sent the *Aud* loaded with antiquated rifles (mostly Russian in manufacture). Scuttled off the coast of Galway, the *Aud's* existence was enough to guarantee the execution of Roger Casement and Patrick Pearse.[30] German support for Irish rebellion in the explicit form of arms supply does not appear to have been taken very seriously by British authorities. Rather, it seems that British officials involved in dealing with arms during the years preceding the Easter Rising preferred to ignore this threat, and focus instead on controlling other means by which arms were brought into Ireland.

Legal regulation of arms imports, falling under DORA, had improved greatly since the surprising abolition of the Royal Proclamation of December 1913 on 5 August 1914. Both the National Volunteers and Irish Volunteers took advantage of the lack of laws to begin importing arms in the autumn of 1914, and to combat this, the Dublin Metropolitan Police were confidentially ordered in November 1914 to begin confiscating weapons being imported into Dublin despite lacking legal backing.[31] Legal measures produced in the early months of the war were directed against the Irish rather than the National Volunteers – by the end of November, for example, pending amendment of the Defence of the Realm Regulations at the request of British government in Ireland, Lord Aberdeen, the Lord Lieutenant of Ireland, authorised Chief Commissioner Davies of the Dublin Metropolitan Police to begin seizing all arms and ammunition consigned to the Irish Volunteers in Dublin and the ports within the city limits. The Board of

Customs and Excise, directed by Sir Laurence Guillemand, also agreed to help take up arms found outside the supervisory area of the DMP.[32] On 28 November 1914, sparked in large part by the recent seizure at the North Wall Customs Deport in Dublin of 54 rifles, 4 revolvers, 154 bayonets, and 36,000 rifles intended for the Irish Volunteers,[33] the Defence of the Realm Regulations were modified: Competent Military Authorities were now permitted to prohibit, at their discretion, the sale, transfer, or disposal of any firearms, explosive substances, or ammunition. A week later, Major-General Friend issued two warrants authorising Competent Military Authorities to seize all warlike equipment landed in Ireland, and banning the sale of all firearms except shotguns and ·22 calibre hunting rifles without the express permission of the local District Inspector of the Royal Irish Constabulary, who would take his cue from the regional Competent Military Authority.[34]

Although these new regulations had been directed against the Irish rather than the National Volunteers, it was the National Volunteers who were first affected by the new laws. A close study of the bureaucratic shenanigans surrounding the seizure of some National Volunteer arms shipments between November 1914 and November 1915 serves to illuminate the functioning of the Dublin Castle administrative machine, ponderous and slow, with a distinct lack of co-operation in this arena. It also demonstrates the Machiavellian machinations of the Redmondites, following every regulation when they saw fit, and completely circumventing the bureaucratic chain of command if this were more to their advantage and liking. Finally, this detailed exploration shows how the necessarily close relationship between Dublin Castle and representatives of the Irish Parliamentary Party, and the British reliance on the support of the Irish Parliamentary Party in the recruiting campaign, crippled the ability of the British government in Ireland to stop firearms being imported into a smoldering tinderbox of an island in the midst of a world war.

On November 24, a shipment of 48 Martini-Metford rifles[35] intended for the National Volunteers arrived in Dublin. The Dublin Metropolitan Police and the Royal Irish Constabulary had been given warrants four days earlier ordering them to seize any arms and ammunition bought for the Irish Volunteers.[36] The Martini-Metfords, still in their crates, were immediately seized.[37] Straightaway, Laurence Kettle, who had been responsible for ordering the weapons, wrote to William Davies, the Chief Commissioner of Police, Major-General Friend, and Augustine Birrell at both his Irish address, and redundantly, at the Irish Office in London (via A. P. Magill). He requested that the arms be released, as all necessary paperwork had been completed beforehand.

The entire problem was quickly given to Sir Matthew Nathan who attempted to mollify Kettle by informing him that the police were holding the arms while waiting for the military authorities to come to a decision about whether or not to seize them for military use.[38] In the meantime, Nathan dined with John Dillon, who warned him that 'there would be great resentment if arms were prevented from coming to the Nationalist Party',[39] and Colonel Maurice Moore, who was told that military calibre weapons seized by the police would certainly be retained by the army for military use. Aware that keeping National Volunteers' rifles without reimbursement would greatly antagonise the Volunteer leadership, a conference was held on 28 November in Nathan's office between Friend, Greenfield, Davies, Attorney-General Pim, and Assistant Under-Secretary Edward O'Farrell. They decided that if Major-General Friend chose to keep the rifles, Italian models would be issued to replace them until the end of the war.[40] Already here we can see the British conceding points to the Redmondites. No British official was pleased to have armed men roaming about Dublin, but the support of the Redmondite party, and thus, by extension, the Redmondite Volunteers, was so crucial that the British were willing to arm the men themselves.

The National Volunteers' desire to continue importing arms caused problems on both sides of the Irish Sea. Under pressure from the War Office to curtail their Irish sales, the Birmingham gun-makers, Hollis, Bentley, & Playfair, wrote to Kettle on 1 January 1915 explaining that they could no longer sell him guns. Kettle replied:

> In applying for the licence to sell to us you might make it perfectly clear that it is the National Volunteers, whose president is Mr. J. E. Redmond, M.P. We mention this for the reason that there happens to be an organisation with a somewhat similar name, which has got more or less into conflict with the Authorities.[41]

Kettle appeared to be certain that the National Volunteers were in a good enough position with the government that they would be able virtually to dictate their demands, using the contacts, parliamentary and otherwise, which were theirs throughout the British Isles. How accurate was Kettle in this somewhat arrogant letter? Using his parliamentary connections, Kettle managed to get permission for four more shipments of arms. Major-General Friend grew more and more concerned about the importation (albeit under legal permit) of arms by the Volunteers, and on 10 January he wrote to the War Office, asking it to decide whether or not the Volunteers should be allowed to import ·303 calibre service ammunition. After hearing nothing for almost a month, Friend and his adjutant, Brigadier-General Greenfield, went to see Nathan on 6 February in an attempt to get his imprimatur upon a new letter to the War Office, but Nathan refused; more than six weeks later, on 27 February, B. B. Cubitt replied on behalf of the Army Council, ordering Friend to make his own decision in this matter. In future, all General Officers in Britain who dealt with arms manufacturing would be warned that nobody could send arms to Ireland without written consent from Irish Command.

The bureaucratic snarls that surrounded Kettle's constant requests for arms permits demonstrate two important problems with the National Volunteers' importation of weapons during the First World War. By scrupulously obeying every regulation issued by the British, the Redmondites forced Dublin Castle into an administrative trap of their own making. Reams of papers flowed between the offices of the National Volunteers, Irish Command, and Dublin Castle, as the multitude of men involved with asking and granting permission for rifles to land in Dublin struggled to keep pace with one another. British administrative organisation, which was so effective when departments co-operated with one another,[42] here fell apart. Major-General Friend and Under-Secretary Nathan squabbled with each other, and little help was given by the Irish Office or War Office in London. More importantly, the constant attention which had to be paid to arms shipments by men at the very top of the British hierarchy distracted them from other, perhaps more important, tasks. Nathan, who was working an average of 58 hours a week in 1915,[43] was forced to discuss replacing Anglo-Italian rifles with older Italian rifles at conferences which were planned to focus on the issue of the seditious press.[44] Major-General Friend occupied much of his time arguing with Matthew Nathan and drawing up contingency plans for stopping arms shipments, instead of focussing on the dispatch of the first Irish Division, the 10th, which left for Egypt *en route* to Gallipoli in February 1915.

The number of arms being imported into Ireland by the National Volunteers was very small, and the National Volunteers were not viewed as a threat to the British government before the Easter Rising transformed the political scene on the island. An examination of the importation of arms from 1914 and 1916 by the Redmondites stands apart therefore from an examination of how the British coped with the Irish Volunteers' and other advanced nationalist groups' arms smuggling. A study of Redmondite arms importation is useful primarily because it illuminates both how bureaucracy can break down, and how the Redmondites were able to exploit their special relationship with Dublin Castle to fulfil their own ends.

What, then, of the more problematic volunteers? Troublesome though they might be, the National Volunteers had thrown in their lot with the British, and were more concerned with saving face in volunteer displays than with actively threatening to overthrow the British government. The Irish Volunteers, and other advanced nationalist groups in Ireland, were a completely different matter. The Irish Volunteers were well aware of the propagandistic value of the rifle. The masthead of the *Irish Volunteer* newspaper featured a stylised volunteer clutching a prominent rifle, and the pages of advanced nationalist newspapers were full of poems singing the praises of the gun. Before 1916, the practical threat from the few antiquated rifles was minimal, but even Birrell was aware of their potential for danger in the wrong hands. 'Firearms are our worst enemies,' he wrote to Nathan in December 1914.[45] This final section of the chapter will examine three ways in which the Irish Volunteers acquired arms before 1916, and the varying levels of success of British counter-measures in stopping the flow of arms to the Volunteers. Unlike with the National Volunteers, British efforts against the Irish Volunteers' gun smuggling met with relatively clear success in two of the three areas, and only failed in one due to the well-intentioned meddling of National Volunteers.

British authorities had the most difficulty preventing advanced nationalists purchasing or stealing arms from the legally imported stocks held by the National Volunteers. This was a great concern for Dublin Castle from the very early days of the war. A robbery of 100 rifles by Sinn Féin from a group of National Volunteers parading through Dublin in late November 1914 was perhaps partly responsible for the tightening of import regulations that month.

Nathan met with Colonel Maurice Moore, who had been technically responsible for the shipment, and warned him that such robberies represented 'a very dangerous state of affairs'.[46] Maurice Moore was disliked and mistrusted by Dillon, Devlin, and the officers of Irish Command with whom Nathan dealt. At dinner on 26 November, Dillon and Nathan discussed Moore, whom Dillon characterised as 'not ... a person of great strength'. It was impossible, however, for a good assistant to be found for Moore, as 'all good men were now at war'.[47] Devlin doubted that Moore was wholeheartedly with the Parliamentary Party, and doubted as well that his security arrangements for weapons were adequate.[48] Major-General Friend in his turn, had grave doubts about both Moore and Laurence Kettle, and wondered whether arms which went through their hands were even reaching the National Volunteers, or just being sent on to the Irish Volunteers at a profit. Furthermore, Friend doubted Moore's complete loyalty to Redmond since Moore was 'somewhat of a disappointed man'.[49] Friend believed that Moore and Kettle were selling the arms imported by the National Volunteers to Irish Volunteers in the 'provinces' for a profit. Birrell agreed with Friend to a point. He also disliked Moore and Kettle, considering Moore a 'soldier with some old military grievance festering', and condemning Laurence Kettle for the activities of his more famous brother, Thomas, complaining that he was 'a literary gent, with a congenital thirst, & as vain as he is thirsty'.[50]

Bulmer Hobson, new editor of the *Irish Volunteer*, claimed in print on 5 December that the Irish Volunteers had nothing to do with this robbery. If they had without his knowledge obtained arms this way, he stated bluntly that 'their duty is, without hesitation and without delay, to do what they can to have the arms restored to their former possessor'.[51] Little evidence remains of the extent to which robberies of arms actually took place in Ireland before 1916. An examination of one particular incident, in August 1915, will serve to demonstrate both how well the advanced nationalists could function at times, and how the meddling of the Redmondites, attempting, as victims, to solve their own crime, harmed British efforts at recovering weapons.

At the beginning of August 1915,[52] National Volunteers' Headquarters in Dublin was notified by the police that they had released for delivery a shipment of 100 Martini-Enfield rifles ordered a few months previously by Laurence Kettle. The rifles were stored in crates in the shipping depot of the London & North-West Railway Company on the North Wall in Dublin. When the call was made, cartage hours for the day had already ended, so the National Volunteers decided to wait until the morning to take delivery. Later that same day, a man went to the Railway depot, and, claiming to be from 44 Parnell Square (National Volunteers' Headquarters), asked if the rifles had yet been delivered. Informed that they remained in the depot, he left. Moore later claimed that this man had nothing to do with the National Volunteers, and was clearly a spy from an advanced nationalist group. That night (14–15 August), after midnight, the depot was raided by six masked men. While two of their party drew revolvers and held up the watchman, the remaining men removed the crates, dragged them 200 yards down the rail line, over a low wall, and into waiting motor cars, which then drove off into the night. The police were informed, and newspaper accounts were published, but no immediate arrests were made.

John Redmond and John Dillon came to see Nathan on 21 August, and complained about the loss of the 100 rifles. Redmond claimed that this loss was causing 'very great irritation' among his volunteers, and that if the police did not find the culprits, the volunteers would have to find them themselves. The reason the guns were stolen, Redmond said, was that the military unnecessarily impeded their delivery, and the police were inefficient. Dillon seized the opportunity to slip in a remark on the uselessness of keeping 12,000 policemen in Ireland if none of them could do his job. Nathan snapped at this point, and declared that not only were the police doing everything they could, but that furthermore the custody of the rifles was the responsibility of the London & North-West Railway Company. Redmond and Dillon left in disgust.[53]

Colonel Maurice Moore went even further when he came to see Nathan a week later. No progress had yet been publicised, so Moore had decided to act on his own. He was convinced that the reason the police were doing nothing was that Chief Superintendent George Lowe, who he believed had charge of the case, was opposed to the National Volunteers, and had taken on the case specifically to destroy the investigation and to stop the National Volunteers from retrieving their weapons. Nathan tactfully pointed out that

Moore's information was incorrect, as not only had Lowe never demon-strated the said political opinions, but he had also retired six months previ-ously.[54] Moore, however, had already written to an acquaintance of his who used to work at Scotland Yard and was now employed by the War Office, and asked him to help since the Dublin Metropolitan Police had refused. Moore offered this gentleman the full assistance of the National Volunteers, who he claimed were 'making every endeavour to get information privately and will give all help'.[55] Moore was careful to insist that helping him in this matter was not an issue of helping the National Volunteers, but rather an issue of public safety. While he had a valid point there, he ruined the strength of this argument by whining at the end of his letter:

> It seems to me very dangerous that such like people should be permitted to seize arms undetected. We always ask permission to import arms but the Sinn Féin Volunteers smuggle them in considerable quantities and have more arms than are permitted to us. It seems to me the Military Authorities ought to take the matter up very seriously.[56]

Both Moore and Redmond felt certain that the arms had been stolen by the Citizen Army. Moore pointed out that only three groups in Ireland had the resources or desire to steal the rifles: the Ulster Volunteer Force, the Irish Volunteers, and the Citizen Army. Quickly discounting the first, Moore believed as well that the leaders of the Irish Volunteers would not condone such a robbery. If it had been the Irish Volunteers, then it would have been a job done by a small 'extreme Fenian Party'[57] connected with the Volunteers. The Citizen Army was thus the only plausible suspect. Not only did Moore think the Army was likely to commit such a crime, but it had 'special facili-ties', as 'all the men who work on the dock and railways belong to them'.[58] Redmond and Dillon wanted the buildings at Liberty Hall and Croke Park, the Headquarters of the Irish Citizen Army, to be raided.[59]

In the event, no progress was made in the investigation. As late as October 1915, Nathan and Friend were still discussing whether or not to raid Liberty Hall for arms. Major-General Friend wanted to do this, but they decided that it would be better to avoid potentially starting a conflict.[60] Maurice Moore was brushed off in November by Nathan, who told him that nothing further had been heard about the rifles taken back in August.[61] It is unlikely that members of the Citizen Army stole the rifles, as close tabs were kept on the arms carried by volunteer organisations, and no rise was seen in numbers in August or September 1915.[62] The allegiance of the masked men who broke into the London & North-West Railway depot on August 14–15 1915 may never be known. What can be gleaned from studying the incident, however, is enlightening. The ease with which the action was carried out shows that the advanced nationalists in Ireland were highly co-ordinated at times. The interference of the Irish Parliamentarians in police business, well-meaning though it may have been, further muddied the waters, and increased the chances of the advanced nationalists getting away with their rifles.

Waiting for the chance to steal weapons from National Volunteers could not, however, supply enough arms to have any possible effect on British rule. Therefore, advanced nationalists quickly turned to other means of procuring firearms. Following the repeal of the Royal Proclamation on 5 August 1914, the Irish Volunteers, just like the National Volunteers, could for a brief time legally import arms. The British were seriously concerned about the Irish Volunteers receiving arms after the Woodenbridge split. Detectives of the crack 'G' Division within the Dublin Metropolitan Police (DMP) believed that seceders had kept many of the weapons brought in at Howth, and they were also aware that arms were being brought in by various means early in the war, including via parcel post, sorters employed on the Mail Boat, and inside passengers' luggage.[63] In an effort to combat this, Sir Matthew Nathan encouraged inter-departmental co-operation. Lists of known Sinn Féin Volunteer leaders were put together from intelligence files, growing postal censorship lists, and information gleaned from 'G' Division inform-ants and interrogations.[64] This co-operation, which was to prove so effective with postal censorship, was slightly more difficult to introduce here. In November 1914, when the British government in Ireland was attempting to get DORA amended to allow for greater latitude in controlling arms impor-tation, Nathan travelled to London to discuss co-operation with the Board of Customs and the Ministry of Munitions. Sir Laurence Guillemand at Customs was willing to help, but General Von Donop, the Master of Munitions, refused to 'do police work'.[65] Once the departments began to co-operate, however, British officials could take advantage of intelligence gath-ered from different areas. In late 1914, the Lord Lieutenant issued a warrant based on inter-departmental intelligence, authorising the police to seize any arms or ammunition addressed to a leader of the Sinn Féin Volunteers whose name appeared on intelligence lists. This warrant backfired, for the advanced nationalists simply put other people's names down on the boxes of arms that were being brought in. Nevertheless, it is an important early sign of co-oper-ation that the names of the leaders were made known to all so early in the war.[66]

Once the Defence of the Realm Regulations were modified in December 1914, banning the import of any arms or warlike stores without permits, the advanced nationalists had to turn to more indirect routes of arms importa-tion. British intelligence discovered during 1915 that revolvers were being shipped from the Clan-na-Gael in America to Glasgow, wrapped in socks and mufflers and declared as woolen goods. From Glasgow they would be brought into Ireland in the same form within passenger luggage.[67] Major I. H. Price, British intelligence chief in Ireland, received an anonymous letter in December 1915, informing him that gun dealers in England were smuggling arms to Ireland concealed in hardware packages.[68] The DMP, RIC, Irish Command, and Customs officials all worked closely together to try to stop arms smuggling. DMP constables and detectives watched the ports in Dublin and Kingstown, and in November 1915, the RIC reported to Nathan that the level of co-operation between it and the Customs officials in Ireland was 'very high'.[69] Sir Matthew Nathan hosted a joint conference in December 1915 between officials of the Board of Customs, the DMP, and Irish Command's intelligence wing. There, it was decided that tighter controls should be kept in England as well as Ireland, as most of the arms that were smuggled into Ireland came from England. This conference was considered very successful by both Nathan and Major-General Friend.[70] More imaginative methods of smuggling were also uncovered by the British. Three weeks before the Rising, on 3 April 1916, the manager of the 'Irish Cutlery Company', an Irish Volunteer, was briefly detained after police discovered that a crate marked 'cutlery', which had been delivered to the North Wall, actually held 500 new bayonets.[71]

Arms smuggling was well combatted by the co-operative efforts of British intelligence, the police, and customs officials. While not all arms could be stopped from reaching dangerous hands, the actual number of arms held by the advanced nationalists was kept very low. An estimate produced by British intelligence in December 1914 found that only 2,000 rifles were in the hands of the Irish Volunteers. Before the grand review of the Volunteers on St Patrick's Day, 1916, the most rifles that had been seen in public were 700, and even at the review, only 800 rifles were carried. The situation was even grimmer in the Citizen Army, where it was noted in April 1916 that the Army had greatly increased its weaponry, an additional twenty shotguns and rifles being seen on display.[72]

Although DORA gave the British the right to seize arms being smuggled into the country, it was still virtually impossible to prosecute individuals for smuggling. Surprisingly, given the relatively high level of British awareness about Casement's activities in Germany, there seems to have been little concern about arms being imported *en masse* from Germany. Anti-smuggling campaigns were mainly organised to stop the flow of arms from Britain, Holland, and the United States. Where prosecutions of individuals involved in smuggling came into play was in the final method of arms procurement by the advanced nationalists, the use of legitimate gun dealers and hides throughout Dublin to hold their weapons. This method was virtually predestined to fail, especially in Dublin, where most of the weapons were brought. Dublin was a small city, and both the advanced nationalist leaders and the important gun dealers in Dublin were well known to the British government. Nevertheless, prosecutions rarely succeeded, and despite the wide range of DORA regulations under which individuals could be prosecuted for possessing and selling arms, relatively few attempts were made by the British before 1916. According to Nathan's testimony to the Royal Commission on the Easter Rebellion in May 1916, only 34 of the 496 cases tried under DORA up to that point had been for possession of arms or ammunition. Nathan blamed this on the amendation of DORA in February 1915, which allowed British citizens to choose a jury trial rather than a court martial if they committed an offence under DORA more serious than a Court of Summary Judgement could handle.[73] Irish juries were notoriouly reluctant to convict anyone accused by the government, and this was almost certainly what led to the infamous (for the British) acquittals of James Hegarty and James Bolger, who had been found in bed together at the home of Laurence de Lacey[74] surrounded by gelignite in 1914, and Alexander McCabe, a Sligo schoolteacher who was arrested on a train platform with a bag full of TNT and grenades.[75]

The DMP continued to raid the homes of well-known advanced nationalist leaders in Dublin up to the Easter Rising, but these raids rarely turned up any evidence. When they did, such as a raid on the Countess Markievicz in January 1916 which discovered 950 ·22 cartridges, a rifle, a hand press, and seditious literature,[76] prosecutors rarely bothered to act. This is especially surprising when one notes that the firearm regulations in Ireland were further modified by an act of council in December 1915 to ban the sale of all weapons without a permit. Eoin MacNeill considered this action 'nothing short of an edict of slavery', which would not permit Irishmen to even hold weapons 'such as would be effective for the defence of their houses and their lives'.[77]

Yet, despite the general inability to prosecute, British intelligence still managed to keep close tabs on the advanced nationalist leaders and their suppliers, and would confiscate what weapons they found. With the National Volunteers, a lack of co-operation and the need to keep the Redmondites happy crippled the efforts of Dublin Castle. No such deficiency was found in their dealings with the advanced nationalists, and so when words turned to deeds on 24 April 1916, and the gun turned from a propaganda tool to a deadly weapon, the men and women who marched out to confront the British Empire were armed with a grab-bag assortment of outdated weapons brought into Ireland by various means. In military terms, the Easter Rising was a total defeat for the rebels. Outmanned and outgunned by the British Army, defences in Dublin crumbled in less than a week. But the Easter Rising was more than just a battle – it was an act of propaganda in action, a supreme moment in the long war of words against the British, and enough rifles were used for the most advanced nationalists to learn the full truth of the old motto of the Volunteers. The rifle *was* the keystone of liberty, and liberty from the British, it was believed, could only be won once the talking ceased and the firing began.

Notes

1 *Irish Volunteer*, 31 October 1914.

2 Bodl., Nathan Ms. 449, Letter 23, fl. 40v, Birrell to Nathan, 6 December 1914.

3 *Irish Volunteer*, 5 December 1914.

4 See A. Jackson, 'Unionist Myths, 1912–1985', *Past and Present*, vol. 136 (August 1992), for an illuminating discussion of UVF activities and mentality.

5 Bodl., Nathan Ms. 467, fls. 182–5, Memoranda of Interviews (Ireland), vol. I: October 1914 to March 1915, Interview with Prime Minister Asquith, 16 March 1915.

6 *Éire-Ireland*, 23 November 1914.

7 *Ibid.*

8 *Irish Freedom*, December 1914.

9 *Sinn Féin*, 8 August 1914.

10 For press censorship see: L. O'Broin, *Dublin Castle and the Easter Rising* (London, Sidgwick and Jackson, 1970), and V. Glandon, *Arthur Griffith and the Advanced-Nationalist Press: Ireland, 1900–1922* (New York, Peter Lang, 1984). For postal censorship see: E. O'Halpin, 'British intelligence in Ireland', in C. Andrews and D. Dilks (eds), *The Missing Dimension: Governments and Intelligence Communities in the Twentieth Century* (London, Macmillan, 1984), and B. Novick 'Postal censorship in Ireland, 1914–16', *Irish Historical Studies*, no. 123 (May 1999).

11 C. Townshend, *Political Violence in Ireland: Government and Resistance since 1848* (Oxford, Oxford University Press, 1984), p. 264.

12 By the summer of 1914, six months later, it is estimated that the UVF could field 85,000 men, and the Irish Volunteers 185,000 men. Though poorly armed, these numbers compared favourably to the regular British army, which sent 160,000 men in the BEF to France in August 1914.

13 *Hansard*, 64 H.C. Debs. 5 s., 9 July 1914, 1214–5.

14 Townshend, *Political Violence*, p. 266

15 Townshend cites Count Gleichen's (General Officer Commanding Belfast) account of his 'wry amusement' upon discovering a cache of arms in the croquet box of a country house where he was a guest. *Ibid.*, p. 273.

16 PRO, CO 904 120/1, fl. 14, Chief Secretary's Office (Judicial Division): Précis of information received from Crime Special Branch, January 1914.

17 *Ibid.*, fls. 23–4.

18 PRO, CO 904/28/3a, Arms: Importation and Distribution, 1914. From November 1914 to January 1915, Sir Matthew Nathan received a slew of letters from the Belfast solicitors Caldwell & Robinson, demanding that their clients be reimbursed for this 'illegal' seizure. Nathan refused to do so, and refused even to acknowledge their letter, a rare practice indeed for such a conscientious civil servant.

19 PRO, CO 904/28/2b Arms: Importation, Exportation, and Distribution, 1914.

20 Harrel thus ended his career with the Dublin Metropolitan Police, but during the First World War remained in Ireland as an agent for Captain Sir Reginald Hall's Naval Intelligence.

21 Cited in T. Denman, *Ireland's Unknown Soldiers* (Dublin, Irish Academic Press, 1992), p. 20.

22 M. Cavanagh, 'Requiem' from *Sheaves of Revolt* (Dublin, Private Publisher, 1914), p. 22.

23 Bachelor's Walk was used throughout the war by advanced nationalist propagandists as a counter to pro-war accounts of German atrocities in Belgium. For more information, see B. Novick, *Conceiving Revolution: Irish Nationalist Propaganda During the First World War* (Dublin, Four Courts Press, 2001), ch. 2.

24 For information on this see: Denman, *Unknown Soldiers*, and P. Callan, 'Voluntary

recruiting in Ireland during the First World War' (unpublished PhD Thesis, National University of Ireland, University College, Dublin, 1986).

25 The repeal of the December 1914 Royal Proclamation was done very quietly. No mention can be found in Hansard, or in private papers of British government officials in Ireland. Townshend as well feels that the repeal of the Royal Proclamation was 'a gesture that is difficult to explain at the commencement of war'; Townshend, *Political Violence*, p. 280.

26 NLI, Ms. 15259, John Redmond Papers, Memoranda on Recruiting, 1914–1918.

27 As the Irish Volunteers grew in power through the summer of 1914, Redmond grew increasingly nervous that this group would supersede the Irish Parliamentary Party in nationalist circles. Aware that Eoin MacNeill's politics were far more extreme than his or his party's, Redmond used his position to force the Volunteer executive to accept more than thirty of his nominees for the executive council. This move effectively guaranteed his control of the group, but did much to heighten tensions between factions within the Volunteers. Until the outbreak of the war, however, the need to keep a coherent group together to resist unionist machinations outweighed the ideological differences.

28 The men who split off took the name 'Irish Volunteers' with them – the majority that stayed reconstituted themselves as the 'National Volunteers' (or occasionally, 'Irish National Volunteers').

29 R. R. Doerries, *Prelude to the Easter Rising: Sir Roger Casement in Imperial Germany* (London, F. Cass, 2000), p. 18.

30 See: M. Foy and B. Barton, *The Easter Rising* (Stroud, Sutton, 1999), for evidence that Pearse's knowledge of the *Aud* tipped the balance at his court martial in favour of a death sentence.

31 PRO, CO 903/19/1, fls. 28–9, Chief Secretary's Office (Judicial Division): Intelligence Notes, 1915, 'Measures Taken to Prevent Hostile Organisations Obtaining Arms and Ammunition'.

32 *Ibid.*, fl. 28.

33 PRO, CO 904/28/4, fl. 646, History of Sinn Féin Arms Imports to Ireland, 1914–1916: Chart, 'Arms and Ammunition seized at Port of Dublin by Police' n.d. [January 1916?].

34 PRO, CO 903/19/1, fls. 28–30, Chief Secretary's Office (Judicial Division): Intelligence Notes, 1915, 'Measures Taken to Prevent Hostile Organisations Obtaining Arms and Ammunition', orders in council dated 5 and 8 December, 1914.

35 These rifles, a common choice of the National Volunteers throughout the war, were made in Great Britain from an Italian design. Falling block action rifles, they fired a slightly smaller cartridge than the Lee Enfield .303 used by the British army. Relatively reliable, and more importantly, cheap, these weapons were popular all over the British Empire. My thanks to Mr Dave Laufer for parts of this information.

36 PRO, CO 903/19/1, fl. 28, Chief Secretary's Office (Judicial Division): Intelligence Notes, 1915, 'Measures Taken to Prevent Hostile Organisation from Obtaining Arms and Ammunition'.

37 There is no evidence in the files that remain in the Public Record Office to demonstrate that the British wished to seize arms going to the National Volunteers, who were no longer considered a threat. Why, therefore, these arms were seized is slightly unclear. Most likely, they were addressed to the 'Irish National Volunteers', a form of address that was still very popular among the National Volunteers early in the war.

38 Bodl., CO 904/29/2a, fl. 233, Arms and Ammunition for Volunteers: Cases, 1914–17, Nathan to Kettle, 25 November 1914.

39 Bodl., Nathan Ms. 467, fls. 36–7, Memoranda of Interviews (Ireland), vol. I:, October 1914 to March 1915, Interview with John Dillon, 26 November 1914.

40 *Ibid.*, fls. 42–5, Conference, 28 November 1914.

41 PRO, CO 904/29/2a, fl. 228, Arms and Ammunition for Volunteers: Cases, 1914–17,

Kettle to Hollis, Bentley and Playfair, 3 January 1915.

42 As was the case with the censorship of the post in Ireland during the war; see Novick, 'Postal censorship'.

43 Number based on Nathan's own calculations of the hours he worked in Bodl., Nathan Ms. 50, Diary, 1915. Nathan's fanatical record-keeping is a boon to historians once his hand-writing can be deciphered, for he wrote down every day the people he saw, where he ate, the hours he worked, and to whom he wrote. Every year he also kept a list of the books he read and the dates upon which he read them.

44 Bodl., Nathan Ms. 467, Memoranda of Interviews (Ireland), vol. I: Conference, 28 November 1914. The majority of this conference was spent discussing final plans for the shut down of 6 'seditious' Dublin newspapers, scheduled to take place the following week.

45 Bodl., Nathan Ms. 449, letter 23, fl. 40v, Birrell to Nathan, 6 December 1914.

46 Bodl., Nathan Ms. 467, fls. 46–7, Memoranda of Interviews (Ireland), vol. I: October 1914 to March 1915, Interview with Colonel Maurice Moore, 28 November 1914.

47 Ibid., fls. 36–7, Interview with John Dillon, 26 November 1914.

48 Ibid., fls. 155–6, Interview with Joseph Devlin, 19 February 1915.

49 Ibid., fls. 144–8, Interview with Major-General Friend and Brigadier-General Greenfield, 6 February 1915. Given the Georgian coyness of the phrase a 'disappointed man', it is somewhat difficult to tell what exactly Friend meant. Moore was extremely upset through-out 1915 at being refused a commission in the army and employment in the War Office. However, 'disappointed' usually refers to a loss in financial affairs.

50 Bodl., Nathan Ms. 449, letter 63, fl. 117v, Letters from Birrell, 1914–1916, 8 February 1915.

51 Irish Volunteer, 5 December 1914.

52 Information in the following paragraph is drawn from: Bodl., Nathan Ms. 468, Memoranda of Interviews (Ireland), vol. II: April to September 1915, primarily from an interview with Maurice Moore on 28 August.

53 Bodl., Nathan Ms. 468, fls. 243–4, Memoranda of Interviews (Ireland), vol. II: April to September 1915, Interview with John Redmond and John Dillon, 21 August 1915.

54 Ibid., fls. 256–7, Interview with Col. Maurice Moore, 28 August 1915.

55 Ibid., fls. 258–58A, Moore to Melville, 20 August 1915, inserted with interview of Moore, 28 August 1915.

56 Ibid.

57 Ibid.

58 Ibid. Moore is certainly exaggerating here. The Citizen Army had approximately 400 members when they marched out on Easter Monday of 1916; however it is likely that they enjoyed greater support from the working class than did the Irish Volunteers.

59 Bodl., Nathan Ms. 468, fls. 243–4, Memoranda of Interviews (Ireland), vol. II: April to September 1915, Interview with John Redmond and John Dillon, 21 August 1915.

60 Bodl., Nathan Ms. 469, fls. 18–9, Memoranda of Interviews (Ireland), vol. III: October 1915 to May 1916, Interview with Major-General Friend, 11 October 1915.

61 Ibid., fl. 69, Interview with Col. Maurice Moore, 1 November 1915.

62 PRO, CO 904/28/4, fls. 648–52, History of Sinn Féin Arms Imports to Dublin, 1914–1916. Memo, 'Importation of Arms, etc. by the Sinn Féin Party', 12 May 1916, Brien to Nathan.

63 Ibid.

64 For Intelligence 'Personality Files', see CO 904/209 series at the PRO; for an example of postal censorship lists, see CO 904/164/2: Postal Censorship, 1915–1916; for 'G' Division records, see Brien's memo in CO 904/28/4.

65 Bodl., Nathan Ms. 467, fl. 23, Memoranda of Interviews (Ireland), vol. I: October 1914 to March 1915, Interview with Major-General Von Donop, London, 20 November 1914.

66 PRO, CO 904/28/4, fls. 648–52, History of Sinn Féin Arms Imports to Dublin, 1914–1916: Memo, 'Importation of Arms, etc. by the Sinn Féin Party', 12 May 1916, Brien to Nathan. For list of known leaders see: Bodl., Nathan Ms. 470, fls. 26–31v, Notebook, vol. I: October to December 1914.

67 PRO, CO 904/28/4, fls. 648–52, History of Sinn Féin Arms Imports to Dublin, 1914–1916: Memo, 'Importation of Arms, etc. by the Sinn Féin Party,' 12 May 1916, Brien to Nathan.

68 Bodl., Nathan Ms. 469, fls. 135–6, Memoranda of Interviews (Ireland), vol. III: October 1915 to May 1916, Conference, 16 December 1915.

69 PRO, CO 904/28/4, fls. 648–52, History of Sinn Féin Arms Imports to Dublin, 1914–1916: Memo, 'Importation of Arms, etc. by the Sinn Féin Party,' 12 May 1916, Brien to Nathan.

70 Bodl., Nathan Ms. 469, fls. 135–6, Memoranda of Interviews (Ireland), vol. III: October 1915 to May 1916, Conference, 16 December 1915.

71 PRO, CO 904/28/4, fls. 648–52, History of Sinn Féin Arms Imports to Dublin, 1914–1916: Memo, 'Importation of Arms, etc. by the Sinn Féin Party,' 12 May 1916, Brien to Nathan. Events grew slightly more confusing three days later, when Sir Matthew Nathan met Mr. W. A. Evans, Chairman of the Irish Cutlery Company. He admitted that the knives, a variant on 'those ordinarily used for sticking pigs', were very much in 'the nature of bayonets'. They had been ordered without his knowledge by the Manager, but he claimed that this Manager was not a Sinn Féiner. Knowing him to be usually loyal, Nathan agreed to release the Manager, and permit the Chairman to be present when his premises were searched; see also: Bodl., Nathan Ms. 469, fl. 369, Memoranda of Interviews (Ireland), vol. III, October 1915 to May 1916, Interview with W. A. Evans. Interestingly, these bayonets are still listed as seized weapons despite this plausible explanation of their use and origin.

72 PRO, CO 904/28/4, fls. 648–52, History of Sinn Féin Arms Imports to Dublin, 1914–1916: Memo, 'Importation of Arms, etc. by the Sinn Féin Party,' 12 May 1916, Brien to Nathan.

73 Testimony of Sir Matthew Nathan to the Royal Commission on the Rebellion in Ireland, Parliamentary Papers 1916, vol. 11, 106–32.

74 Erstwhile editor of the *Irish Volunteer*.

75 PRO, CO 903/19/1, fls. 31–4, Chief Secretary's Office (Judicial Division): Intelligence Notes, 1915, Cases of unlawful possession and larceny of high explosives.

76 *Ibid*. Police were acting on intelligence gathered from the RIC in Glasgow. There, two men had been arrested for the theft of explosives from a quarry. One of them, a man named Reader, had taken weapons and explosives to Dublin when he travelled there in early January 1916 to attend an Irish Volunteer's Convention. Upon his arrest he admitted that he had distributed weapons to houses within Dublin, and the police searched these places, finding incriminating evidence at the homes of Markievicz, T. J. Fitzgerald and Edward Murray; (see: Bodl., Nathan Ms. 478, fls. 136–9, Rebellion in Ireland: Documents for Royal Commission and Report, vol. III, May & June, 1916).

77 *Irish Volunteer*, 18 December 1915.

6

'You might as well recruit Germans': British public opinion and the decision to conscript the Irish in 1918

ADRIAN GREGORY

At 4.40 am on Thursday 21 March 1918, ten thousand German artillery pieces began a precisely registered bombardment with gas and high explosives along a seventy mile section of front held by the British Third and Fifth Armies. Less than two hours later, half a million German infantry, many of them transferred from the Eastern front since the collapse of Russia, advanced through fog into the shattered British positions. It was the greatest single offensive operation of the First World War. By the end of the day each army had suffered approximately 40,000 casualties, the bloodiest single day of the war. In terms of permanent losses the British Expeditionary Force (BEF) had suffered worst: more than three quarters of the British casualties were dead, prisoners or permanently maimed. Dozens of battalions had entirely ceased to exist, and the war diary of the 12th Royal Irish Rifles succinctly stated, 'Battalion surrounded. Twenty two officers and 566 men missing.'[1]

This traumatic assault continued over a period of two months. The Fifth Army, commanded by General Sir Hugh Gough, was to all intents and purposes destroyed. Gough, notorious as a Curragh 'mutineer', was dismissed, arguably as a scapegoat for deeper failings in the army. When, with French assistance, the initial German assault in the Somme Valley was held in front of Amiens, Ludendorff mounted a second massive assault on the British in the vicinity of Ypres. The BEF was haemorrhaging, losing a quarter of a million combat troops in less than a month.

The British War Cabinet was thrown into crisis. For the first time since August 1914 the prospect of losing the war on the battlefield had become imminent. Unless the British army could be provided with manpower to rebuild the shattered divisions, the BEF would cease to exist. In these circumstances the War Cabinet took the most contentious decision of the war; they extended compulsory military service to Ireland. In doing so they guaranteed the failure of any attempt to settle the Irish question on the basis of Home Rule as recommended by the Irish Convention, wrecked the credibility of the Irish Parliamentary Party and permanently alienated a wide swathe of Irish opinion.

The causal link between the two events seems clear enough. The decision to conscript Ireland was, in the words of Winston Churchill, 'a battlefield decision'. Britain had reached, 'the bottom of the barrel' in terms of manpower. Lloyd George wrote in his memoirs, 'Our final Military Service Act did not achieve any very striking increase in the number of recruits; apart from Ireland, no such increase was possible.' Extending conscription to Ireland was the only way that the BEF could be rebuilt.[2]

Except that it wasn't. From the passing of the new Military Service Act to the end of the war, Ireland yielded less than 5,000 recruits for the British Army,[3] less than one eighth of the permanent casualties sustained on 21 March alone and far less than the 8,102 men 'combed out' from Churchill's Ministry of Munitions in the single week ending 5 April 1918.[4] Furthermore, as will be seen, conscription was never really applied to Ireland; these Irish recruits were yielded by a last-minute voluntary recruiting campaign designed to stave off the implementation of conscription. Judged in isolation as an act of military value, conscripting the Irish was a massive failure. Indeed in terms of the military balance it was probably negative, pinning down British forces to deal with the resultant disorder, which could have been better used elsewhere.

The decision to extend conscription to Ireland was apparently a blunder. But was it? What was the reasoning of the decision-makers at this critical moment in 1918? There are several competing explanations. The obvious answer was that the War Cabinet was misinformed, that there was a genuine belief that extending conscription to Ireland would yield a significant number of men.[5] Whilst this is not impossible, an examination of the discussions surrounding the decision demonstrates that it is a rather unlikely explanation. The second explanation rests with the machiavellian mind of David Lloyd George. In this view Irish conscription was an ingenious attempt designed to cut through the Gordian knot of the 'damnable question' of Ireland.[6] There are several variants of this and it should not be ruled out entirely, but it is equally implausible as a fully viable explanation of the 'battlefield decision'.

To understand the decision to conscript Ireland it is important to remember that the extension of conscription to Ireland was just one part of a comprehensive, indeed draconian, extension of military service in the whole of the British Isles and that this is the key to understanding why it occurred.

The minutiae of the unfolding of the decision, from the first inception of the extension of military service to the passing of the act, helps to unlock the reasoning behind it. The first meeting of the War Cabinet to discuss the specific manpower crisis created by the German offensive was on 23 March 1918. But the issue of manpower had been a persistent difficulty for the War Cabinet for many previous months. Manpower policy had been evolving on an *ad hoc* basis since the outbreak of the war. Applying conscription to a nation which had generally opposed compulsory military service had never been easy, and conscription had developed in a way which was hardly optimum judged purely in terms of military efficiency. Historians have rather tended to accept at face value the view of politicians that Britain was running out of manpower by the end of 1917.[7]

The argument is that Britain was unable to release more men for the army without seriously jeopardising munitions output. This contention is not particularly viable. The example of France is instructive. By March 1918, France had suffered at least three times as many permanent casualties from a male military age population which was substantially smaller than Great Britain's. The French manpower pool was genuinely depleted. Yet at the same time France was sustaining a larger army on the Western Front than Britain *and* producing significantly more munitions.[8] Of course, this is not the whole story: Britain did have manpower commitments that France was spared. Britain was manning the world's largest navy, producing large numbers of naval and merchant ships and maintaining a substantial output of coal. Yet to a large extent these represented priority decisions rather than objective constraints. For example, the arrival of American battleships gave the allied fleets a superiority in the North Sea that amounted to overkill. There was no objective obstacle to diminishing the substantial manpower demands of the main British battle fleet. This was not done. In the first systematic manpower budget, the British government deliberately chose to give the army the lowest priority on manpower.

Just as serious were the political and administrative constraints on rational deployment of manpower. The greatest critic of manpower policy was the minister in charge of implementing it. Sir Auckland Geddes, a medical doctor by training, took the view that the rational deployment of manpower should be determined by the criteria of fitness and vital irreplaceable skills.[9] Instead the system he inherited was complicated by institutional infighting, trade union defence of vested interest, age restrictions, compassionate exemptions and bureaucratic inertia. Even before his appointment, replacing Neville Chamberlain, he had sent a sharp memorandum in July 1917 damning the existing system. When appointed in October 1917 he took an overview of the situation. There was no doubt that there was a shortage of men in Category A, those fit for infantry service between the ages of 18 and 25 remaining in civilian life. Geddes believed that the maximum availability was 270,000. He estimated that there were a further 700,000 men between the ages of 25 and 41, the existing parameters of conscription. In both categories many of these men were genuinely irreplaceable. There were two possible further sources, each politically sensitive: men in Great Britain between the ages of 41 and 50 and the extension of conscription to Ireland. Both categories would yield a further 150,000 fit men. Geddes recommended that the first action should be a comb out within the existing parameters and that the government should seek to raise the maximum age to 45. He also advocated conscripting Ireland. But at a War Cabinet meeting, all of these proposals were rejected. Manpower policy had reached an impasse.

The problem was exacerbated by several crucial informal, but very real, constraints. The first was a government pledge not to send 18-year-olds to France. The second was that Trade Union opposition to combing out was intense. In particular, the Amalgamated Society of Engineers had raised the cry of industrial conscription, claiming that conscription was being used to break the union. Informal strikes were the response to attempts to conscript physically fit engineers. By the spring of 1918 it appeared that the coal miners would follow suit. Finally there was the tribunal appeal procedure. This neglected aspect of conscription policy was a devastating constraint. It not only denied men to the army, it seriously delayed those who were called up.

Extracting fit men of military age from war industry had become an administrative nightmare. First of all a case had to be made to an advisory committee that the man was replaceable, and he had to be proved fit to serve. Assuming that the employer did not appeal there would then be the risk of an unofficial strike which might involve time-consuming arbitration. If the man's conscription was upheld he would almost certainly appeal to the over-worked local tribunal, possibly on conscientious grounds, more probably on grounds of domestic responsibility. Assuming that the tribunal upheld his conscription, which was by no means automatic, he had the right to take his case to an appeal tribunal, and subsequently, if he chose, to the Central Tribunal. In all likelihood the local tribunal would grant a temporary exemption: this might be appealed by the military representative but that was time-consuming and by no means guaranteed to succeed. Even getting a fully fit non-unionised man in non-essential industry actually into uniform could take months. In a nominally conscriptionist Great Britain, the government's ability to make someone serve against their will was, at least in the short term, almost non-existent.[10]

Taken together these constraints meant that by 1918 Britain had put a significantly lower proportion of its available manpower into the army than most other combatants. Furthermore a large number of men were still not being sent over to France. Significant numbers of men could be found to meet the German offensive if some of these constraints were removed or modified, but the risks of such action were high in terms of home front morale.

This was the context of the War Cabinet meeting on 23 March. The first actions were to apply emergency measures to adjust priorities and release immediately available manpower. These were not insubstantial: 5,000 officer cadets were drafted as infantry and 88,000 men on leave were instantly recalled; 45,000 trained soldiers working in agriculture and 16,000 in munitions were made available as were 27,000 men from Home Defence. Nevertheless it was clear that these forces would only replace losses for a very short time. The first contentious decision was taken that day. The pledge not to send 18-year-olds to France was revoked. It had been stated that they would only be sent in an emergency. The War Cabinet concluded, 'the emergency has arisen'. 30,000 18-year-olds were immediately released. This was the first step on the road to Irish conscription.[11]

Geddes was charged at the meeting with putting forward proposals with a view to 'increase the total amount of manpower available'. He warmed to the task: it was an opportunity to remove, 'obstacles which stand in the way of the full mobilisation of our manpower and for tapping such new sources as still remain'. Both clauses of this statement are vitally important.

Two days later the War Cabinet discussed Geddes's proposals. They were far reaching. Top of the list was a bill to 'cancel all exemptions' and 'do away with tribunals'. He further advocated raising the age limit. If it was raised to 45 then 50,000 more men could be made available to the army and if raised to 50 then a further 60,000 would be made available. Nearly 300,000 more men would be available for 'General Service'. It was stated that this 'involved a large question of policy, before any decision the whole position should be carefully considered'. It was only after this that the issue of extending the Military Service Act to Ireland was discussed. Viscount French, commander of Home Forces, gave an optimistic view of the Irish situation based on a recent visit.[12] Geddes was asked to respond. He estimated that 150,000 men could be recruited. He then made a crucial addition: 'as tribunals would not be possible in Ireland, it would be necessary if compulsory recruiting was made applicable to that country, to abolish tribunals in England'. Geddes had revealed a two-track agenda. The meeting went on to discuss the comb out of government departments, conscripting ministers of religion, the recruitment of Russian subjects, reduction of time for the call-up notice and the cutting down of medical boards.[13] In addition Ireland was now under discussion. The Prime Minister invited the Chief Secretary of Ireland, the head of the Irish Constabulary and the General Officer Commanding the British Army in Ireland to report on the practicalities of Irish Conscription.

On 26 March the Prime Minister delivered their opinions to the War Cabinet. His first interview was with the Chief Secretary, H. E. Duke, who expressed grave doubts about the proposal. Then he spoke to the head of the RIC, General Byrne, who told him that conscription was a mistake: 'by passing and enforcing such a measure: both the whole of the Catholics and nationalists in Ireland would be united against the British Empire'. He claimed that there would be the greatest difficulty enlisting men, that there would be riots and that he was very doubtful what the worth of the recruits would be. The Prime Minister had finally interviewed the army commander

Sir Bryan Mahon whom Lloyd George reported to be 'on the whole favourable' even though he had expressed the opinion that there would be 'considerable trouble'.[14]

The Cabinet was presented with a memorandum, written by Mahon, amended by Byrne and signed by Duke, presenting a composite view, although Duke expressed reservations about it. The memorandum, with Byrne's additions italicised, made grim reading. 'Conscription can be enforced, but with the *greatest* difficulty. It will be *bitterly* opposed by the *united* Nationalists and clergy'. There would be '*organised* strikes *dislocating the life of the country*'. It would require additional troops, 'at least two brigades, *I think considerably more*'. For the first fortnight 'there would be bloodshed'. Mahon believed that 160,000 or more men could be extracted, but Byrne added that '*a considerable number would be likely to give trouble*'.[15]

Even on the most optimistic basis this was hardly a resounding endorsement. The best interpretation was that at least 10,000 soldiers would need to be sent immediately to Ireland, at a time of critical shortage in France. Furthermore the country would descend into chaos and that in the long term about 160,000 men might be extracted, many of them of questionable military value.

Duke was clearly horrified at the proposal. On his watch he believed that the situation in Ireland was gradually coming under control. At the start of the year he had sent an optimistic memorandum based on postal censorship which suggested that Sinn Féin was losing ground. Localised agrarian discontent was a nagging worry, but on the whole the picture was improving and would continue to do so as long as the government did not do anything stupid, stupidity defined specifically as applying the Military Service Act to Ireland. Since then IPP success at by-elections had apparently confirmed his view.[16]

Yet the situation in Ireland was not to be foremost in the minds of the Cabinet. After the report was submitted, Lloyd George reminded them, 'the enforcement of a drastic application of compulsory military service in Great Britain was contemplated' and that this, 'would be very difficult if Ireland was exempted'.

What followed was in fact to be an elaborate pretence at considering the Irish situation. In truth the decision had clearly already been taken in the mind of the Prime Minister. He knew that 'very difficult' was an understatement – in political terms it would be impossible. He was fighting for his political life, trying to stave off military defeat and maintain a domestic consensus in Great Britain. Ireland was about to be sacrificed to the cause.

Over the next three days the fate of both islands was placed in the balance. The case was presented to the War Cabinet on 27 March. The proposals of the new Military Service Bill, if all materialised, would furnish 555,000 men from

Great Britain and 150,000 from Ireland. The major components were as follows: the abolition of tribunals would immediately release 75,000 grade 1 men and 75,000 others; raising the age to 50 would provide 110,000; more, and lowering the effective age of conscription to seventeen, through compulsory volunteer force membership, would provide another 120,000. A 'clean cut' comb out of exempted men would release about another 270,000. Ireland might thus provide additionally about 30 per cent of the manpower that was to be found from Britain.

Yet the view of the man in the best position to know was that this was a complete fiction. Duke stated, 'It would be impossible to extend the Military Service Act to Ireland in such a way as to help the war ... General Mahon believed that sooner or later, 150,000 men could be got out', but in his view, 'we might as well recruit Germans.' He believed that the result would be 'the loss of Ireland'.[17]

Desperately, Duke suggested instead a Militia ballot declared through Order in Council solely for the purpose of maintaining Irish regiments. The Cabinet considered Duke's jeremiad. Walsh indicated that conscription was sure to be opposed by Dillon and his party, 'but he did not believe that the manpower proposals now put forward could be applied to England unless at the same time conscription was applied to Ireland'. Geddes explained the general provisions of the bill once more and Addison put a spoke in the wheels by opposing the abolition of tribunals. The Labour representative, George Barnes, concurred and also expressed doubts about the inclusion of Ireland. Memoranda submitted on the Irish issue showed chaos in official thinking. Byrne and Mahon were sceptical that Duke's scheme offered substantial advantages: Duke was proposing that conscription should be extended to 'paramilitary volunteers'. Byrne and Mahon insisted that there could be no half measures in suppressing the inevitable protests.

Soundings continued; the next day the Chief Justice of Ireland was called. He was unambiguous. There would be bloodshed. The Cabinet then received one of the most remarkable opinions of the entire crisis. Sir Edward Carson responded to the Chief Justice's comments, 'the result of conscription in Ireland would be such that its introduction [was] not worth contemplating'.[18] In the general discussion that followed, the War Cabinet thought through the implications. They discussed the growth of Sinn Féin numbers since the uprising. Then they considered the Imperial dimension. It was concluded that broaching conscription would destroy the Irish convention. In apocalyptic terms it was suggested that the Irish, if conscripted, would not fight, that they would be 'a weakness rather than a strength' and that they might even 'shoot their officers'. Only French seems to have been optimistic that once under military law the Irish could be compelled.[19]

The Cabinet turned to the Convention report, concluding that without Irish conscription, neither parliament nor public would accept it. This part of the discussion has given rise to substantial historiographical speculation. But the real key was the conclusion, the summing up by Geddes. He stated, 'the British public would not accept the extension of the military age to 50 *with no tribunals* unless conscription was applied to Ireland'[20](my italics).

Lloyd George's next action was eloquent testimony to his thinking. He arranged to discuss the conscription of Ireland with interested parties. Not, as one might imagine, the IPP. They had been excluded all along from the decision making. Instead Lloyd George arranged to meet leaders of British Labour. In formal terms the Labour Party was opposed to the conscription of Ireland as well as deeply suspicious of the extension of military service in Britain. The next day Lloyd George reported back. Officially Labour would not oppose Irish conscription as an emergency measure. Furthermore one prominent figure had pressed his opinion that 'he would not feel justified advocating on the platform the raising of the Military Age to fifty unless some form of conscription was applied to Ireland'. It was this, not the wildly optimistic opinion of French that conscription in Ireland would actually work, which was the green light to legislate.[21]

In the meantime objections from the Board of Trade and the Local Government Board were forcing Geddes to back down on the complete abolition of tribunals. But tribunals would remain a key piece in the Military Service Bill jigsaw, because of the difficulties in creating a uniform practice between Britain and Ireland.[22]

A committee was now formed. In their first minutes Geddes was reported as stating that there were 900,000 fit men still in civil life – whether he was including Ireland is unclear. He insisted that in practical terms Irish tribunals would have to be nominated bodies, the implication being that this would have to be true in Britain as well. The exact solution for Ireland was left indeterminate – either the extension of the new act or an Order in Council.

But the decision of principle had clearly be taken no later than 30 March. A telegram from Lloyd George to the Dominion Prime Ministers reveals this, as well as another dimension to the crisis, 'The fundamental problem is manpower ... We are also prepared to face trouble in Ireland because we feel it is vital to prove ourselves stronger than the Germans this summer ... we trust that your Government will do its utmost to get as many men to Europe as it possibly can.'[23]

Discussion now moved to a Cabinet sub-committee with the responsibility of creating a draft bill. A series of submissions was made. The Chief Secretary and the Lord Chief Justice of Ireland again protested against Irish conscription. Duke once more pointed out that recent by-elections had seen the nationalists defeat Sinn Féin and that this trend would continue in the imminent King's County election unless something occurred 'to excite strong public feeling'. The Lord Chief Justice pointed to the unviability of a tribunal system in Ireland.[24]

The Committee sat for three days. A memorandum on 2 April 1918 by the Attorney General of Ireland was the most vigorous and detailed protest lodged to that date. Conscription was a 'blunder' which would 'inevitably lead to rebellion'. Furthermore 'the essence of the consideration, it would prove ineffective'. The practical objections were clearly laid out. The practical difficulties were 'immense', operation would 'be slow and involve the employment of a great number of troops'. The conscripts, when obtained, 'would have a consuming hatred of the cause they were conscripted to serve'. He predicted, 'several priests would be shot defending their flocks'. All of this would hold good even if conscription were accompanied 'by any measure of Home Rule'.[25]

The Chief Secretary again weighed in with a memorandum rhetorically asking a series of 'grave questions'. These cut to the essence of the issue. Would parliament 'consent to place further burdens of service on the British population without requiring service from Ireland?' Duke concluded no. Would Home Rule pass without conscription? Likewise no. Would parliament pass conscription of Ireland in the face of the resistance of the IPP and the people of Ireland? Duke felt that it depended on the handling. If passed, could conscription be enforced? This was a matter for the military and police, although his scepticism was clear. If conscription were enforced would these Irish troops be of any use? Duke was immensely doubtful.[26]

Duke had acknowledged the fatal truth. The only one of his grave points that really mattered was the first. As the committee sat the pressure mounted. An ominous memorandum from the Army Council pointed to a deficit of 282,000 men for the army. It was highly critical of past manpower policy and deeply threatening. The military had in effect issued an ultimatum, demanding immediate action. Included in this was Irish conscription.[27]

On 3 April Geddes again vigorously protested against the retention of tribunals in Britain, claiming that he had understood his instruction had been to implement a 'levy en masse'. To his frustration, other members of the committee prevailed and tribunals were retained. But extending military service to Ireland in the same bill meant that the powers of tribunals would inevitably have to be watered down in Britain.

The final full War Cabinet discussion on the bill returned once more to the issue of tribunals. At the meeting, 'the opinion was very strongly expressed that the system of tribunals in England had proved very unsatisfactory', in all probability by Geddes. Lloyd George responded that it was, 'essential that the same rules regarding tribunals should apply in both countries'. Once again the apparent necessity of imposing conscription on Ireland was proving useful in forcing through an unpopular change to the operation of conscription in Britain. Geddes's attempt to scrap them altogether had failed and tribunals would survive in a very watered down form, but the impracticality of genuinely representative tribunals in Ireland would be used to reduce the independence of British tribunals.[28]

On 6 April 1918, the Prime Minister gathered together all ministers, both those inside and outside the War Cabinet. The meeting was to begin with a classic oration. He summarised the dire military emergency. This justified the sending overseas of boys under the age of nineteen. He reviewed the delay in recruiting miners and engineers, commenting that despite the Local Government Board's faith in tribunals, they meant 'delay and the first thing that 50,000 miners released for military service have done is to put in applications to tribunals'. To meet the emergency two things had to be done – call up every available man and draw on the Americans.

After this long preamble he turned to 'a highly controversial question'. Ireland was to be conscripted. No doubt there would be trouble, 'perhaps bloodshed'. This had weighed on his mind. Two considerations had settled his view. First he gave a cursory nod to the political long game, 'even if Home Rule was carried tomorrow, the army and navy would still be under the control of the Imperial parliament'. Then a long and impassioned explanation:

> I do not believe it is possible in this country to tear industry about, to break up single businesses, to take fathers of 45 and upwards from their homes to fight the battles of a Catholic nationality on the continent without deep resentment of the spectacle of sturdy young Catholics in Ireland spending their time in increasing the difficulties of this country by drilling and by compelling us to keep troops in Ireland, I do not know any grounds of justice and equity on which conscription could not be applied to Ireland. We have now decided that we cannot apply these drastic and devastating proposals to England, Scotland and Wales, without applying conscription to Ireland where there is not even a rationing system. We cannot go to the House of Commons and ask our people to make sacrifices, sacrifices which the Irish in America are making and leave the Irish at home out.

The Prime Minister touched on Home Rule again and then admitted, 'It will take time to put conscription in place in Ireland. We have not the machinery.' The Cabinet began to question the Prime Minister on the implications for Home Rule and spent some time discussing it. It was only at the end of the discussion that H. A. L. Fisher asked the obvious and crucial question, 'Are you definitely satisfied that there is a military advantage in applying conscription to Ireland?'

Lloyd George replied, 'That is the consideration that chiefly worried me. Is it worthwhile in a military sense? You will get 50,000 at any rate, a minimum who will fight.' Churchill supported him, citing the views of the Generals in France, it was 'a battlefield decision, but a wise one'.[29]

The decision would be presented then and ever afterwards as a military necessity. It was, but not primarily in the sense that Lloyd George ever expected to get any men from Ireland. The speech makes this abundantly clear. In advocating the controversial measure he did not mention once that a single Irish recruit would be forthcoming. He spoke at length of equity of sacrifice, even introducing an utterly irrelevant comment about the lack of rationing in Ireland. He admitted that conscription would cause chaos and because of the total lack of machinery it would take time, time which was at a premium, but until quizzed by Fisher he avoided giving a number. When one was given, it was plucked out of the air. There was no evidence for it and the mass of informed opinion gathered in the previous two weeks did not support it. The Cabinet may have believed it, but whether it did or not was secondary. Indeed there is even some doubt as to whether the Prime Minister really gave a number at all: according to Fisher's diary it was Derby and not Lloyd George who claimed Irish conscription would produce 50,000 good troops.[30]

Churchill, ever belligerent, might have believed the generals he cited, although he rarely believed them about anything else. But Churchill was Minister of Munitions and responsible for combing out men for the army. He too had every reason to require that a sense of equity of sacrifice should be sustained. Two Cabinet memoranda illustrate this concern. A report on the labour situation by the Ministry of Munitions for the week ending 10 April described the situation as 'distinctly tranquil', but warned that this should not 'obscure the likelihood of organised opposition to the manpower proposals'. It went on to state that, 'the conscription of middle aged men is bound to be unpopular with all classes and that it is not confined to the working classes is shown by the vigorous protest of London solicitors.' A report for the same week on Pacifist and Revolutionary organisations was more explicit: 'Men between forty and fifty are inclined to raise again the cry of industrial conscription. I believe that if they knew conscription was to be introduced in Ireland, they would be inclined to accept the position, but as long as they see Irishmen of military age coming over to jobs in this country, it is difficult to get them to believe that their national existence depends on every fit man taking his share of the danger.'[31]

The bill that would be put before parliament would hopefully furnish the manpower to stave off defeat and it would do so by an unprecedented call-up of the population of Great Britain. It might furnish some men from Ireland, more likely it would not. It would certainly have grave political consequences, possibly including Duke's predicted loss of Ireland. But that could not be helped. A letter from Robert Cecil put it clearly. Regarding conscripting Ireland, 'the necessity exists'. No member of Cabinet, 'or indeed anyone else disputes this'. He continued, 'It is felt by many, including myself, that to ask the English, Scots and Welsh to submit to very drastic provisions ... while leaving the Irish free would be so unjust as to imperil the whole war spirit of the county.'[32]

The passage through parliament was turbulent. From the first introduction of the bill on 9 April 1918, the Irish nationalists met the bill with a genuine sense of moral outrage and a keen realisation that they were fighting for their political lives. Yet this vehement opposition to the Irish clause served the Government well by focusing attention upon it.

The Prime Minister's speech introducing the bill bore some relationship to that he had given to ministers, but in parliament it was heckled and interrupted by Irish members. He introduced the bill as involving 'extreme sacrifices on the part of large classes of the population' as a matter of 'extreme necessity'. There would be a clean cut of munition workers, miners, civil servants and transport workers. Local tribunals would be replaced by nominated bodies. Ireland was to be conscripted because, 'an emergency has arisen which makes it necessary to put boys of eighteen and men of fifty in the Army'. Dillon's response was ,'You will not get any men from Ireland by compulsion – not a man.'[33] Asquith, the official leader of the largest opposition group, wanted to know if the military results would justify the act and deliberately avoided going into the question of Ireland. His voice of calm consideration was lost in the tumult. Devlin asked pointedly if a single representative of Ireland had been consulted, a question Dillon would repeat. Almost unnoticed, the Prime Minister was able to slip in the fact that local tribunals were to become nominated bodies, an announcement which under normal circumstances would have been highly contentious.[34]

Things got very ugly, the extreme 'patriot', Joynson-Hicks stating that he had seen the sacrifices made by England, Scotland and Wales whilst Ireland refused to play her fair part and that he was glad that the IPP had been exposed as traitors. Another MP endorsed Irish conscription as 'even-handed justice'. Irish MPs responded both emotionally and rationally. J. O'Connor described how a Dublin constituent had said that the district was 'becoming alright' as long as the government did not 'by some act of stupidity drive them back to chaos'. Another nationalist wanted to hear, 'the candid opinion of the Chief-Secretary', which was one thing that the Prime Minister would certainly not allow. That refrain would echo over the next few days as Irish MPs rightly smelt a rat. William O'Brien stated that he was renouncing his 'dreams of reconciliation'. The government was digging a gulf that 'no one alive would ever see bridged over'.[35]

There was a little support for the IPP from other quarters. One English member did concur that conscripting Ireland was 'an insane proposal'. A Welsh MP gave notice of his intention to oppose the whole act.[36] Even on the first day one nationalist, Tim Healy, saw straight through Lloyd George:

> He has two arguments. Both repugnant. His first argument was – and this was in his 'Daily Mail' style – How can we – when we are increasing the age up to fifty for the Britisher, allow fine strapping papists of twenty-one to idle about in Ireland. A splendid argument – and so convincing to this House – though not the Irish portion – that what other argument can you want?[37]

Healy claimed that it was the uneasy conscience of an ex-Home Ruler at work. This was not an argument Lloyd George believed in, and Healy also pointed to the lack of the Irish Chief Secretary's name on the foot of the bill. In fact Healy's comment was so close to the tone of the Prime Minister's earlier speech to the ministers and his appreciation of Duke's doubts were so acute that one might suspect a tip off.

But the argument of equity of sacrifice was one that was biting hard in the commons. Even a Scottish member who was somewhat sceptical about the bill pointed to resentment on the Clyde when young Irishmen had come to fill the places of the sons and brothers of Scottish workers.[38]

The summing up on the first day was by a man guaranteed to provoke nationalist outrage. Whether this would have been increased or lessened had they known that he had advised against conscripting Ireland is a moot point. In the House of Commons, Edward Carson supported the bill. As an 'Irish member' he would not stand up when calls were made, 'for sacrifices of the most terrible and harassing nature on the inhabitants of Great Britain were being made and ask that my own part of the United Kingdom should be spared'.[39]

The next day, the Home Secretary spoke. In an exchange with Dillon he touched on tribunals. There were of course, none in Ireland, so time would have to be taken to appoint them. Dillon stated that no one would serve on them. Cave insisted that they would be appointed, a chorus of nationalists claimed that they could not be. Cave then stated that they would be, 'under the machinery which would be applied to the whole country'.[40]

A Scottish MP who served on several tribunals spotted the point. The Home Secretary had passed over them in a few sentences. 'I am sure he will excuse me if I take a greater interest.' Under Clause 4 of the bill, reorganising tribunals, 'the Government may do whatever it likes'. Asquith picked up the theme: Clause 4 was 'not in conformity with our traditions or indeed with the interests of the nation'. Nield, the chairman of the London appeal tribunal urged the government to reconsider.[41]

When Geddes rose to speak, announcing that the bill would involve real clean cuts, he came under attack from the political right and left. Thomas, speaking on behalf of Labour, claimed that the act would break the agreements with the trade unions, whilst the maverick 'patriotic' independent MP, Pemberton Billing, attacked the policy as allowing 'aliens to pinch British businesses'.[42]

The next day both resumed their attacks. Billing asked, 'Are the whole of the English population to suffer without having a voice in this very important matter?' Thomas demanded that, 'We should be able to put down reasoned amendments to protect the people that we represent.' He added, 'Anyone listening to the debate so far would assume that we were discussing a purely Irish bill.' Another MP, Ryland Adkins, claimed that the bill, 'proposes at one stroke to abolish all the constitutional regulations and safe guards which at present hedge in enlistment and recruitment.'[43] The bundling together of Irish conscription with the British measures now served a useful purpose for the government; it had divided the potential opposition. Time was limited. Adkins demanded time to debate Clause 4. Dillon rose and expressed sympathy, but emphatically demanded that the time be used to discuss the Irish provision.[44]

The first reading of the bill passed. The next day Pemberton Billing rose to demand that the British and Irish clauses of the bill be separated to give adequate time. This was rejected. On 15 April the bill went to committee. Again the issue of tribunals was raised. When quizzed on whether, 'the same class and character of tribunals' would be set up in Britain and Ireland, Fisher was evasive.[45]

Healy pounced. 'The tribunal will still be there, but the body will be a corpse ... Of all the extraordinary declarations I ever heard made, that ... is the most extraordinary.' This was how the Irish issue was being used, 'one of the great safeguards' of the Military Service Act for the English was being removed 'because you cannot have one law for England and another for Ireland and therefore the tribunal is to be nominated. You could not set up any in Ireland except by nomination, and accordingly poor England is to have the same system.' Healy was desperately trying to rally British support for Irish opposition, but he was very close to catching the precise reasoning of the War Cabinet. Devlin followed through:

> Everyone knows why conscription has been introduced to Ireland. There is not a single man on these benches who believes that this measure will be of the slightest military advantage ... Ireland has been brought in because you want to create a series of battalions of English grandfathers ... They want to obscure the issues and chloroform British opinion.[46]

One or two MPs took the point. The measure was, according to Thomas, 'to deceive the British democracy' and Smallwood admitted, regarding tribunals, 'My Irish friends have seen something in view which we did not see before.' Nevertheless the new Military Service Act was overwhelmingly passed, by a vote of 276 to 134.

The calculation regarding parliament had proved correct, but was Irish conscription required to sell the new act to the British people? There is every indication that it was.

The best selling weekly newspaper in Britain, *John Bull*, the mouthpiece of the demagogue (and crook) Horatio Bottomley, devoted a long editorial to conscription in its edition of 13 April, which was on sale during the parliamentary debate. Entitled, 'No panic call up' it stated bluntly:

There must be no more nonsense about Ireland ... You cannot justify calling up the men of England, Scotland and Wales of middle age while lusty young men in Ireland are living off the fat of uncouponed towns and drilling, not to fit themselves to fight the Hun, but to fight each other ... Is it fair and reasonable – is their any meaning in 'equality of sacrifice', so long as these young fellows dodge their duty ... the Government will have the people of Great Britain behind them in any measure which will make it obligatory for Ireland to assume its rightful place in the fight for civilization ... I think I know the British public as well as most men. I know their thoughts and hopes to-day. I know their sufferings and their sacrifices. They must be treated fairly; they will deeply resent anything like a humbugging scheme, which, while it makes a further and far reaching call on the manhood – and the middle aged manhood of this country, leaves Ireland for all effective military purposes the happy land of the neutral, free from every one of these restrictions which press heavily if necessarily upon the homes of England and able to pursue the path of uninterrupted prosperity which without the money and support of this country they could never enjoy.[47]

Sometimes misery demands company. The British people by April 1918 were conscripted, tired, hungry, intermittently bombed and more than a little war weary, and were in no mood to tolerate a neighbour which appeared to be treacherous, shirking and profiteering.[48] Conscripting Ireland was punishment; a vindictive act to ease the pain.

The nadir was reached in a comment in the comic weekly *The Passing Show* where it was argued that Britain had the right to conscript Ireland, because the Irish were fed by the British Empire, a statement of breathtaking historic insensitivity. Such commentary which is also apparent in private letters and diaries, demonstrates the extent to which the government was backed into a corner on the question and explains why it persisted with a policy which was instantly revealed as a failure. Attempts to back down were met with violent rhetorical opposition on 4 May 1918, when it appeared that the government would shelve Irish conscription in favour of a renewed voluntary scheme. *John Bull* headlined, 'Why Lloyd George will go'.[49]

Nevertheless the government rode the storm. By conscripting Ireland, the government survived the great challenge on the manpower question when it came. It is a moot point whether the Coalition would have held together during the Maurice Debate without it.

The view that Lloyd George was pursuing an agenda related to the Irish question does not stand up. There was much talk about the relationship of conscription to Home Rule, but conscription was not introduced to guarantee unionist acquiescence to the Convention proposals. Nor was it introduced as part of a complicated double game to permanently shelve both Home Rule and conscription as a temporary solution to the Irish question. If Lloyd George was intending to take the sting out of Irish politics it is hard to understand how he could advocate the use of aircraft to disperse anti-conscriptionist protests as he did on 29 April 1918 according to a shocked H. A. L. Fisher. In the same diary entry Fisher stated that Lloyd George felt English public opinion, 'would applaud the violent enforcement of conscription'.[50]

As it turned out conscription was not violently enforced – it was not enforced at all. After May 1918 it was no longer needed to mollify public opinion: the British public simply had to think that the government intended to conscript Ireland, the government did not have go to the trouble of doing so. But in the highly symbolic world of Irish politics, the damage had been done. If a solid body of Irish nationalist MPs in Westminster was entirely unable to prevent the imposition of a massively unpopular measure on Ireland, then the entire point of representation in Westminster was removed. Sinn Féin abstentionism became more attractive. Furthermore, 'constitutional' nationalist claims that they could prevent conscription were falsified and 'advanced' nationalist predictions that conscription would be forced on Ireland were borne out. Home Rule was permanently discredited, it was made clear that a Home Rule parliament would lack the power to decide what was literally a life and death issue for its constituents, and Home Rule was linked in the popular mind with conscription. The rout of the IPP in December 1918 was rendered a certainty.

Even in the long unhappy history of Anglo-Irish relations, the application of the Military Service Bill to Ireland was an unusually cold-blooded piece of cynicism. A policy which could not work in Ireland and which may not even have been intended to work, was introduced in order to force through a workable conscription policy in Britain. The extent to which the policy had been pushed through in the face of informed opinion is best indicated not by the inevitable opposition of nationalists but by the fact that it had led directly to the resignation of Chief Secretary Duke, Lord Lieutenant Wimborne and army commander, Mahon.[51] It is difficult to think of any other piece of British policy towards Ireland carried out in the face of such overwhelming opposition from Dublin Castle. Lloyd George's mission was to pacify England; to buy time and some consent from his critics to the right and to the left and to head off the developing attack by his military commanders which would focus on the manpower question. He had to prevent the government from falling and needed to sustain national morale. Above all he had to deliver the troops in time for the battle not to be lost.

It worked far better than anyone could have anticipated. In August and September 1918, middle-aged Britons, industrial comb outs and above all the vital 18-year-olds, not only kept the British army in the field, they smashed the Imperial German Army and broke the Hindenburg line. The German army, bulked out by discontented industrial workers who had been drawn without consent or consultation from a dispirited home front, suffered a catastrophic collapse in morale. It had been a near-run thing and a slight edge in what Cecil had described as the 'war spirit' had been dispro-portionately significant.

On 16 April 1918, Duke had reported to the War Cabinet that Ireland was falling apart, there were massive protests in Belfast, including Protestants; preparations were being made for the formation of a provisional government and that conscription was unenforceable with 15,000 troops, probably unenforceable with any number. Lloyd George responded that they would stand firm: 'Lincoln had to face a similar situation'. Duke angrily responded that Lincoln had had the country behind him, whilst 'Ireland was united in opposition'. But Lloyd George was doubtless aware of another Lincoln analogy, not conscription, but the Emancipation Proclamation. On that occasion Lincoln had freed the slaves in precisely the areas he did not control, he was mocked for doing so and his critics attacked it as an empty gesture. But gestures can be crucial and decisive – Lincoln used the procla-mation to silence his critics, to show the war was being fought with every possible means, no matter how uncomfortable. For Lloyd George, Irish conscription had served the same purpose.[52]

When the issue was national survival, the 'loss of Ireland' was a price that would be paid. With nice irony, Churchill in a similar crisis in 1940 would take another 'battlefield decision' and offer de Valera reunification. On that occasion it was de Valera's cynicism which changed history.

By chilling coincidence the crucial meetings of the War Cabinet had occurred over Easter Week in 1918. Once again a passion play was enacted, but this time in secret. The War Cabinet washed its hands of the Irish ques-tion and the constitutional nationalists were sacrificed to appease the British public demanding a sacrifice.

Notes

1 There are many accounts of 'Operation Michael'. For an evocative summary see M. Brown, *The Imperial War Museum Book of 1918: The Year of Victory* (London, Pan, 1998), pp. 45–82.

2 For Churchill see PRO, Cab 23/6/385, War Cabinet Minutes (hereafter WCM), 3 April 1918; and Bodl., H.A.L. Fisher Mss, Box 11, H. A. L. Fisher, Carbon copy of diary, entry for 3 April. Fisher described Churchill as 'vehement'. For Lloyd George's retrospective assessment, see D. Lloyd George, *War Memoirs*, Vol. 2 (London, Odhams, 1936), p. 1601. These memoirs are very carefully constructed on such points. Lloyd George was not only defending a controversial decision regarding Ireland, but also covering himself from the charge of withholding British manpower from the army, a charge that would soon surface in the Maurice debate.

3 For a full discussion of the last phase of Irish recruiting see K. Jeffery, *Ireland and the Great War* (Cambridge, Cambridge University Press, 2000), pp. 6–9. The figure given here might be slightly misleading as it refers specifically to recruitment to the army. In the last three months of the war 56 per cent of Irish volunteers entered the newly formed RAF. But it was the army, particularly the infantry, which was undergoing the manpower crisis and

the Irish contribution to overcoming this was negligible.

4 PRO, Cab 24/GT 4238, Ministry of Munitions memorandum to War Cabinet week ending 10 April. This was exclusive of the 'substantial' number of munition workers who volunteered.

5 A certain amount of credence is given to this view in R. J. Q. Adams and P. Poirier, *The Conscription Controversy in Great Britain 1900–1918* (London, Macmillan, 1987), pp. 230–7. The undoubted deviousness of Lloyd George makes such interpretations very tempting, but it is notable that this distrust that he inspired could lead to precisely the opposite conclusion. John Dillon believed that Lloyd George had cold bloodedly attached conscription to Home Rule precisely in order to 'let HELL loose in Ireland' which would allow him to wriggle out of Home Rule altogether; Cited in T. Hennessey, *Dividing Ireland: World War I and Partition* (London, Routledge, 1998), p. 221.

6 G. Dangerfield, *The Damnable Question: A Study in Anglo-Irish Relations* (London and New York, Quarter, 1976).

7 See for example K. Grieves, *The Politics of Manpower* (Manchester, Manchester University Press, 1988). From a different angle see also J. M. Winter, *The Great War and the British People* (London, Macmillan, 1985) which stresses that by 1918 the pool of men fit for frontline service was shrinking fast.

8 See for example J. J. Becker, *The Great War and the French People* (Leamington Spa, Berg, 1985). Various objections could be raised to this comparison. The French population was more rural and a lot of anecdotal evidence suggests that standards of health and physique were higher in the French population. Likewise the French made much more systematic use of Prisoners of War, foreign workers and colonial populations in both industry and agriculture. This should be balanced against the fact that a significant proportion of the more densely populated territory where some at least of the available manpower had been lost to the French government had been occupied by the Germans.

9 See PRO, Cab 24/GT 1481, memorandum by Geddes, 'The theory and practice of recruiting', July 1917, in response to the memoranda of June 1917, 'Position and prospects of recruiting' PRO, Cab 24/GT 1057, and July 'Recruiting dissatisfaction' PRO, Cab 24/GT 1445. Geddes' memorandum states, 'Individual, domestic and financial interests should not *per se* be a ground for exemptions.'

10 The actual operation of military service tribunals in Britain has not yet been given sufficient attention by historians. This is largely because the records of Local and Appeal Tribunals have generally been destroyed. Where they are available they present a surprising picture of generosity and widespread exemption. This could be particularly true in rural areas. This is not the place to discuss this in detail, but a small illustration might prove helpful. In a single diary entry for 16 May 1918 the Reverend Andrew Clark, the vicar of Great Leighs in Essex mentions no less than 5 young men who had only just been called to the colours (including the twin sons of a farmer). In the two months of April and May, 10 names are mentioned in this context. In the entire war 67 men from Great Leighs served. This rather suggests that in this village a significant proportion of those fit to serve had been exempted until March 1918 and this was almost certainly typical of the English countryside. See A. Clark, *Echoes of the Great War* (ed. J. Munson, Oxford, Oxford University Press, 1988), p. 235.

11 PRO, Cab 23/5/371, WCM, 23 March 1918.

12 The apparent optimism of French which flew in the face of most of the expert opinion is surprising. One possible interpretation is that his argument was essentially political, that the real agenda for French was to gain the power for a military crackdown on dissent in Ireland which would be aided by the enforcement of conscription. French also believed that if young Irishmen could be removed from the pernicious influences of advanced nationalist troublemakers by being brought into the army it would be possible to undermine the

opposition. Such a view seems consistent with some of his comments during these discussions. See C. Townshend, *Making the Peace: Public Order and Public Security in Modern Britain* (Oxford, Oxford University Press, 1993) and D. Fitzpatrick, *The Two Irelands, 1912–1939* (Oxford, Oxford University Press, 1998), p. 74

13 PRO, Cab 23/5/372, WCM, 25 March 1918.

14 *Ibid.*, Cab 23/5/374, 27 March 1918.

15 *Ibid.*, Appendix, Cab 23/5/374.

16 This important memorandum is PRO, Cab 24/GT 3233, dated 5 January 1918. Duke commented that any attempt to conscript Ireland seemed 'unlikely'. A report on postal censorship dated 21 January 1918 quantified sentiment in Ireland. 22 per cent of the population was assessed as 'violently' pro-Sinn Féin, 18 per cent moderately sympathetic and 60 per cent were 'loyalist'; PRO, Cab 24/GT 3407. Whilst this cannot be taken as a precise 'opinion poll', it would be wrong to discount it entirely. Dublin Castle had every incentive in 1918 to try to get the picture right.

17 PRO, Cab 24/5/375, WCM, 27 March 1918.

18 Carson's attitude towards Irish conscription was much more complex than has generally been realised. His public pronouncements were in favour and this has sometimes misled historians regarding his considered opinion in March. A. J. P. Taylor however must have noticed Carson's dissent to the War Cabinet and mentioned it although he didn't footnote his evidence. It is highly probable that he based his opinion on CAB 24 (which had just been released at the time). See A. J. P. Taylor, *English History 1914–45* (Oxford, Clarendon Press, 1965), p. 147.

19 PRO, Cab 23/5/376, WCM, 28 March 1918.

20 PRO, Cab 23/4/376.

21 PRO, Cab 23/5/377, WCM, 29 March 1918.

22 PRO, Cab 24/GT 4058–4059, Memoranda by Fisher and Stanley, 28 March 1918.

23 PRO, Cab 24/GT 4098, Telegram to Dominion Prime Ministers, 30 March 1918.

24 PRO, Cab 24/GT 4099, GT 4101, Memoranda, 30 March 1918.

25 PRO, Cab 24/GT 4129, Memorandum by the Irish Attorney General (James O'Connor).

26 PRO, Cab 24/GT 4133, Chief Secretary, Memorandum 2 April.

27 PRO, Cab 24/GT 4132, Army Council, Memoranda.

28 PRO, Cab 23/6/383, WCM, 5 April 1918.

29 *Ibid.*, Cab 23/6/384, 6 April 1918.

30 Bodl., H. A. L. Fisher Mss, 11, Diary, 3 April 1918, p. 61.

31 PRO, Cab 24/GT 4197, 'Labour situation week ending 10 April 1918'; PRO, Cab 24GT 4199, 'Report on Pacifist and Revolutionary Organisations week ending 10 April 1918'.

32 R. Cecil letter, 7 April 1918, Cab 24/GT 4166, PRO.

33 *Hansard*, vol. 104, 9 April 1918. Prime Minister, cols 1337–8; Dillon, col. 1358; Devlin; col. 1372; Dillon, col. 1378.

34 *Ibid.*, Prime Minister, col. 1356.

35 *Ibid.*, Joynson-Hicks, col. 1374; Peto, col. 1379; O'Connor, col. 1382; Farrell, col. 1386; O'Brien, col. 1397.

36 *Ibid.*, Mason, col. 1398, Llewelyn Williams, col. 1417.

37 *Ibid.*, col. 1435.

38 *Ibid.*, R. Cooper, col. 1410.

39 *Ibid.*, Carson, col. 1444.

40 *Ibid.*, 10 April 1918, exchange between Cave and Dillon, cols 1481–2.

41 *Ibid.*, Maclean, cols 1493–4; Asquith, col. 1523; Nield, col. 1565.

42 *Ibid.*, Geddes, cols 1583–5; Thomas and Billing, col. 1584.

43 *Ibid.*, 11 April, Billing, col. 1698; Thomas, col. 1715; Adkins, col. 1719.

44 *Ibid.*, 11 April, Dillon, col. 1719.

45 *Hansard* vol. 105, oral answers, col. 26.

46 *Ibid.*, 15 April 1918, Healy, col. 82; Devlin, col. 94.

47 *John Bull*, 13 April 1918, pp. 6–7.

48 The precise state of morale in Britain at this time is open to debate. It was probably not as bad as the rather apocalyptic interpretation recently put forward by Brock Millman, which he bases on some of the more alarming internal surveillance reports, but there was certainly a strong undercurrent of middle class war weariness. See B. Millman, *Managing Domestic Dissent in First World War Britain* (London, Frank Cass, 2000), pp. 258–63.

49 *John Bull*, 4 May 1918.

50 Bodl., H. A. L. Fisher Mss, Fisher Diary, 11 and 29 April, p. 73. In the same meeting he had been 'furious against the Priests'.

51 See Fitzpatrick, *The Two Irelands*, p. 71

52 PRO, Cab 23/7/392, WCM, 16 April 1918.

7

Mobilising the sacred dead: Ulster unionism, the Great War and the politics of remembrance

JAMES LOUGHLIN

At the end of his study of nineteenth-century Britain, in which the tension between the centripetal and centrifugal tendencies in British society is discussed with great originality, Keith Robbins concludes that, despite internal divisions, the Great War demonstrated that a British nation did authentically exist.[1] Robbins does not include Ireland in his study, but a comprehensive approach to British identity could hardly exclude Ireland, especially as in Ulster a Protestant community existed for whom a vociferously expressed British state patriotism was its main form of national identity. Moreover, despite its contribution to the British war effort, at war's end that community would find its membership of the British state seriously at risk. This chapter is concerned with exploring how unionists employed their war experience as part of the struggle to maintain the union between Ulster and Britain in the post-war years and its place in the unionist mindset thereafter.

It has recently been argued that, unlike Britain, the Great War and the memory of it in Ireland was, and is, 'politicised'. From the beginning it was a symbol of the battle between unionism and nationalism.[2] But at its outbreak at least – before it became 'Great' and was still being assessed within the perspective of the small wars of the Victorian era – politicians in Britain, no less than in Ireland, were tempted to define its meaning in domestic political terms. Winston Churchill, for instance, hoped that a unifying struggle involving Britain and Ireland would create bonds of cohesion that would dissolve Anglo-Irish enmity.[3] Even as late as January 1916, Bonar Law could interpret the voluntary enlistment of John Redmond's Irish National Volunteers as evidence that imperial patriotism had indeed been growing in pre-war Ireland,[4] thus validating, implicitly, the policy of 'constructive unionism' which unionist governments had pursued up to 1905. 1916 is significant as the year in which the Irish question, as it had existed since Parnell had mobilised nationalist Ireland in pursuit of Home Rule in the 1880s, was dramatically transformed by the Easter Rising. The sequence of events it initiated impacted detrimentally, though differently, on both Ulster unionists and Redmondite nationalists.

Both had engaged in the war from a combination of party and wider national motives. The nationalists did so because almost all the nationalist leaders believed the aims for which it was fought were morally righteous;[5] enlistment in the British army was consistent with the objective of Home Rule within the United Kingdom; and because Redmond hoped that war service would both demonstrate Irish loyalty and remove the fears of Home Rule entertained by Ulster unionists.[6] However, the realisation that the war would not be short and that the cost in human lives was appalling, went together with a diminishing of Redmond's influence at Westminster. The Liberal Prime Minister, Herbert Asquith, created a coalition government in May 1915 that included Sir Edward Carson as well as Tory leaders. But Redmond, bound by his party's traditional policy of distance from British parties until the Irish question was resolved, would not participate. In the run-up to Easter 1916 Redmond's loss of influence went together with a perception in Ireland that the cost of Home Rule – still to be actually implemented – was fast outrunning the benefits. Accordingly, the ground was well prepared when the Easter Rising initiated the series of developments that destroyed constitutional nationalism by 1918. The historian who drew a parallel between the number (inaccurate) of Irish 'Wild Geese' who fought *against* Britain on foreign fields in the eighteenth century and those who fought *for* her in the Great War,[7] might have added that for both groups the ultimate Irish objectives for which they fought were never achieved.

Ulster unionists appeared much better placed to take advantage of a prolonged conflict. Their aggressive strain of British identity found a natural outlet in the heightened emotional context of war patriotism, appearing to personify the spirit of the British nation. So far had this tendency developed by early 1916 that Sir Edward Carson was being seriously talked about as a war leader for the British people.[8] His national prominence in this respect was pithily, if unsympathetically, indicated by a young Aldous Huxley, who in deploring the proliferation of unsightly war memorials in Britain, remarked: 'perhaps we had better imitate the Germans and build a series of Carson-turms [towers] in every town in the country, all of exactly the same pattern of bull-necked hideousness.'[9] As aggressive British patriots, Ulster unionist emotions were engaged by the war uninhibited by the qualifications and mental reservations that beset many Irish nationalists reared on a diet of anti-British propaganda. And if suspicions did persist about possible Westminster 'treachery' after the war, military training would be a good preparation for meeting it.[10]

At first sight the Easter Rising was a gift to Ulster unionists, allowing them an opportunity to counter southern treachery with demonstrations of their own loyalty. Nevertheless, the Rising also had a detrimental effect on unionist fortunes. In forcing the Irish question back on to the Westminster agenda as an issue requiring immediate attention, it compelled Carson to re-position himself as a sectional, Ulster unionist, rather than British national, leader.[11] Thereafter, while their influence at the centre of government in the immediate post-war years would still be felt, the safeguarding of their consti-tutional position would be, to a large extent, at the mercy of political devel-opments the direction of which was difficult both to gauge and direct. Unlike the pre-war period, Ulster unionism now lacked pressure groups and politi-cians either lobbying for or against it,[12] while on the Irish question the British national interest was being shaped chiefly by the pressures of the present. In this context, the war service rendered by Ulster unionists, and how it could be exploited, would be of considerable importance.

Shortly after the Rising the Ulster Division was presented with an oppor-tunity to distinguish itself when, on 1 July 1916, the first day of the four-month-long battle of the Somme, the Division lost 5,000 men in a heroic, but fruitless, assault on German lines. Imbued with a simple religious piety and ideological cohesion, singular among the various British regional and national formations,[13] the Division was almost wholly Protestant,[14] while the location and date of the battle – along the banks of the river Ancre, on the original date of the battle of the Boyne – allowed it to be easily framed within the Ulster unionist mythic tradition, encouraging the belief that, as in 1690, a great victory would be won, in the pursuit of which the Division managed to advance further than accompanying formations.[15] Yet it was not just the heroism of the Ulster Division or the appalling losses it suffered that would give the Somme importance to unionism as a bond of identity with the population of Britain in the post-war years. Over the course of the battle British losses in general were appalling – 60,000 on the first day and 419,654 overall.[16] The battle, moreover, could be as historically resonant for main-land troops as it was for the Ulster Division. After three months their slow advance brought them within reach of Crecy and Agincourt.[17]

The political context within which Ulster unionists sought to capitalise on their war experience, however, was a complex one, certainly not one in which their contribution to a glorious victory could be triumphantly cele-brated. At one level a victory had been won by 1918: 'the Kaiser was displaced, Belgium restored, Anglo-French honour vindicated and a good bag of territorial spoils acquired into the bargain.'[18] These gains, however, paled in comparison with the losses of war. Economically Britain was almost bankrupt. In four years the British contribution had cost the country £11,000,000,000, with her savings exhausted, foreign securities sold, and with debts owing to her unpaid.[19] Constitutionally, the sequence of events that would see the state reduced by the independence of southern Ireland in 1922 was already in train. But it was the human losses that cast a 'pall of death'[20] over the inter-war years. A total of 722,785 British servicemen lost their lives.[21] Over 41,000 servicemen had limbs amputated and a further 272,000 suffered other injuries, while in the late 1930s almost 640,000 servicemen were still receiving disability pensions.[22]

It was, accordingly, extremely difficult in the post-war years to establish a satisfactory rhetoric of commemoration for a conflict in which the costs could seem to have far outweighed the gains. It has been argued that in fact two, fundamentally incompatible, rhetorics of commemoration emerged; one framed in the traditional language of 'victory' and 'glory', and another, determined by the need to convey the reality of war, with both rhetorics occupying 'the same space'.[23] In a context where the traditional rhetoric of national patriotism proved incapable of expressing mass grief it was inevitable that some higher meaning to the conflict would be sought; and a consistent theme of post-war commemoration was the view that it was up to the living to invest the conflict with retrospective meaning by living better lives. The sacred dead had set the ultimate ideal of citizenship – that of sacrifice for the greater good – which the living were, as best they could, urged to emulate;[24] an argument made repeatedly by Stanley Baldwin, who, in his public persona, sought to embody British national values.[25] But to what extent did the Ulster Protestant and unionist community share the mainland reaction to the war and how its meaning might be defined?

At one level, there was no difference. For ordinary people the sense of personal loss was as profound in Belfast as it was in Bristol, or any other British city. However, the public, or 'national', context that shaped the meaning of the war in Ulster in the post-war years was quite distinctive. In particular, the Ulster Protestant community was unique in the extent to which historical myth, religio-ethnic identity, and the unresolved dilemma of their constitutional future provided an interpretative framework within which the meaning of the war was defined. To a large extent, its meaning was determined by the degree to which Ulster's contribution furthered the unionist objective of maintaining their membership of the United Kingdom; and that issue was not resolved substantially until 1922, and more completely, though far from entirely, in 1926.

The unionist exploitation of their war experience should be seen in the context both of the popular British view of Ireland as a place apart, and of Ireland's overall contribution to the British war effort, which was proportionately lower than that of Britain. It has been argued that the Irish contingent represented only three per cent of the British armed forces; just three per cent of the Irish population, and eleven per cent of its eligible men.[26] As a part of the Irish contribution to the war effort, the Ulster Protestant element was impressive, though not outstanding. Estimates in this area are inevitably imprecise, but it is known that the UVF contributed 30,000 men to the Ulster Division in a province where Catholics were just as likely to enlist as Protestants,[27] and which contributed 75,000 enlisted men from 1914–18.[28]

The total Irish figure is difficult to arrive at conclusively, but might have exceeded 200,000, with a Roman Catholic element of about 58 per cent.[29] Moreover, Ireland, North and South, had a similar experience of an early, enthusiastic, rush to the colours, followed by a tapering off as the available pool of recruits dried up and as news of the horrors on the Western Front filtered back.[30]

But if the Ulster Protestant contribution to the war has to be seen in the context of Ireland generally, post-war developments would allow them to exploit it to the full. Sinn Féin's boycott of Westminster following its great election victory of 1918 left the Ulster unionist contingent, which included six army officers,[31] in a strong position to make their case. The discrediting of constitutional nationalism in Ireland meant that there was no significant competition for the unionist exploitation of Ireland's war experience, republicans viewing the latter as a disgrace best forgotten. As both the dominant unionist and republican movements framed the war experience according to their own political agendas, Ireland, unlike Britain, was less affected by the traumatic question of what the war was fought for. With Catholic ex-servicemen politically marginalised in a now hostile environment,[32] that section of Irish society for whom the question had most relevance lacked an effective voice. It was the case that in Ulster a remnant of Redmond's Party did survive the electoral collapse of 1918. But its efforts to contest the Ulster unionist exploitation of the province's war sacrifice were too feeble to be effective.

For our purposes the most crucial period is 1919–21, during which the Irish War of Independence was fought and when, in its struggle to come to terms with Irish republican violence, the Westminster Government was moved to consider increasingly radical options, including the inclusion of Ulster in an all-Ireland parliament.

Nevertheless, fortuitously, some of the most dangerous phases of the Anglo-Irish struggle for Ulster unionism coincided with war commemorations, allowing unionists the opportunity to counterpoint any tendency of Westminster to 'betray' Ulster with a powerful reminder of the province's sacrifice in the British national interest, and, accordingly, the debt owed by Britain. The nature and scope of the Peace Day celebrations in Belfast on 9 August 1919, for instance, have to be seen in just such a context. The threat of the implementation of the Home Rule Act of 1914 – suspended for the duration of the war – had hung over Ulster since November 1918. Then, on 7 August, the Prime Minister, Lloyd George, declared his intention of giving effect to the Act by implementing it regardless of the views of any Irish party.[33] Most worrying, it was rumoured that 'county option' would be employed to solve the Ulster difficulty, which would mean the loss to unionism of the counties of Tyrone and Fermanagh, with their small, but significant, nationalist majorities. And despite their war service unionists were only too aware that the climate of opinion in Britain towards Ulster had changed since 1914, evidenced clearly in the newspapers that were now prepared to favour an Irish parliament. As the *Belfast News-Letter* noted: 'even among unionists it is not always easy to distinguish between friends and enemies'.[34] Of politicians, Walter Long, leader of the Irish unionist group at Westminster from 1906–10, was now a federal devolutionist, heading a committee that would, in November 1919, propose a scheme of Irish government consisting of two parliaments, together with an all-Ireland council intended to facilitate Irish unity and the creation of a state with quasi-dominion powers.[35]

The Belfast celebration was originally intended to take place as part of the nation-wide Peace Celebration held across the United Kingdom on 19 July. But what the *Belfast News-Letter* – in a reference, apparently, to the politically volatile situation in Belfast – described as 'circumstances that are local',[36] caused the Belfast activities to be postponed. But even without Belfast's official participation the occasion still functioned to serve Ulster unionist interests. It was marked by parades across the state, except in southern Ireland, indicating the extent to which it was alienated from British rule. In Dublin the Irish administration did manage to organise a parade of 20,000 service personnel in the presence of the Viceroy, Lord French, and with the support, at least, of the unionist population of the city.[37] In his report to the king Lord French put the best construction on the occasion, declaring that the parade was received with acclamation by 'your Majesty's Irish subjects'.[38] However, ample evidence existed to support a quite different interpretation.

The nationalist-controlled Dublin city corporation had previously decided that, as Ireland was being held down by British bayonets, there was nothing to celebrate and that the occasion would be ignored.[39] It was a position generally adopted by nationalist-controlled municipalities in the south. In Dundalk and Cork black flags were flown, while Cork, Dublin and Limerick also experienced serious disturbances with a number of policemen suffering bullet wounds.[40] Peace celebrations in Britain were not entirely without incident either, especially in Luton where ex-servicemen used the occasion to air disruptively their grievances about war pensions and other aspects of their treatment by the state.[41] The import of the Irish disturbances, however, was entirely different, symptomatic of a fundamental crisis of legitimacy facing the British state. But while this situation was of great concern to southern loyalists, it nevertheless provided Ulster unionists with a congenial environment in which to demonstrate their own loyalty to the state; for despite the official postponement of the Belfast dimension to the celebration the north still participated in the national event. Belfast had a parade of 1,100 soldiers of the Cornwall, Norfolk and Somerset regiments, through a city bedecked in flags and bunting and attended by enthusiastic crowds. Across the region, Derry, Antrim, Bangor, Portadown, Ballymena, Larne, Portstewart, and other places, participated in the celebration;[42] though in areas where nationalists and unionists were strongly represented, such as Enniskillen, disputes over the celebration could function to thwart involvement.[43] From a nationalist point of view, however, the extent of Ulster's participation in the celebration of 19 July could well seem sufficient to satisfy the requirements of a great national occasion. Certainly plans for another celebration in Belfast aroused their suspicions about the reasons behind it, and when it became known that the occasion would be recorded on film suspicions were aroused that what was being planned was little more than a great Orange demonstration against Home Rule. As the *Derry Journal* asked rhetorically: 'What will the show in Belfast be presented as afterwards? What will the cinematograph operators' record be used for?'[44]

Arrangements for a 'Civic Reception and Review of Ulster Troops' in Belfast on 9 August were published a few days after the national occasion of 19 July.[45] These were in the hands of a 'Citizens Committee' established by the Lord Mayor and Corporation of Belfast, a body under the control of the Unionist Party whose leader, Sir Edward Carson, was in the process of organising a campaign against the government's Irish plans. Carson had caused great offence in Britain by a speech at an Orange demonstration on 12 July in which he threatened the British people with a 'call out' of the Ulster Volunteers.[46] In this context the Belfast celebration could easily be read as a reminder to Britain of what it owed to the wartime service of the UVF in its manifestation as the Ulster Division. The intention was to assemble the largest number of ex-service personnel connected with Ulster and/or its wartime service. Participation was open to all ex-service personnel, combatants and non-combatants, men and women, including all who had served in Ulster regiments; all demobilised officers and men, and all women with war-related service, 'now residing in Ulster'. Everyone qualified to take part and travelling from 'WITHIN the boundaries of Ulster' would be entitled to a free return railway voucher and be given a public dinner and a memento of the occasion.[47] The unionist MP, T. E. M'Connell, would boast that outside London no city in the kingdom had attempted anything on the scale of the Belfast celebrations.[48] The *Londonderry Sentinel* enthused that Belfast would see 'the most impressive peace celebration possible to conceive'.[49]

But if the conditions for participation were construed so as to attract the largest possible participation, indications soon emerged that the particular focus of the occasion would be more narrowly framed – on the war service of the Ulster Division. Nationalist ire was aroused when a travel warrant issued to a Catholic ex-servicemen in Derry stated erroneously that the bearer had served with the Ulster Division.[50] Thereafter a controversy ensued between the leading nationalist and unionist papers in the city, with the former exposing the sectarianism of a regiment that barred Catholic membership until circumstances forced their admission, and the latter carrying an interview with a deputation of Catholic ex-servicemen who had served in the regiment, and denying charges of unionist deception.[51] But despite the *Londonderry Sentinel*'s claim that there would be no undue focus on the Ulster Division at Belfast,[52] the charge would be difficult to refute. The Citizens Committee admitted as much, justifying it on the ground that 'a large percentage' of Ulster ex-servicemen had served with the Division.[53] But that there was more to it than this was evident in Sir Edward Carson's contribution to the commemorative booklet for the occasion produced by the Citizens Committee. Ulster mourned her dead, he noted, 'but is proud of the glory and honour they have won for the Imperial Province'[54]. The term 'Imperial Province' was a long-standing unionist description for Ulster, the comparative reference of which was to the allegedly disloyal three southern provinces. But perhaps the most significant indicator of unionist intentions for the Belfast celebration was the political initiative that provided the background to it. On the day before the event Carson presided at a meeting of the Standing Committee of the Ulster Unionist Council, at which it was decided to revive the Unionist Clubs and other pre-war political organisations that had been in abeyance during the conflict, and to initiate a series of 'great political demonstrations' with Carson as the principal speaker.[55] In this context the Peace celebration, with Carson and the region's unionist MPs forming a substantial element of the platform party, would have an inescapable political complexion. At the same time, however, the susceptibilities of the audience which the occasion was primarily addressing – British public opinion – had to be kept in mind.

If the Belfast peace celebration was to carry a powerful anti-Home Rule message, it would have to do this while remaining firmly within the parameters of reverent homage that was already the established mien of war commemoration: the political message would have to be effectively, but implicitly, rather than explicitly, made. It would be an exercise of some delicacy but not impossible to effect successfully. The scale of human loss may have undermined the credibility of patriotic triumphalism; nevertheless, it has been argued persuasively that cenotaphs and tombs of unknown soldiers are 'the most arresting emblems of the modern culture of nationalism' because they are 'saturated with ghostly *national* imaginings'.[56] They are inescapable reminders that it was for the nation that the dead had been sacrificed, but most importantly, the nationalist messages they convey are expressed, not publicly and audibly, but privately and silently through the imagination.

It was another, perhaps the most important, advantage to Ulster unionists of the national Peace celebrations on 19 July that they provided a point of departure – a point of comparison – by which to frame the Belfast celebrations in such a way that their propaganda point could be established most effectively. The centrepiece of 19 July was the London commemoration with its march-past of 18,000 servicemen with the war leaders of France, Britain and the USA – Marshal Foch, General Haig, Admiral Jellicoe and General Pershing – taking the salute at Sir Edwin Lutyens' great abstract memorial to 'The Glorious Dead' of the Empire that had been erected at Whitehall.[57] The Belfast activities, taking place three weeks later, and after Glasgow held a Peace Day involving 10,000 soldiers, were deliberately constructed to make a statement that went beyond celebration *per se*. In the event, they ran over five days, involved the festive decoration with flags and bunting of, it was claimed, 'practically every street within the boundaries of the city', and in scale, at least, dwarfed the London event. The centrepiece was a commemorative march-past of 36,000 men and women who had seen war service – exactly double the number involved in London – and a number that inescapably invoked the memory of the Ulster Division. Forming a procession eleven miles long, they took three hours to pass a Cenotaph erected at the City Hall similar to that designed by Lutyens in Whitehall,[58] where a salute was taken by the Irish Viceroy, Lord French, accompanied by one of Ulster unionism's most staunch defenders, Sir Henry Wilson, Chief of the Imperial General Staff, together with Sir Edward Carson and the region's unionist MPs. The British Navy acknowledged the occasion with the arrival at Bangor of Vice-Admiral Sir Reginald Tupper with three warships.[59] And if the Citizens Committee could not produce a saluting panel to compete with London, it compensated by bringing together a communication from the king praising the wartime efforts of the Ulster Division with similar communications from General Haig, Admiral David Beatty and Winston Churchill.[60]

The Belfast commemoration was impressive testimony to Ulster's wartime contribution, and resonated with similar events in Britain. In itself this made it an occasion of great significance. Since the Home Rule issue had become one of practical politics in the mid-1880s Ulster unionists had struggled to establish a true identity of interests between themselves and a mainland population that was increasingly alienated from Ulster's toxic mix of religion and politics. War commemoration allowed them simultaneously to share authentically in a profound British national experience *and* to address their own political concerns. At once an act of homage to the sacred dead, the Peace Day commemoration was also an act of solidarity in the face of political and constitutional difficulties still unresolved. Accordingly, its importance transcended the occasion itself, and in this context the prominence given to the activities of the Ulster Division reflected a central theme of unionist exploitation of the war in their interest – the reduction of the service of all Ulstermen to that of the Division.

As the last redoubt of constitutional nationalism it was just possible that a contingent of nationalist ex-servicemen might have participated in the Belfast commemoration, and by their presence frustrated the intentions of the Citizens Committee. But even in Ulster nationalist ex-servicemen were in a state of alienation and confusion, regarded as traitors by republicans and finding it impossible to participate in celebrations of peace when the Irish freedom for which they fought was unrealised and the country held down by British bayonets.[61] Against this background, the decision of nationalist ex-servicemen in Derry to boycott the Belfast parade in the wake of the railway warrants controversy[62] is hardly surprising. The boycott, however, merely facilitated unionist purposes. The *Belfast News-Letter* declared:

> the celebrations in Belfast today are representative of loyal Ulster as a whole, and we venture to claim for them, therefore, a general character, and to look upon them as the expression of joy and thankfulness of a loyal and united people for the conclusion of peace.[63]

Yet impressive as the Belfast event was, the political environment it sought to influence was, as we have noted, one in which the interests of Ulster unionism were a variable. The issue of *The Times* which reported the impressive occasion in Belfast also carried an editorial in favour of an all-Ireland parliament: 'the English people are entitled to remind Ulster Unionists that the blessings of Irish unity would not ... be reserved for non-Ulster Unionists alone.'[64] To forestall that outcome a sustained campaign would be needed, and as part of it sustained exploitation of war service. The post-war years were to see this pursued in a variety of ways, especially in books,[65] and unionists continued to benefit by fortuitous circumstances which facilitated such exploitation. For example, the third reading of the Government of Ireland Bill in 1920 – which conferred on north-east Ulster a parliament that unionists did not initially want, together with a Council of Ireland to deal with areas of common concern between north and south – took place on the same day, 11 November, when the tomb of the Unknown Warrior was unveiled in London. In a context where unionists continued to view the intentions of the Westminster Government with the greatest concern, Belfast was once again the scene for a massive gathering in commemoration of the province's war dead. Employing a now established rhetoric of commemoration that managed both to resonate with the wider British commemorative experience at the same time as it reflected more local concerns about Irish developments, the *Belfast News-Letter* intoned:

> The war is now, happily, a thing of the past, but we can profit by its lessons, and one of the most important of these is that no community can be deprived of its birthright if it is sufficiently firm in its determination to defend and maintain it.

The two minutes of silence was an act of solemn remembrance – remembrance of the men who were faithful until death and recollection of the duty laid upon us, for whom they died, to see that their sacrifice was not in vain.[66]

In 1920, however, the Anglo-Irish conflict had entered an acute phase, together with an intensity of sectarian conflict in Ulster; and in both respects war sacrifice and the rituals of its remembrance became enmeshed with them. Reflecting on the month of November, Beatrice Webb regarded the public funerals it had included as emblematic of depressing times: 'The public pageant of the "unknown warrior" symbolising the ten million white men killed in the war, the funeral of the martyred Lord Mayor of Cork, and as a reprisal, the military parade through London of the corpses of the English officers murdered in Dublin.'[67] In Ulster war commemoration was not just becoming the preserve of the unionist community, but the Orange Order and the other loyal orders were taking control of the remembrance rituals.[68] As war commemoration became increasingly sectarianised Catholic shipyard workers found that war service was no protection against expulsion, a form of persecution excused on the ground that their jobs would be taken by good loyalist ex-servicemen.[69]

The Ulster unionist resistance to compromise on the exclusion of north-east Ulster from Dublin rule determined that Ireland would have two self-governing jurisdictions in 1921. The Northern Ireland parliament was opened on 21 June 1921 with all the dignity conferred by the presence of the king who, in his speech, made a triadic connection between Ulster's war sacrifice, patriotism and her parliament.[70] But the conferring of parliamentary government on the North did not remove the constitutional danger for unionists. Lloyd George still had the republican campaign for complete independence to deal with, and on 24 June he abandoned the military struggle against the IRA, arranged a truce, and initiated the process of negotiation that would lead, on 6 December 1921, to the signing of the Anglo-Irish Treaty.[71] At one point, however, the process of negotiation included a plan by Lloyd George whereby Ireland would have one parliament within the Empire. It was a prospect that appalled Ulster unionists. In their opposition to it, however, they were facilitated once again by the fact that this latest crisis also coincided with war commemoration, one of greater significance than any of its predecessors.

The climax of the crisis was the week of 10–17 November 1921. On 10 November Lloyd George appraised Sir James Craig of his plan for an Irish parliament. An indignant Craig immediately enlisted the assistance of the former Tory leader, Bonar Law, who used his influence with the die-hard section of the party to ensure that at the party conference on 17 November – held in Liverpool, the bastion of Ulster unionist support in Britain – the inclusion of Ulster in Lloyd George's plan was effectively buried.[72] The opposition of this section of the party to the 'coercion' of Ulster was undoubtedly given point by the significance of the war commemorations undertaken by Ulster unionists. Concern about government plans ensured 'one of the most impressive spectacles ever' in Belfast on Armistice Day. The sacrifice of the gallant men 'has not been forgotten ... at the present time, when the security of Ulster is even more seriously threatened than it was in the momentous years preceding the outbreak of war.'[73] And war commemorations in Ulster were now more extensive, as many towns and villages were constructing their own memorials.[74] Moreover, to ensure that the unionist message registered in London the Whitehall service at Lutyens' Cenotaph saw wreaths laid representing Craig and the Northern Ireland Government, and with Lady Carson and Sir William Allen – who had commanded a battalion of the Ulster Division – themselves present.[75] In the days leading up to the Liverpool conference a series of loyalist demonstrations were held, while on conference day itself, Sir Edward (now Lord) Carson published a letter in the British press expressing his intention to be at the opening at Thiepval, in northern France, on 19 November, of a battlefield memorial to the dead of the Ulster Division. To make the necessary political point the circumstances required, Carson included quotations from messages sent to the Belfast Peace Day celebration in 1919 from British national and war leaders, to counter 'the abuse, misrepresentation, and cruel attacks which are being made upon Ulster'.[76]

As it turned out, with the abandonment of the plan to include Northern Ireland in an all-Ireland parliament, the opening was less freighted with political anxiety than it would otherwise have been. The Thiepval monument was, nevertheless, the most impressive of unionist exploitations of Ulster's war dead. It was made possible by the necessity of allowing a battlefield monument to the dead of the Indian sub-continent, given the non-Christian aversion to the exhumation of bodies once buried; and since India was to have a separate monument it would have been difficult to prevent others being erected. In fact, of all the governments of the Empire, it was the newly formed Northern Ireland Government that was first in the field.[77] The same constitutional anxieties that moved Ulster unionists to construct the largest Peace Day celebration in the United Kingdom in 1919 also moved them to construct the first battlefield memorial. A replica of Helen's Tower – built in 1861 by the first Marquis of Dufferin and Ava on his Clandeboye estate in honour of his mother – the Thiepval memorial is certainly impressive. Constructed in stone, it stands seventy feet high on raised ground that formed part of the line along which the Ulster Division advanced on German trenches on I July 1916.[78] As such, it is a conspicuous landmark offering commanding views of the surrounding countryside.

The patina of time has lent the Thiepval monument an aura of dignity and political non-contentiousness. So much so that the Ulster poet, Michael

Longley, could describe the erection of a memorial to Ulster's *Orange* dead in its vicinity in 1993 as a sectarian contamination of a sacred site.[79] In fact, from the beginning it was as much a political, as a war, monument. The opening ceremony was conducted by that most fanatical supporter of Ulster unionism, Sir Henry Wilson, while the Revd Dr Lowe, Moderator of the Presbyterian General Assembly, declared that *all* Ulstermen 'would have preferred to belong to the Ulster Division'.[80] But perhaps most significantly, on Armistice Day, the third Marquis of Dufferin and Ava, President of the Ulster Ex-Servicemen's Association and Speaker of the upper chamber of the new regional parliament, publicly rejected the political neutrality that post was supposed to embody, adding that when he 'saw enemies trying to filch from Ulster what belonged to her he must ... protest with all his might and all his power'.[81]

The war commemoration of 1921 was the last on which such an occasion coincided with a serious crisis involving Ulster's constitutional position. In a context where their influence over a settlement of the Irish problem had waned since 1914, the commerative rituals, coinciding with acute phases in the Anglo-Irish crisis, allowed Ulster Unionists to effectively counterpoint apparent political duplicity and 'betrayal' with reminders of an authentic experience of Protestant blood sacrifice in the British national interest. Accordingly, the rituals were important elements of the moral case against the inclusion of north-east Ulster in an all-Ireland parliament. With that objective substantially secured in 1922 the unionist government consolidated its position until 1925, when the Boundary Commission[82] completed its work. In that year a constitutional crisis did coincide with the Armistice Day commemoration, but this time it involved the Irish Free State, not Northern Ireland. On 7 November the *Morning Post*, the most consistent and uncritical of Ulster unionism's press supporters in Britain, leaked the Commission's findings and immediately created a crisis in Irish politics. It was revealed that, against the expectations of a large section of Irish opinion, not only would Northern Ireland remain virtually intact, but the Irish Free State would lose part of east Donegal. The upshot was that the Commission's report was quickly buried and the existing border confirmed,[83] the Free State's Minister of Finance, Ernest Blythe, declaring that north and south could not be forced together.[84] Unlike the Free State, where Armistice Day was, as in 1925,[85] frequently associated with violence, the occasion in the north was now an established and unproblematic occasion in the ritual calendar of the regime. Indeed, the *Belfast News-Letter* went so far as to claim, erroneously, that the two minutes silence originated in Belfast, from whence it spread to the rest of the United Kingdom and the Empire.[86]

With the constitutional question settled for the foreseeable future, and with Westminster having already established the convention of non-interference in its affairs, Northern Ireland became a distinctive region within the United Kingdom. Its government would pursue a range of policies – many of them contentious and the cause of later, justifiable, criticism – that they liked to believe was consistent with the 'British' values of the mainland. But while Westminster's non-interference was the crucial, negative, factor that made this possible, the Armistice Day ritual was one of the few, positive, occasions that facilitated this belief. Especially in the inter-war period, when the shadow of the war hung so heavily over the kingdom, Armistice Day was a profoundly poignant national experience across the whole British state. But it was not only in the practice of government that Northern Ireland differed from Britain, a difference can also be detected in the way that the post-war population responded to the experience of war.

It has been suggested that one area of difference lay in the fact that, unlike Britain, the exclusion of Catholics ensured that the commemorative experience in Northern Ireland was fundamentally sectarian.[87] But in Britain, as in Northern Ireland, Catholics were likely to be excluded, partly through Church policy affecting services over which it had no control and partly due to community dislike and suspicion of a perceptibly disloyal minority.[88] Nor was it the case that Northern Ireland managed to avoid the controversies that surrounded the process of local memorial building in Britain.[89] It could also be argued that if the memory of the war in Britain was determined by 'existing predilections in the culture, political, religious and "communitarian"',[90] in regard to the Protestant community at least, this was no less the case in Northern Ireland.

Where it can be argued that Northern Ireland did differ significantly from Britain, was in the extent to which it was possible to answer the question of what the war was fought for. The cultural chasm identified by Samuel Hynes, between a traditional form of commemorative explanation focusing on glory, and a popular experience of war's horrors which undermined the validity of that explanation, did not apply as well to Northern Ireland as it did to Britain. Certainly, the horrors of war were felt as strongly in the north, and it is possible to find individual loyalist cases of personal grief expressed as a rejection of 'England's wars'.[91] Nevertheless, in the main, the historical grand narrative of Ulster unionism proved capable of subsuming the war within its explanatory myths, so that its meaning as a struggle to free Ulster of the menace of Irish nationalism was as least, if not more, important than other, wider, British concerns. That objective was largely secured by 1922. Nevertheless, it was unfortunate that the interpretation of the war that came to have substantial currency in Britain – 'an ethical triumph over evil, rather than a military triumph over other people'[92] – could not register significantly in Northern Ireland. This was difficult in a region where images of the Somme sat back-to-back with depictions of William III's victory at the battle of the Boyne on Orange banners. It would be fifty years – 1966 – before any sustained critical debate on the war took place in Northern Ireland,[93] and even then this did not include the local, Ulster, dimension of the conflict.

The fiftieth anniversary of the battle of the Somme was significant for a number of reasons. The Queen marked the occasion with a review of veterans during only her second visit to Northern Ireland since her coronation.[94] A loyalist terrorist group calling itself the UVF was formed and began the killing of Catholics that would be the chief feature of loyalist terrorism four years later.[95] The Prime Minister, Terence O'Neill returned from the Somme commemoration in France to proscribe the UVF as an illegal organisation under the Special Powers Act, denying that there was any connection between 'a sordid conspiracy of criminals' and men who had fought and died for their country.[96] O'Neill's action was consistent with his reformist project of encouraging Catholic loyalty to the state, a project that faced considerable opposition from within the Protestant community.[97] Nevertheless, it is somewhat surprising that he should overlook the opportunity to extend the ideological basis of his project by widening the commemoration of the Somme to include the many thousands of Ulster Catholics who also fell in the Great War. Such a move could have been expected to appeal, not only to those Catholics prepared to make an accommodation with the state, but also to Protestant opinion, as an effective riposte to the extensive – and to unionist minds, highly offensive – celebrations of the Easter Rising that had occurred in the North in April. That O'Neill failed to so exploit the Somme commemoration suggests the extent to which Ulster's sacrifice had, by 1966, become firmly entrenched in the mindset of even liberal unionism as the sacrifice of the Ulster Division. O'Neill did attempt to employ the Somme commemoration to further his reform project, but only in a general sense, identifying 'the courage and real bravery' of the Ulster Division as the qualities needed for the tasks that faced unionists in the 1960s.[98] As the Ulster conflict developed from 1969, however, it was always more likely that the commemoration would be associated with reaction than reform. Certainly the connection between remembrance and loyalist paramilitarism was enhanced.

While O'Neill's concern to deny a possible link between the Ulster Division and the UVF of the 1960s is understandable, their differences were perhaps not quite as significant as he claimed. Many members of the original UVF came out of service in the Ulster Division to find a place in the B Specials, an auxiliary police force that became engaged in pogroms against the Catholic community in the early 1920s.[99] With the outbreak of civil conflict in 1969 the UVF would remerge to engage in similar activities, claiming a legitimising connection with the Ulster Division.[100] More generally, over the course of the conflict unionist perceptions of the Second World War have been added to that of the First to provide a mode of understanding – and added legitimisation – for their struggle with militant republican-

ism, with the scope of the remembrance ritual itself being extended to
include security force personnel and civilians killed by republican paramili-
taries.[101] This development must, in part at least, be responsible for the fact
that sales of the poppy in Northern Ireland each year are usually the highest
of all regions in the United Kingdom.[102]

Of atrocities affecting the unionist community one of the most devastating was the Remembrance Day bomb of 1987, which killed eleven and
injured sixty four people gathered around the war memorial at Enniskillen.
The nature of the atrocity caused outrage throughout the British Isles and
beyond, with messages and visits of condolence from public figures from the
Irish Republic and Britain, including the Prime Minister, Mrs Thatcher, and
the Prince and Princess of Wales. What became known as the 'Spirit of
Enniskillen' – a spirit of forgiveness and tolerance – was expressed by
Gordon Wilson, whose daughter Marie was killed in the blast. A number of
cross-community initiatives followed and also, but more controversially, a
reshaping of the town's war memorial to include the names of those killed,
together with eleven sculpted doves around the base of the memorial
expressing the spirit of forgiveness. The addition of civilian names made the
Enniskillen memorial exceptional among British war memorials, while the
doves were offensive to some whose concept of the sacred dead included IRA
victims, the remembrance of whom was freighted with emotions that were
too recent and raw to include forgiveness. That one of the doves was muti-
lated in protest[103] is not entirely surprising.

The controversy over the Enniskillen memorial, while singular at one
level, can also be seen as indicative of how Great War remembrance moved
to a more central position in the Ulster problem in the 1980s, especially in
the aftermath of the Anglo-Irish Agreement of 1985, and in association with
Orange marches. In fact, in the summer of 1985, before the Agreement was
signed, the right of Orangemen to march through nationalist areas of
Portadown, county Armagh – the heartland of Ulster loyalism – was
restricted. Since then, the controversy over Orange marches in the town, and
across Northern Ireland, has intensified, but the primary focus of the controversy is the annual crisis in Portadown over the Orange march to Drumcree
Parish Church on the first Sunday in July to commemorate the dead of the
Ulster Division. Uncontroversial on its outward route from the centre of the
town, the traditional route homeward takes the marchers through the once-
rural, but now heavily nationalist, area of the Garvaghy Road; a route
strongly contested by the residents since the early 1990s. The Orange argument that the march is not sectarian as it is conducted for the purpose of a
religious service, is countered by the nationalist view that the essentially
sectarian nature of the organisation undertaking it, and the paramilitary
trappings often associated with the marches, invalidates this argument.[104]
Nevertheless, to further their moral claim to take the traditional route the

Portadown Orangemen have sought to enhance the Somme dimension, with their spokesman, David Jones, working on a history of the UVF in Portadown, its subsequent membership of the Ulster Division, and the losses the town suffered at the Somme.[105] The war service dimension in general has been enhanced by highlighting the numbers of ex-servicemen who belong to the Portadown Lodge,[106] while the Orange refusal to negotiate with the Garvaghy residents on the issue is justified on the ground that their spokesman, Breandan MacCionnaith, is a former republican paramilitary who has served a prison term for bombing the office of the Portadown branch of the British Legion.[107] When the Parades Commission held a public forum in Portadown in 1998 to discuss the Drumcree problem the overwhelmingly loyalist audience was primarily concerned with 'who had fought hardest in the First World War'.[108] Since 1998, when the marchers were prevented from walking the Garvaghy Road, the sectarian violence associated with the issue has increased considerably. It has, moreover, taken on wider significance for unionists and loyalists opposed to the Good Friday Agreement. Faced with the reality of republicans in government, the exclusion of Orange marches from the Garvaghy Road is increasingly regarded as symbolic of the success of the 'pan-nationalist agenda' to destroy unionism.[109]

Rejectionist unionists, however, cannot claim a monopoly of Somme remembrance occasions. Indeed the era when these were solely unionist occasions is clearly ending. That had been a function of the triumph of republicanism over constitutional nationalism, and frosty Anglo-Irish relations on contentious issues. But with the demise of southern irredentism since the early 1980s, and especially since the signing of the Good Friday Agreement – which, in the context of the Anglo-Irish Council, places as much importance on Anglo-Irish rapprochement as conciliation between political parties in Northern Ireland – a new era is opening. It has been signalled, perhaps most significantly, in the area of Great War commemoration. A joint initiative by a former loyalist paramilitary and a southern Irish parliamentarian has led to the building of a new Irish war memorial at Messines in Belgium. A replica of an Irish round tower designed to commemorate not only the Ulster Division, but also the nationalist 16th (Irish) Division, its opening in November 1998 was attended by the Queen, the Irish President Mary McAleese, and the Belgian king, Albert II.[110] The background to the monument's erection is one in which nationalist – though not republican[111] – attendance at Remembrance Day events has steadily increased in recent years.[112]

The speeches made by pro-Agreement politicians associated with the event were heavily freighted with the lessons the Great War and the forms of its commemoration had for the people of Ulster today. In this context, a British reporter noted that David Trimble's contribution – which expressed the hope that the occasion would signal the demise of the anti-British element in Irish culture – brought the occasion 'perilously close to a political event'.[113] This reaction reflected the mainland British experience, in which the dead of the Great War have occupied a hallowed place in the popular mind, uncontaminated – apart from the controversy over Michael Foot's attire at the Remembrance service at Whitehall in 1981[114] – by association with party politics. But as we have seen, this has never been the case in Northern Ireland. Nor, it can be argued, is it desirable that the political association be broken now if Great War commemoration facilitates the resolution of the Ulster problem.

Notes

This chapter occasionally uses the contentious term 'mainland' in reference to unionism and Britain. It is employed solely for the purpose of illuminating the unionist mindset. I am grateful to Adrian Gregory for suggestions on improving the text.

1 K. Robbins, *Nineteenth-Century Britain: Integration and Diversity* (Oxford, Clarendon Press, 1988), pp. 174–5.
2 D. G. Boyce, 'Ireland and the Great War', *History Ireland* (Autumn 1994), p. 48.
3 Churchill to Bonar Law, 14 September 1914 in M. Gilbert, *Winston S. Churchill: Volume III: 1914–16* (London, Heinemann, 1971), p. 79.
4 Law, *Hansard 5*, vol. 77 (17 January 1916), cols 55–6.
5 M. McDonagh, *The Home Rule Movement* (Dublin, The Talbot Press, 1920), p. 282.
6 N. Mansergh, 'John Redmond', in C. C. O'Brien (ed.), *The Shaping of Modern Ireland* (London, Routledge and Kegan Paul, 1960), pp. 44–6.
7 H. Harris, *The Irish Regiments in the First World War* (Cork, Mercier Press, 1968), p. ii.
8 See, for example, H. A. Gwynne, editor of the *Morning Post*, to Lord Derby, 20 January 1916 in K. Wilson (ed.), *The Rasp of War: The Letters of H. A. Gwynne to Countess Lady Bathurst 1914–1918* (London, Sidgwick and Jackson, 1988), p. 159.
9 Aldous Huxley to Julian Huxley, 30 June 1916, in G. Smith (ed.), *Letters of Aldous Huxley* (London, Chatto and Windus, 1969), pp. 103–4.
10 See, for example, *Ulster Gazette*, 19 September 1914.
11 R. J. Scally, *The Origins of the Lloyd George Coalition: The Politics of Social Imperialism 1900–1918* (Princeton, Princeton University Press, 1975), p. 295.
12 D. G. Boyce, *Englishmen and Irish Troubles: British Public Opinion and the Making of Irish Policy 1918–1922* (Cambridge, Mass., MIT Press, 1972), p. 103.
13 J. G. Fuller, *Troop Morale and Popular Culture in the British Dominion Armies* (Oxford, Clarendon Press, 1990), pp. 16 and 155–7; P. Orr, *The Road to the Somme: Men of the Ulster Division Tell Their Story* (Belfast, Blackstaff Press, 1987), pp. 29–30.
14 Only fourteen of its soldiers were Catholics, and even they, it seems, had to sign Carson's anti-Home Rule covenant; T. Denman, *Ireland's Unknown Soldiers: The 16th (Irish) Division in the Great War 1914–1918* (Dublin, Irish Academic Press, 1992), p. 27.
15 Orr, *Road to the Somme*, pp. 199–200.
16 N. Ferguson, *The Pity of War* (London, Penguin Books, 1998), p. 293.
17 R. Blythe, *The Age of Illusion: Some Glimpses of Britain Between the Wars* (Oxford, Oxford University Press, 1983), p. 3.
18 R. Holland, *The Pursuit of Greatness: Britain and the World Role 1900–1970* (London, Fontana Press, 1991), p. 53.

19 *Ibid.*, pp. 63–4.
20 D. Cannadine, 'War, death, grief and mourning in modern Britain', in J. Whaley (ed.), *Mirrors of Mortality: Studies in the Social History of Death* (London, Europa, 1981), p. 233.
21 J. M. Winter, *The Great War and the British People* (London, Macmillan, 1985), p. 71.
22 Ferguson, *Pity of War*, p. 437.
23 S. Hynes, *A War Imagined: the First World War and English Culture* (London, Bodley Head, 1990), p. 283.
24 B. Bushaway, 'Name upon name: the Great War and remembrance' in Roy Porter (ed.), *Myths of the English* (Cambridge, Polity Press, 1992), p. 148.
25 See S. Baldwin, *On England* (London, 1926; 11th impression, Hodder and Stoughton, 1939), pp. 73 and 244–6.
26 N. Ferguson, 'New myths for old in Ireland', *Sunday Times*, 15 November 1998.
27 K. Jeffery, 'First World War', in S. J. Connolly (ed.), *The Oxford Companion to Irish History* (Oxford, Oxford University Press, 1998), p. 196.
28 *Belfast News-Letter*, 11 August 1919.
29 Jeffery, 'First World War', p. 196. Ferguson, however, puts the Irish figure at 172,104 ('New myths for old in Ireland'); D. Fitzpatrick, *The Two Irelands 1912–1939* (Oxford, Oxford University Press, 1998), p. 54.
30 D. Fitzpatrick, 'Militarism in Ireland 1900–1922' in K. Jeffery and T. Bartlett (eds), *A Military History of Ireland* (Cambridge, Cambridge University Press, 1996), p. 388.
31 Fitzpatrick, *Two Irelands*, p. 76.
32 J. Leonard, 'Facing "the finger of scorn": veterans' memories of Ireland after the war', in M. Evans and K. Lunn (eds), *War and Memory in the Twentieth Century* (Oxford, Berg, 1997), pp. 60–1.
33 *Belfast News-Letter*, 9 August 1919.
34 *Ibid.*
35 J. Kendle, *Walter Long, Ireland and the Union 1905–1920* (Dun Laoghaire, Glendale, 1992), pp. 176–84.
36 *Belfast News-Letter*, 21 July 1919.
37 *Ibid.*; *Londonderry Sentinel*, 22 July 1919.
38 *Belfast News-Letter*, 22 July 1919.
39 *Londonderry Sentinel*, 15 and 19 July 1919.
40 *Belfast News-Letter*, 21 July 1919.
41 *Ibid.*
42 *Ibid.*
43 For disputes about the commemoration in both Enniskillen Urban District Council and the Board of Poor Law Guardians, see *Derry Journal*, 11 July 1919.
44 *Ibid.*, 4 August 1919.
45 *Belfast News-Letter*, 24 July 1919.
46 Boyce, *Englishmen and Irish Troubles*, p. 107.
47 *Londonderry Sentinel*, 24 July 1919.
48 *Belfast News-Letter*, 9 August 1919.
49 *Londonderry Sentinel*, 24 July 1919.
50 *Derry Journal*, 14 August 1919.
51 *Ibid.*, 6, 8 and 11 August 1919; *Londonderry Sentinel*, 2, 7 and 9 August 1919.
52 *Londonderry Sentinel*, 7 August 1919.
53 Citizens Committee, *The Great War 1914–1918: Ulster Greets Her Brave and Faithful Sons and Remembers Her Glorious Dead* (Belfast, 1919 [reissued, Pretani Press, in 1991]), p. 5. Copies of this publication were the mementoes presented to ex-service personnel participating in the Belfast celebration.

54 *Ibid.*, p. 127.
55 *Londonderry Sentinel*, 9 August 1919.
56 B. Anderson, *Imagined Communities: Reflections on the Origins and Spread of Nationalism* (London, Verso, 1983), p. 9.
57 Hynes, *A War Imagined*, p. 279.
58 *Belfast News-Letter*, 9 August 1919; *The Times*, 11 August 1919.
59 *Belfast News-Letter*, 8 August 1919.
60 *Ibid.*
61 K. Jeffery, 'The Great War in modern Irish memory', in T. G. Fraser and K. Jeffrey (eds), *Men, Women and War: Historical Studies XVIII* (Dublin, Lilliput Press, 1993), p. 148; K. M. Gormley, 'The memory of the Great War, with particular reference to nationalists in the north west of Ireland' (MA Thesis, University of Ulster, 1997), pp. 37–42.
62 *Derry Journal*, 6 and 8 August 1919.
63 'Ulster's peace day', editorial, *Belfast News-Letter*, 9 August 1919.
64 'The case of Ulster', editorial, *The Times*, 11 August 1919.
65 See, for example, H. S. Morrison, *Modern Ulster: Its Character, Customs, Politics and Industries* (Belfast, H. R. Allenson, 1920); C. Falls, *The History of the 36th (Ulster) Division* (Belfast, M'Caw, Stevenson & Orr, 1922); R. McNeill, *Ulster's Stand for Union* (London, J. Murray, 1922), ch. 20; James Logan, *Ulster in the X Rays* (2nd edn, London, A. H. Stockwell, 1924), ch. 17.
66 'Belfast's Noble tribute', editorial, *Belfast News-Letter*, 12 November 1920.
67 Diary entry, 29 November 1920 in N. and J. McKenzie (eds), *The Diary of Beatrice Webb: Vol. Three: 1905–1924* (London, Virago, 1984), p. 371; Hynes, *A War Imagined*, p. 281. The Lord Mayor of Cork, Thomas McSwiney, died on hunger strike on 25 October in Brixton Prison, where he was incarcerated for possessing an RIC cipher. On 21 November the IRA killed thirteen British intelligence agents in Dublin.
68 N. Jarman, *Material Conflicts: Parades and Visual Displays in Northern Ireland* (Oxford, Berg, 1997), p. 72.
69 Fitzpatrick, *Two Irelands*, p. 96.
70 *Belfast News-Letter*, 22 June 1921.
71 K. O. Morgan, *Consensus and Disunity: The Lloyd George Coalition Government 1918–1922* (Oxford, Clerendon Press, 1986), pp. 130–1.
72 R. Blake, *The Unknown Prime Minister: the Life and Times of Andrew Bonar Law* (London, Eyre & Spottiswoode, 1955), pp. 430–5; R. J. Q. Adams, *Bonar Law* (London, John Murray, 1999), pp. 302–5.
73 'The armistice anniversary', editorial, *Belfast News-Letter*, 12 November 1921.
74 *Ibid.*, 14 and 25 November 1921.
75 *Ibid.*, 12 November 1921.
    'Lord Carson and Ulster' in *ibid.*, 17 November 1921.
77 M. Heffernan, 'For ever England: the Western Front and the politics of remembrance in Britain', *Ecumene*, vol. 2 (1995), p. 307.
78 *Belfast News-Letter*, 21 November 1921.
79 M. Longley, 'A monument to bad taste', *Belfast Telegraph*, 16 July 1997. The article was Longley's contribution to G. Lucy and E. McClure (eds), *The Twelfth: What It Means to Me* (Lurgan, Ulster Society, 1997).
80 'Thiepval', editorial, *Belfast News-Letter*, 21 November 1921.
81 *Ibid.*, 12 November 1921.
82 Established by the Anglo-Irish Treaty of 1921 to re-define the border between north and south, it ostensibly came into operation when Northern Ireland exercised its right to opt out of the Treaty settlement, which it did in January 1922. However, due to a number of delays, it did not begin work until April 1924.

83 See *Report of the Boundary Commission*, introduction by G. Hand (Shannon, Irish University Press, 1969), pp. vii–xxii.
84 *Belfast News-Letter*, 10 November 1925.
85 *Ibid.*
86 *Ibid.*,'"Remembrance Day": its duties', editorial. In fact, it was a practice that originated in South Africa and was then approved by King George V (Blythe, *Age of Illusion*, p. 6; A. Gregory, *The Silence of Memory: Armistice day 1919–1946* (Oxford, Berg, 1994), p. 9).
87 D. Officer, 'The Ulster Division's unburied dead', *Peace Review*, vol. 8, (1996), pp. 251–2.
88 See A. Gaffney, *Aftermath: Remembering the Great War in Wales* (Cardiff, University of Wales Press, 1998), pp. 127–8; Gregory, *Silence of Memory*, pp. 199–201.
89 See A. King, *Memorials of the Great War in Britain: the Symbolism and Politics of Remembrance* (Oxford, Berg, 1998), chs 3 and 4; C. Moriarity, 'Private grief and public remembrance: British First World War memorials', in Evans and Lunn (eds), *War and Memory*, p.127; Jeffery, 'Great War and Irish memory', pp. 146–7.
90 Gregory, *Silence of Memory*, p. 5.
91 See, for example, J. Y. Simms, *Farewell to the Hammer: A Shankill Boyhood* (Belfast, White Row Press, 1992), p. 95.
92 King, *Memorials of the Great War in Britain*, p. 176.
93 Orr, *Road to the Somme*, pp. 217–19.
94 See 'Fiftieth anniversary of the Somme', in *Ulster Commentary*, no. 245 (June 1966), p. 10. This magazine was a government propaganda organ.
95 D. Bolton, *The UVF 1966–73: an Anatomy of Loyalist Rebellion* (Dublin, Gill and Macmillan, 1973), pp. 48–50.
96 T. O'Neill, *Autobiography* (London, Hart-Davis, 1972), pp. 80–2; O'Neill at Stormont, 28 June 1966 in T. O'Neill, *Ulster at the Crossroads*, introduction, by John Cole (London, Faber and Faber, 1969), p. 121.
97 Sunday Times Insight Team, *Ulster* (Harmondsworth, Penguin Books, 1972), ch. 3; M. Mulholland, *Northern Ireland at the Crossroads: Ulster Unionism in the O'Neill Years 1960–9* (Basingstoke, Macmillan, 2000), chs 5–6.
98 See speech on community relations in Northern Ireland at Corrymeela, 8 April 1966, *ibid.*, p. 119. For a more pointed connection between the Somme commemoration and the reform project by the editor of the O'Neillite *Belfast Telegraph*, see A. Gailey, *Crying in the Wilderness: Jack Sayers: a Liberal Editor in Ulster 1939–1969* (Belfast, Institute of Irish Studies, 1995), p. 107.
99 M. Farrell, *Northern Ireland: the Orange State* (London, Pluto Press, 1976), pp. 56–7 and 95; S. McKay, *Northern Protestants: An Unsettled People* (Belfast, Blackstaff Press, 2000), p. 56.
100 *Ibid.*, p. 57.
101 *Ibid.*, pp. 18, 88–90, 135 and 164–5.
102 On poppy sales, see Denziel McDaniel, *Enniskillen: The Remembrance Sunday Bombing* (Dublin, Wolfhound Press, 1997), p. 112.
103 *Ibid.*, pp. 135–9; McKay, *Northern Protestants*, p. 217.
104 J. Loughlin, *The Ulster Question since 1945* (Basingstoke, Macmillan, 1998), ch. 4. The residents' case is presented in Garvaghy Residents, *Garvaghy: a Community Under Siege* (Belfast, Beyond the Pale, BTB Publications Ltd., 1999). For an account of the Drumcree issue from a pro-Orange perspective, see R. Dudley Edwards, *The Faithful Tribe: An Intimate Portrait of the Loyal Institutions* (London, Harper Collins, 1999).
105 See Jones's contribution to Lucy and McClure (eds), *The Twelfth*, p. 73.
106 'Veterans campaign for the right to march', *Belfast Telegraph*, 9 July 1998.
107 *Ibid.*, 12 July 1996, Clifford Smyth, 'This is a territorial conflict'.
108 McKay, *Northern Protestants*, pp. 145 and 177–8.

109 See reports of Orange speeches at Drumcree in *Belfast Telegraph*, 10 July 2000.
110 See Eric Waugh in *Sunday Times*, 8 November 1998.
111 See interview with Marie Moore, Sinn Féin Deputy Mayor of Belfast, *Belfast Telegraph*, 19 June 1999; report of newly-elected Sinn Féin Lord Mayor of Derry rejecting attendance at Remembrance Day ceremony (*Belfast Telegraph*, 6 June 2000). Having accepted the compromises on Irish unity entailed in the Good Friday Agreement, the Sinn Féin leadership is clearly using the boycotting of the Remembrance Day ceremony as an important symbolic assertion of republican principle.
112 For insightful comment on this subject, see Gormley, 'Memory of the Great War', pp. 69–79.
113 A. Hamilton, 'Side by side in tribute to the fallen', *The Times*, 12 November 1998.
114 See P. Wright, *On Living In an Old Country: The National Past in Contemporary Britain* (London, Verso, 1985), pp. 135–40.

8

Shell-shock, psychiatry and the Irish soldier during the First World War

JOANNA BOURKE

War and insanity are inextricably linked. The tedium of army life and the terror of battle are just two aspects of military service that create intense psychological stress, sometimes resulting in madness. During the First World War, Irish soldiers were no more exempt from the stresses and strains of warfare than were their English, Scottish and Welsh counterparts. The fear of mutilation or death haunted these men. The drift into a nervous disorder such as neurasthenia or hysteria could provide some sort of escape. The diagnosis of 'shell-shock' would at least take a man behind the lines, often permanently. However, as this chapter will argue, for Irish soldiers such an escape could be particularly short-lived. Their 'sacrifice of nerves' did not end in 1918. Long after the battlefields had reverted to farmland, their nightmares continued. They discovered that they had returned to an Ireland that no longer valued their actions in wartime, and the fact that they had broken down psychologically only served to reinforce their shame.

Although the subject of this chapter is insanity, it is crucial to draw attention to the fact that the vast majority of Irish soldiers who managed to survive the bullets and bombs also managed to come through the war emotionally and psychologically 'intact'. Indeed, the great surprise for many commentators was precisely the fact that psychiatric collapse was relatively limited. For instance, Dr Graham, Resident Superintendent of the Belfast Asylum, was surprised to discover that the number of admissions into insane asylums in Ireland had declined in the first year of the war. In his words:

This contrast ... would be worthy of notice at any time, but it becomes almost an enigmatic paradox when we recall that the nation since August, 1914, has been plunged in common with nearly all the great civilized Powers, in a struggle more terrible than any of which our earth has been the scene since the fall of the Roman Empire. The very foundations – moral, social, intellectual, and economic – of European society are being shaken, and in such a period of upheaval it is natural to suppose that mental suffering, ending in collapse of the brain, should be the order of the day, yet up to the present this has not been the case. ... Why is it that the shock of the world conflict has not worked the mental disaster to be expected, either in the case of the heroes who have survived or in that of the relations of those who have died so magnificently?

Of course, he was speaking prematurely – in 1915, Irish soldiers still had their greatest trials ahead. However, it was a paradox that interested commentators even after the war. The explanation given by Graham was typical. For him, the answer lay in that 'profound psychological law' that it was not the 'great tragedies of life that sap the forces of the brain and wreck the psychic organism'. On the contrary, what caused the human psyche to collapse was 'the dull drab of a life without joy and barren of all achievement'. He continued: 'It is often said that war brutalizes the soldier and so opens the door for the ingress of all sorts of mental disorders. To this it suffices to reply, not all war degrades, and whether a given war degrades or not depends on the motives which sustain the soldier.'[1]

While the importance of 'motives' or belief in the cause was crucial in enabling men to deal with fear states arising in the course of battle, it would be wrong to assume that all (or indeed, most) instances of psychiatric collapse while in the army were the result of combat. Lieutenant-General Sir Charles Burtchaell was right when he reminded the Royal Academy of Medicine in Ireland that large numbers of men had broken down despite never being in the firing line. He was not surprised by this, explaining that this was 'only to be expected seeing that a large number of men who joined the Army were temperamentally unfitted for a soldier's life. Such men got into a nervous state before they came under fire'.[2]

Indisputably, though, a significant proportion of men became psychiatric casualties, whether because of the stresses resulting from being catapulted into a very different military environment, the terror of combat, or more long-term predisposition to insanity. The *extent* of the problem is unknown since there are no reliable statistics telling us what proportion of Irish soldiers suffered psychiatric collapse during the First World War. The chief problem is that the data provided by medical personnel is highly unreliable. Officers in all units strenuously avoided the use of psychiatric terms, preferring 'safer' diagnoses based upon organic categories. Poor (and often non-existent) psychiatric training and the hurried nature of diagnosis in wartime conditions, dampened enthusiasm for accurate record-keeping. The statistics were also distorted by variations in nomenclature (a headache might be labelled concussion, shell shock, or malingering); differences in evacuation procedures, variations in climatic conditions and terrain (for instance, a sudden increase in cases of trench foot might cause wholesale eviction of psychiatric patients from the hospital); and the presence of a wound in addition to emotional collapse (in which case, the wound would take precedence). If we assume, however, that the risk of breakdown amongst Irish troops *during the war* was no different from that of other soldiers in the

British army, then around one-quarter of all Irish discharges from the army were the result of psychiatric illness.

Coping with war was particularly difficult for Irish servicemen in a number of ways. For the Irish soldier, the radical disjunction between the myths of war and their experience of it could be especially disorientating. Many had been raised on stories of the Irish as a 'martial race'. Myths associated with the Irish at war were legendary and continued to be recycled throughout the war itself. For instance, according to Samuel Parnell Kerr in *What the Irish Regiments have Done* (1916), the Irish positively enjoyed battle and 'would not have missed it for "lashins [sic] of money"'. The stories told of Irish prowess were outlandish. One of Kerr's tales involved the Connaughts who were being 'sorely pressed by the enemy'. In fact, the Irish soldiers were outnumbered by five to one, which was 'about the odds which best suits an Irishman', Kerr alleged, since it made the fight 'tremendously sporting'. However, he continued, before the Irishmen charged

they did what Irish regiments always do before a fight: they put up a silent prayer – 'a prayer to the Mother of Our Lord to be merciful to the loved ones at home should we fall'. Then they charged with the bayonet, and routed the enemy.[3]

A less pious story, with a similar emphasis on the ubiquitous 'sword' was told by Michael MacDonagh in *The Irish at the Front* (1916). He also believed that Irishmen excelled in the

close and relentless contest, man to man and bayonet to bayonet. ... Furious smithing, gleaming thrust and parry, stab and hack, hack and stab, with the Irish in the trenches and the Germans above; and in the end, it was the Germans running away and the Irish speeding their departure with rifle fire.[4]

This emphasis on the enjoyment of the intimate fight was central to myths about martial races. It made the fight a chivalrous one, between equals, and fought according to age-old rules of honourable warfare.

Of course, war was not like that. Instead of wielding the 'sword' themselves, it was Irishmen who were being hacked to pieces. Or, more likely, blown apart. They were running for their lives. Even worse than the scarlet fear of battle was the utter impotence and anonymity of modern warfare in which soldiers were trapped in their trenches being shelled but unable to hit back. Many men in such a situation must have echoed the plea of the soldier quoted in the book, *The Irish on the Somme* (1917): 'Please, sir, may we go out and bomb the Germans?'[5] Indeed, as I argue elsewhere, medical officers at the front were forced to recognise that more men broke down in war because they were *not* allowed to kill than collapsed under the strain of killing.[6] What was most unbearable about modern warfare was its passivity in the midst of extreme danger. As Tom Kettle (Young Irelander and

Lieutenant in the Dublin Fusiliers) lamented: 'In the trenches death is random, illogical, devoid of principle. One is shot not on sight, but on blindness, out of sight.'[7] The modern soldier was pitted against anonymous agents and his aggression was also incognito. Human emotions could not cope with such frightful impotence. If their sacrifice was said to be worthy because it was 'given for Ireland',[8] how was an Irish soldier to respond if 'Ireland' could not respect it? It was precisely this inability to live up to the myths, and the increasing disassociation between the Ireland they were fighting for and the Ireland they returned to, which made repatriation difficult for all Irish soldiers, but for the soldier tainted with brush of madness, even more so.

This reputation for being a 'martial race' had another negative impact. There was a high price to be paid for being considered a 'martial race'.[9] It was precisely the way writers like Kerr and MacDonagh differentiated Irish courage from that of the English which *harmed* the case for Irish self-government. As Harold Spender explained in 1916:

> there is in the Irish soldier a peculiar quality of electric zeal and dash. 'Missile troops' they have been called; and the phrase is eloquent of much. Those who most doubt the Irishman's capacity in civil affairs are often the readiest to admit his fury and prowess in battle.[10]

Many of the traits said to characterise Irish soldiers were, in fact, also said to be characteristic of other 'martial races', such as black Africans and Indians; Cynthia H. Enloe called this the 'Gurkha syndrome'.[11] The theory behind such characterisations was imbued with popularised interpretations of recapitulation theory. Just as the growth of the embryo 'recapitulated' the evolutionary history of the species, so too nations developed in a biological fashion, passing through the stages of infancy to childhood, to adolescence, to maturity.[12] In this schema, the Irish (as well as Indians and black Africans) were still in the child stage. Thus, MacDonagh wrote in *The Irish on the Somme*:

> It may well be that sometimes the English officers of Irish battalions are puzzled by the nature of their men – its impulsiveness, its glow, its wild imagery and overbrimming expression. It is easy to believe, too, that the changeful moods of the men, childlike and petulant, now jovial, now fierce, and occasionally unaccountable, may be a sure annoyance to officers who are formal and precise in matters of discipline.[13]

This was a surprising comment, perhaps, from a propagandist supposedly arguing *for* the Irish, but officers commanding Irish battalions often agreed. Brigadier W. Carden Roe of the Royal Irish Fusiliers confided that the Irish soldier acted like a 'naughty child' who would 'resent' not being chided by his officers.[14] Rowland Fielding (commander of the 6th Battalion

Connaught Rangers from 1916) wrote to his wife on 14 June 1917, saying that 'Ireland will always be Ireland. It is a land of children with the bodies of men, and politically they do not themselves know what they want.' Fielding believed that like children, the Irish were 'easily made happy' and, equally, 'easily depressed'.[15] Politically, they needed strong leadership from an older and more cautious father-nation.

Consequently, Irish soldiers were often regarded as emotionally vulnerable. Pensioning authorities and the War Office constantly asserted (without reliable statistical verification) that proportionately more Irish servicemen were driven insane during the war than their English, Scottish, or Welsh comrades. Ulstermen were exonerated from this devastating slur. In 'Ireland (South)', otherwise known as the 'South Ireland Pension Area', the proportion of ex-servicemen receiving pensions for neurasthenia (and, indeed, all other forms of disablement) was said to be well over the average.[16]

In attempting to explain this distressing belief, well-known prejudices emerged. Primarily, it was agreed that the Irish were predisposed to insanity. This had been a common assumption even before the war. As Sir Charles A. Cameron, Chief Medical Officer in Dublin for over thirty years, told the Interdepartmental Committee on Physical Deterioration in 1904, Irish levels of lunacy were high (and rising) because of the long-standing 'cerebral excitement' caused by questions about land and politics.[17] According to a writer in *The Lancet* at the end of September 1914, high lunacy levels in Ireland were a 'legacy of mental weakness dating from the sufferings of the famine years'.[18] Indisputably, psycho-neuroses developed in only two types of people, declared the prominent socialist and psychiatrist, Dr Montague David Eder: they were common either in men who were 'inherently below the level of civilization' (that is 'degenerates') or in those who were 'ethically in advance of their age'.[19] There was no question which category Irishmen fell into.

Pensioning authorities added to such negative characterisations of the Irish at war. In defence of the extremely high levels in 'Ireland (South)', the District Commissioner of Medical Services for the region, Dr Boldie, tried to explain that the high percentage of ex-service lunatics in Ireland was not only due to the 'special political conditions' but also to 'a definite Neurasthenic temperament which is prevalent amongst the South Irish'. Another pension authority, Dr Wallace, added that it was 'indisputable' that recruitment practice in Ireland was more lax and that subsequently 'large numbers' of men recruited in Ireland were physically unfit, mentally defective, and subject to a wide range of nervous disorders.[20] In a slightly more sympathetic tone, Dr P. L. Forward pointed out that, in his belief, the problem was simply that Irish Service lunatics were kept on their home treatment allowances or in hospital on 'humanitarian grounds' because they had no prospect of supporting themselves in any other way. Forward went so far as to state that, in the current political circumstances, this action was 'almost justifiable' since if this help was withdrawn the men would 'drift or starve'.[21]

Such assumptions about the social and ethnic characteristics of shell-shocked men translated into poor treatment for the unfortunate men appearing at the Casualty Clearing Stations (and later the hospitals), shaking or screaming. They were assumed to be malingering.[22] Even kindly Medical Officers (such as Dr Eder) who were engaged in gentle persuasion and the 'talking cure', believed that there were 'nice and nasty neurotics'.[23] As Lieutenant-General Sir Charles Burtchaell admitted in an address to the Royal Academy of Medicine in Ireland in 1920, military medicine had no civilian counterpart. While in civilian practice, the individual was paramount, in war 'it was essential to the success of military operations to look at disease and physical non-effectiveness from a collective point of view'. This required 'up-to-date and progressive knowledge of the scientific methods' and an understanding of physiological stress. However, for Burtchaell, there was another necessity, and that was 'knowledge of human nature as seen in a military community', or (as a more cynical interpreter might elaborate this phrase) an awareness that frightened men might shirk, malinger, feign madness, or even 'really' become temporarily insane in order to escape the anticipated slaughter.[24] Servicemen had to be prepared to give not only their lives or limbs for 'the nation', but their nerves as well.

Such attitudes and shifting scientific notions of shell-shock had a major impact upon treatment. In the early years of the First World War, shell-shock was believed to be the result of a physical injury to the nerves. Incidents such as being buried alive or exposed to heavy bombardment were naturally considered to be plausible explanations for nervous collapse, while fear and guilt had little role to play in the development of the neurosis. Increasingly, however, medical officers began emphasising psychological factors as providing sufficient cause for breakdown. Once these factors were admitted, fear and the act of killing itself suddenly became important.

This shift from regarding breakdown as organic to viewing it as psychological had inevitable consequences in terms of treatment. From the start, there was concern about the low levels of 'cure'. Amongst patients in psychiatric wards, four-fifths were permanently unable to return to military service.[25] It was imperative for the military that more efficient ways were developed to restore the maximum number of men to duty as quickly as possible. If breakdown was a 'paralysis of the nerves', then massage, rest, dietary regimes, and electrical treatment were invoked; if a psychological source was indicated, the talking cure, hypnosis, and rest would speed recovery. In all instances, occupational training and the inculcation of masculinity were highly recommended.

Not all doctors made this transition. For instance, in 1920 Dr B. McSwiney of the University of Dublin read a paper before the Royal

Academy of Medicine in Ireland entitled 'Physiological Psychology of Fatigue and Allied Conditions'. While he cautiously rejected explanations for war madness focusing solely on organic categories, he still insisted that there was a physiological component to the disorder. He reminded his audience that the 'functions of our natural life are closely allied to our psychical existence, and so any disturbance of our physiological functions disturbs the working of the mind'. Therefore, if the physical condition of an individual was lowered – by fatigue, for instance – his emotions were much more likely to become 'exaggerated'. The problem with war was that no amount of military training could 'train his emotions ... It is the experience of these emotions, with subsequent expression, which lead later to neurotic conditions. The emotional states will return to the memory, for no stimulus is ever forgotten or the memory lost.' Therefore, it was imperative that further study took place of 'Physiological psychology'.[26]

Other medical personnel were more confident about the usefulness of the new psychology of the mind. Undoubtedly, wartime experiences increased the popularity of psychotherapy in Ireland, as elsewhere in Europe. Cecil P. Smyly, in a speech to the Dublin University Biological Association, was one of the chief champions of psychotherapy, arguing that it was a method of treatment that 'undoubtedly produces beneficial results in some instances' and calling for more research to be dedicated to it in order that it was not 'left to the exploitation of those with more imagination than discretion'. He did express reservations about Freud's almost exclusive emphasis on sexual complexes (despite admitting that sex does occupy 'a large, in some a very large, part in the mind'), preferring to side with W. H. R. Rivers that even these sexual complexes could be 'dethroned by fear and other emotions and interests'.[27]

In practical terms, these shifts worked to the advantage of the insane. In the early years of the war, so called 'emotional Irishmen' and 'weak privates' were given progressively more painful electric shocks in an attempt to effect a 'cure'.[28] Increasingly, however, more sensitive methods of psychotherapy were employed. In the context of Ireland, the most important proponent of these methods was Dr Eder. One of his patients was an Irish soldier (a former plumber) who was suffering from hysterical paralysis after being bayoneted fifteen times. Eder listened carefully as this Irishman explained over and over again that 'in such fighting you must clutch your rifle very firmly and never let it go, guarding yourself all the time'. Psychotherapy led Eder to conclude that, 'Grasping the rifle was the very attitude his hand still assumed; in the unconscious he was still clutching the rifle; he was still fighting the good fight, and this desire was symbolised by the grasping hand.' Eder also observed that the man had not felt the pain of the fifteen bayonet wounds until the fight was over and others drew attention to the blood pouring from his side. In other words, during the fight, his unconscious had refused to allow him to feel the pain. In Eder's words:

The unconscious acted here like Nelson did consciously at the Battle of the Sound. And for a similar motive. Nelson wanted to go on fighting. So did my young Irish soldier – who was as you may imagine, a very highly strung and sensitive individual. Had he allowed himself consciously to feel pain he would either have had to retire from the struggle or perhaps let go his clutch on the rifle and be killed.

Thus, when threatened with pain, at first the unconscious took no notice, but as the pain continued, 'the former memory was revived and the unconscious became on guard. The Turks were at it again; re-living a similar experience, the unconscious developed the same defensive mechanism – that is, the perception did not pass from the unconscious to the conscious.' Explanation and hypnosis provided the cure.[29]

Although some medical officers could show sympathy towards shell-shocked servicemen, the wider, civilian population maintained a sterner stance. This was the case for patients of other nationalities, as well as for the Irish. It was not uncommon for men arriving at Netley Hospital (for British servicemen suffering shell-shock) to be greeted with silence as onlookers hung their heads in 'inexplicable shame'.[30] Officers frequently argued that there were two types of men who were more liable to collapse in combat: cowards and 'womanish' men. Many medical officers believed that psychological breakdown was a form of cowardice.[31] Undoubtedly, some men *did* fake madness in order to get out of combat.[32] For instance, the Cockney-Irishman, Edward Casey was a veteran malingerer who managed to delay further service during the First World War by pretending to be shell-shocked. He described how the medical officer hypnotised him: 'I had to tell him every thing I remembered before the barrage. Talking and telling him lies while he wrote every word I spoke, in a book, telling me my complaint of shattered nerves was becoming very prevalent.'[33]

Even though such dissemblers were exceptional, it was widely thought that diagnoses like shell shock gave 'fear a respectable name' and encouraged the 'weaklings' to malinger. As one 'old stager' told the neurologist to the 4th Army: 'if a man lets his comrades down, he ought to be shot. If he's a looney, so much the better!'[34] Sympathy was rarely forthcoming and sufferers everywhere had no choice but to accept the stigma of cowardice and recognise that their reputations as soldiers and men had been dealt a severe blow.

Although the shell-shocked ex-serviceman did not occupy an enviable position anywhere, the Irish soldier faced a number of special problems. As mentioned, madness was not an escape for the Irish combatant – for where was he to go? In Ireland, men's sacrifices were not simply denied, they were positively derided. As the person in charge of pensions in Ireland, Dr P. L. Forward, noted in March 1921, ex-servicemen who had broken down in war were faced with a 'hostile attitude' directed against them, both individually and collectively. Even sympathetic employers bowed to intimidation and threats. In Forward's words:

> These patients, in addition to their nervous disabilities resulting from the stress of War, all have the super-added anxiety states occasioned by the hopeless outlook for the future in respect to their obtaining employment, and in earning the means wherewith to maintain themselves and their dependants.

Gloomily, he added that 'no amount of psychotherapy' could relieve their sufferings.[35] Officials frequently believed that the ex-servicemen had brought trouble on themselves by being lazy. As one unnamed official put it, complaints about being boycotted in employment were simply 'a facile shibboleth of exculpation from not really seeking work'.[36] Many Irish ex-servicemen found refuge in the Fianna Fáil Party, but even this could not safeguard them from prejudice, particularly (according to a report in 1936) in the western counties of Galway, Clare, and Mayo where the ex-service population was relatively small and unemployment was high.[37] Others agreed that being blocked from employment was desperately painful, going further by observing that neurasthenic patients in Ireland suffered more than their physically disabled comrades because 'in the few who are willing to work the anxiety state is increased, and in those who are unwilling the non-work habit is fostered'.[38] So serious was this state of affairs that some commentators recommended that self-contained 'work colonies' (described identically to prisons in which labour was forced) be established to house any cured service lunatic agonising about his status as 'an outcast and an undesirable'.[39] As one, icy-cold 'Report from Dublin' put it in 1936: 'Every southern Irishman who enlisted did so as a volunteer, and each individual must either bear the responsibility for the results of his voluntary act or look to his employer, the British government, for redress.'[40]

In addition, resources to help such men adapt to civilian life were limited. In comparison with neurasthenic casualties elsewhere, they were shorn of economic resources. The most effective post-war treatment for psychiatric illness arising out of war was thought to lie in the establishment of special workshops dedicated to 'hardening' men through work. As the Director General of Medical Services warned the Commissioner of Medical Services in Dublin in 1921, it was very easy to create neurasthenics or to prolong their disability unless they were given something to do. Work was 'the all important [factor] with the Neurasthenic'.[41] Yet, as those responsible for pensions in Ireland confessed, there were very limited facilities available throughout the island.[42] For instance, only two institutions catered to ex-service lunatics. In September 1917, Mrs Bernard Dunning presented the estate and mansion of Leopardstown Park, County Dublin, to the Ministry of Pensions as a permanent home for neurasthenic servicemen. Also in 1917,

the Craigavon Hospital was handed over by Lieutenant-Colonel James Craig
to the Ulster Volunteer Force Hospital Board of Management to be used as a
Neurasthenic hospital, after it had been argued that forcing Belfast men to
attend the neurasthenic board in Dublin was a 'serious matter for men
shaken by shell-shock'.[43] At the opening ceremony, The Rt Hon G. N.
Barnes (Minister for Pensions) declared that the country 'must not be content
with giving a man a pension; it must build him up and return him a self-
supporting and self-respecting unit to the community'.[44] Craigavon was to
be modelled along the lines of the hospital in Golders Green, London, and
was to be under the guidance of Lieutenant-Colonel Sir John Collie, famous
for his obsession with detecting cases of malingering.[45]

However, both institutions were constantly under threat. As early as June
1920, Craigavon only marginally managed to avoid being turned into a
sanatorium for consumptives[46] and there was a constant (and unforthcom-
ing) scramble for money to increase the opportunities for treatment and
training there.[47] In the south of Ireland three years after the end of the war,
there were still 120 officers and 1,200 men in the other ranks awaiting hospital treatment for neurasthenia. Most of these men were dependent upon
'home treatment allowances' which were costing the Ministry of Pensions
over £100,000 a year.[48] In 1921, the South Ireland Pensions Area had the
highest proportion of ex-servicemen awaiting treatment for neurasthenia in
the United Kingdom, as can be seen in the following table.

Table 5   Proportion of all patients awaiting either in-patient or
out-patient treatment, 1921

Area	Percentage awaiting in- and out-patient treatment	Percentage awaiting in- patient treatment	Percentage awaiting out- patient treatment
Scotland	2.5	21.0	0
North	7.5	0	13.5
North West	37.1	22.5	56.3
Yorkshire	20.9	7.3	24.5
Wales	4.5	5.3	7.6
North Midlands	49.9	22.2	53.1
Midlands	58.6	39.2	64.8
South West	7.6	8.7	7.3
London	7.2	32.8	5.9
Ulster	22.2	42.1	4.3
'South Ireland'	69.0	87.9	48.2

Source: PRO, PIN 15/56.

The Ministry of Pensions for 'South Ireland' pleaded with the Ministry of Pensions in London for help in expanding facilities at the Leopardstown Park Hospital, arguing that 'unless the neurasthenic institutions in England are able to help us, there is little prospect of the waiting list being reduced in less than eighteen months to two years, and then only allowing for a short course of treatment for each case'.[49] But nothing was done.

There were other problems faced exclusively by Irish patients. One important question had been: what should be done with insane ex-servicemen who acted violently and needed to be forcibly admitted to an asylum? As in Britain at this time, there were two ways to admit a person into an asylum: the police could drag the dangerous lunatic before a magistrate and have him committed or the Poor Law Infirmary could admit a patient and, on the first occasion when he or she acted violently, could transfer the patient to an asylum. Neither method worked in Ireland, as the Ministry of Pensions in Dublin explained in exasperated tones to the London office. In the first instance, the arresting of dangerous lunatics by the police was 'in abeyance, owing to other difficulties experienced by them in the discharge of their work'. In the second instance, there was the problem of finance. The Ministry of Pensions in London could meet the cost of certification but, if the Ministry refused to accept that the man's madness was a result of war service, nothing could be done. More seriously, asylums in Ireland were largely run through government grants. However, local authorities refused to recognise the British government and refused to have their accounts audited. Thus, Irish asylums lacked finance and strenuously avoided admitting any patients at all, let alone ex-servicemen.[50]

Problems also arose out of the fact that the Army Council Instruction No. 8 of 1918 was not made applicable to Ireland. This Instruction decreed that soldiers suffering from chronic mental disease for over nine months were to be deemed 'incurable' and were to be 'discharged to the appropriate asylum and handed over as service patients'. The General Commander-in-Chief, Irish Command, made representations against the fact that this Instruction did not include Ireland. Because Ireland was not included, a man from the south might be kept indefinitely in the Belfast Hospital 'where his friends may never be able to visit him'. In addition, as there were only two special hospitals in Ireland for patients with mental illness, it was 'seldom possible to transfer a case to another Military hospital where he would be nearer his friends'. The General asked whether it was possible extend the Instruction to Ireland 'without the men being classified as paupers on admission to the Civil lunatic asylum'.[51] But this caused a further problem. The fear of a 'pauper taint', meant that the Belfast War Pensions Committee opposed the idea that ex-service lunatics be discharged into county asylums.[52]

The position of the relatives of these service lunatics was equally hard, primarily due to a misprint in the Lunacy (Ireland) Act of 1901. Instead of using the word 'person' (as in the British legislation), the Irish Act had inserted the word 'prisoner'. This meant that any soldier consigned to a lunatic asylum in Ireland became technically a 'criminal lunatic' and the State was therefore liable for the whole cost of his maintenance out of Imperial funds. In England, Scotland and Wales, the cost of maintenance fell on local authorities and if those authorities agreed to waive their claim on a man's pension for his maintenance, the Army Council was allowed to pay that pension to his wife or other dependants. In Ireland, however, because ex-soldier lunatics were technically classified as criminal lunatics, the whole cost of their maintenance was transferred from local Irish funds to the Imperial Exchequer. What this meant was that the War Office simply discontinued the man's pension, thus causing hardship to his dependants. In terms of propaganda, this misprint was a disaster. As one commentator noted, it was obvious that much 'hostile use' was made of the fact that Irish ex-service lunatics were technically 'criminal lunatics .... to be kept in an Asylum during His Majesty's pleasure'.[53]

The pensioned, lunatic ex-serviceman also suffered because of the state of ex-servicemen in Ireland more generally. Irish ex-servicemen formed a smaller proportion of the population in Ireland than in Great Britain, they tended to be scattered throughout the island, and they did not possess a large political organisation to lobby for them. Thus, in the words of one report, they were 'less well acquainted with their rights and were less liable to have Pension Regulations brought to their notice'.[54] They were further disadvantaged because of the disturbed state of Ireland between 1918 and 1923 when 'normal postal facilities were not available resulting in loss of letters dealing with their pensions'. This also meant that when the Ministry of Pensions issued statements about how ex-servicemen should appeal against 'Final Awards', Irishmen were not made aware of them.[55] Ireland was also not a party to the King's Roll, whereby grateful employers undertook to employ no less than three-quarters of ex-servicemen in their establishments. In contrast, job priority in government was given to ex-Free State soldiers and while some of these had served in the British Army, this fact was irrelevant and could even be held against them. Irish ex-servicemen also could not take part in the emigration scheme, unless they lived in England for six months.[56]

Clearly, the Irish ex-serviceman faced considerable institutional hurdles. In addition, he was in a more vulnerable psychological position than his English counterpart. The conditions of Irish troops overseas were no different from their British counterparts, and they cannot be assumed to have suffered higher rates of breakdown in battle. However, the psychological resilience of Irish soldiers may have been weakened by a number of factors. Much evidence – most notoriously from the Vietnam War – suggests that negative psychological reactions to war by service-personnel dramatically increase under two conditions. First, the absence of 'purification rites' upon their return home made servicemen vulnerable. Thus, emotional turmoil leading to psychiatric collapse often occurred when hostile crowds greeted the return of servicemen, rather than friendly, grateful crowds willing to confirm the rightness of the slaughter, bestow understanding and forgiveness upon uneasy consciences, and embrace their 'boys' as returning 'men'. Although the extent to which Irish servicemen were instantly rejected upon their return to Ireland has been exaggerated, it is clear that most did not think that their sacrifices had been sufficiently honoured either by word or deed.

Second, psychological collapse was more frequent when servicemen were returning to a country vastly different from the place veterans had left. This caused disorientation and disillusionment. The 1916 Rising brought forcibly home to them the fact that their sacrifices were in danger of being rejected. When the Easter Rising took place, Irishmen in the front lines were generally distraught and bewildered. Driver R. L. Veneables recorded in his diary that 'we also heard that there was a rebellion in Ireland, and we were having to send soldiers there instead of to the war; we thought this was odd, as there were a lot of Irishmen in the firing line'.[57] Humphrey J. Cholmeley was confused. The Rising occurred just three months prior to his being killed during the Battle of the Somme on 14 July 1916. He asked his mother 'What was the Irish rebellion [sic] I only saw one newspaper and that said it was all over [sic] who rebelled? And what for?'[58] Lieutenant-Colonel H. Jack Chappell was recuperating from an injury in Winchester at the time of the Rising. His letter to his parents mentioned that 'poor old Pat' was 'very upset' over the Rising. Chappell explained that Pat was 'a nationalist & feels very grieved for his people whom he feel sure have been incited by German agents. In fact he wanted to send in his papers for sheer shame but I managed to dissuade him.'[59] R. B. Marshall summarised the general feeling in a letter to his mother on 4 May 1916: 'I am glad the rebels in Ireland are getting squashed. I hope they shoot a good many of them. The amusing part is that all these Irish regiments out here would like nothing better than to have a go at them with a bayonet.'[60] Returning Irish soldiers were required to adapt remarkably quickly to dramatic changes in the political culture of their homeland. This was a difficult task and one that led to much resentment and disillusionment.

Irish servicemen who had broken down in war were right to feel bitter about the position in which they found themselves. Not only were they outcasts for having 'fought for England instead of Ireland', their maddened minds debarred them from 'making good' in the War of Independence and the Civil War and, in an increasingly militaristic society, discredited their very masculinity. Even their 'sane' comrades in war turned from them in shame for having disgraced myths of the indomitable Irish martial spirit. Their masculinity was in doubt, their loyalty was derided, and the passivity engendered on the modern battlefield was continued once they returned home when everyone from the bureaucrats at the Ministry of Pensions to local employers seemed to gang up against them. Their activities in the British military were seen as the most shameful fact of all. For such men, the landscape of violence was carried back within them.

Notes

1 Dr Graham, 'The war and insanity', *The British Medical Journal*, 14 August 1915, p. 272. For other discussions of this decline, see 'Lunacy in 1915', *British Medical Journal*, 26 May 1917, p. 698.

2 Lieutenant-General Sir Charles Burtchaell, 'Disease as affecting success in the war', *Transactions of the Royal Academy of Medicine in Ireland*, vol. 37 (1920), p. 540.

3 S. Parnell Kerr, *What the Irish Regiments Have Done* (London, T. Fisher Unwin Ltd., 1916), pp. 55–6.

4 M. MacDonagh, *The Irish at the Front* (London, Hodder and Stoughton, 1916), p. 44.

5 M. MacDonagh, *The Irish on the Somme* (London, Hodder and Stoughton, 1917), p. 63.

6 J. Bourke, *An Intimate History of Killing: Face-to-Face Killing in Twentieth Century Warfare* (London, Granta, 1999).

7 T. M. Kettle, *The Ways of War* (London, Constable and Co., 1917), p. 171.

8 S. Gwynn, *John Redmond's Last Years* (London, George G. Harrop and Co., 1919), p. 201.

9 J. Bourke, '"Irish Tommies": the construction of a martial manhood 1914–1918', *Bullan*, vol. 6 (February 1998), pp. 13–30.

10 H. Spender, 'Ireland and the war', *Contemporary Review*, vol. 110 (November 1916), p. 567.

11 C. H. Enloe, *Ethnic Soldiers. State Security in Divided Societies* (Harmondsworth, Penguin, 1980), p. 26.

12 For a discussion, see P. Bovet, *The Fighting Instinct*, translated by J. Y. T. Greig (London, George Allen and Unwin, 1923), p. 149.

13 MacDonagh, *The Irish on the Somme*, p. 111. Also see Rev R. H. Bassett, 'The chaplain with the West African forces', *Journal of the Royal Army Chaplains' Department*, vol. 7 (July 1950), p. 24 and D. Killingray, 'The "Rod of Empire": the debate over corporal punishment in the British African Colonial Forces, 1888–1946', *Journal of African History*, vol. 35 (1994), p. 202 for West African soldiers. For Indian troops, see E. Candler, *The Year of Chivalry* (London, Simpkin, Marshall, Hamilton, Kent and Co., 1916), pp. 273–4 and Lieutenant-Colonel J. W. B. Merewether and Sir Frederick Smith, *The Indian Corps in France* (London, John Murray, 1917), pp. 110–11.

14 IWM, 77/165/1, Brigadier W. Carden Roe, 'Memoirs', pp. 8–9. Also see Lieutenant-Colonel H. F. N. Jourdain, *Ranging Memories* (Oxford, Oxford University Press, 1934), p. 305.

15 R. Feilding, *War Letters to a Wife. France and Flanders, 1915–1919* (London, The Medici Society, 1929), p. 121, letters dated 25 September 1916 and 14 June 1917.

16 PRO, PIN15/56, 'Memorandum on Conference of Neurological D.Cs.M.S. Held at Headquarters on Friday, June 17th 1921', p. 3.

17 Sir Charles A. Cameron giving evidence in *Interdepartmental Committee on Physical Deterioration*, Parliamentary Papers 1904, vol. 32, pp. 406–7.

18 'Insanity in Ireland', *The Lancet*, 26 September 1914, p. 811.

19 Montague David Eder, *War-Shock. The Psycho-Neuroses in War. Psychology and Treatment* (London, William Heinemann, 1917), p. 17.

20 PRO, PIN15/56, 'Memorandum on Conference of Neurological D.Cs.M.S. Held at Headquarters on Friday, June 17th 1921', p. 3.

21 PRO, PIN15/899, Dr P. L. Forward in 'Provision of Employment for Ex-Service Men in Ireland', 11 March 1921', p. 3.

22 For a detailed discussion, see J. Bourke, *Dismembering the Male: Men's Bodies, Britain and the Great War* (London, Reaktion, 1996).

23 Montague David Eder, 'An address on the psycho-pathology of the war neuroses', *The Lancet*, vol. 2 (12 August 1916), pp. 264–5.

24 Burtchaell, 'Disease as affecting success in the war', p. 527.

25 A study of 731 discharges from the Red Cross Military Hospital at Mughum in the year ending 30 June 1917, in T. W. Salmon, 'The care and treatment of mental diseases and war neuroses ("shell shock") in the British Army', *Mental Hygiene*, vol. 14 (October 1917), p. 525.

26 B. McSwiney, 'Physiological psychology of fatigue and allied conditions', in *Transactions of the Royal Academy of Medicine in Ireland*, vol. 37 (1920), pp. 541 and 547–9.

27 C. P. Smyly, 'Psychotherapy in practice', *The Irish Journal of Medical Science*, 5th series, vol. 33 (November 1924), p. 491

28 For example, see the brutal description in L. R. Yealland, *Hysterical Disorders of Warfare* (London, Macmillan and Co., 1918), pp. 97–101.

29 Eder, 'Psycho-pathology of the war neuroses', pp. 264–5.

30 PRO, PIN15/2502, Undated and untitled typescript by W. D. Esplin, first paragraph.

31 'Malingering', *British Medical Journal*, 28 July 1917, p. 117; PRO, PIN15/2946, 'Minister's Meeting with Representatives of War Pensions Committees. Extract from the Summary of Proceedings of the Meeting Held at Bristol on 25th April 1930'; C. S. Myers, *Shell Shock in France 1914–18. Based on a War Diary* (Cambridge, Cambridge University Press, 1940), pp. 51–3; Salmon, 'Care and treatment of mental diseases and war neuroses', p. 516; R. T. Williamson, 'The treatment of neurasthenia and psychosthenia following shell shock', *British Medical Journal*, 1 December 1917, p. 714.

32 'Ex-Private X', *War is War* (London, Victor Gallancz, 1930), pp. 97–8; PRONI, D3804, J. Hutchinson, 'The early reminiscence of a Royal Irish Rifleman, 1917–1919', 1982, p. 33; *Report of the War Office Committee of Enquiry into 'Shell-Shock'* [Cmd 1734], H. C. 1922, xii, p. 43, evidence by William Brown; E. E. Southard, *Shell-Shock and Other Neuro-Psychiatric Problems Presented in 500 and 89 Case Histories from the War Literature, 1914–1918* (Boston, W. M. Leonard, 1919), pp. 106 and 643.

33 J. Bourke, *The Misfit Soldier* (Cork, Cork University Press, 1998), p. 54.

34 Dr H. W. Wills, 'Footnote to Medical History', n.d., p. 2, Liddle Collection, General Aspects: Shell Shock. Item 1.

35 Forward in 'Provision of Employment for Ex-Service Men in Ireland', pp. 1–2.

36 PRO, PIN15/7558 , 'Report from Dublin', 22 June 1936, p. 3.

37 Ibid., p. 2.

38 PRO, PIN15/899, Note by H. Sugars, Staff, DCMS, Ireland (South Region), 21 March 1921, appended to a letter from C. K. Darnell, Ministry of Pensions, Ulster Region, 14 March 1921.

39 Forward in 'Provision of Employment for Ex-Service Men in Ireland', p. 4.

40 PRO, PIN 15/758 , 'Report from Dublin', 22 June 1936, p. 1.

41 PRO, PIN15/56, Letter from John Harry Hebb for the Director General of Medical Services, to H. Sugars, Commissioner of Medical Services, Dublin, 21 December 1921.

42 Forward in 'Provision of Employment for Ex-Service Men in Ireland', p. 1; PRO, PIN15/56, 'Memorandum on Conference of Neurological Deputy Commissioners of Medical Services Held at Headquarters on Friday, June 17th, 1921', p. 2; PRO, PIN 15/55, Minute from the Commissioner, Medical Services, Ulster Region, 26 May 1921.

43 PRO, PIN15/54, Letter to the Earl of Derby at the War Office by unknown author, 29 May 1917.
44 'Craigavon neurasthenic hospital for soldiers, Belfast', *British Medical Journal*, 28 July 1917, p. 132.
45 *Ibid.*, p. 132.
46 'The proposed sanatorium at Craigavon, Belfast', *British Medical Journal*, 5 June 1920, p. 783.
47 PRO, PIN15/899, Note by H. Sugars, Staff, DCMS, Ireland (South Region), 21 March 1921, appended to a letter from C. K. Darnell, Ministry of Pensions, Ulster Region, 14 March 1921.
48 Forward in 'Provision of Employment for Ex-Service Men in Ireland', p. 2. The Local Government Board *rejected* a request by the Down County Council to borrow £127,000 to purchase Craigavon as a sanatorium for consumptives.
49 PRO, PIN15/56, Letter from H. Sugars of the Ministry of Pensions, Ireland (South) to Dr John Harry Hebb, Ministry of Pensions, London, 24 November 1921.
50 PRO, PIN15/899, Letter from the Ministry of Pensions in Dublin, 24 March 1921.
51 PRO, PIN 15/896, Letter from The Secretary, War Office, to The Secretary, Ministry of Pensions, 15 April 1918.
52 PRO, PIN 15/897, Memo by L. G. of the Medical Services Branch, 21 September 1918.
53 *Ibid.* Also see PRO, PIN 15/896.
54 PRO, PIN15/757, 'Extract from Report on Committee on Claims of British Ex-Servicemen', pp. 4–7.
55 *Ibid.*, pp. 4–7.
56 Captain F. C. Hitchcock, 'Plight of Ex-Service Men in the Irish Free State', *Morning Post*, 19 December 1927.
57 IWM, 76/225/1, R. L. Venables, 'The Great War 1914–1918: Diary', diary entry in 1916, p. 33.
58 IWM, P360, H. J. Cholmeley, 'Letters', letter to his mother, 13 May 1916.
59 IWM, 92/3/1, Lieutenant Colonel H. Jack Chappell, 'Letters and Diary', letter to his parents, 27 April 1916.
60 R. B. Marshall, letter to his mother, 4 May 1916, in the Liddle collection.

9

The road to Belgrade: the experiences of the 10th (Irish) Division in the Balkans, 1915–17

PHILIP ORR

In one of the less well-remembered 'side-shows' of the First World War, a number of Irishmen served with the Salonica Expeditionary Force in the Balkans. A large proportion of these soldiers were in the 10th (Irish) Division, and this chapter examines their experiences. The '10th' had been formed in the first series of Kitchener's new army divisions, prior to the formation of the 16th and 36th Divisions, each of which required a period of political manoeuvring in order for men of the rival volunteer forces of John Redmond and Edward Carson to join up *en masse*. The 10th Division recruited in all four provinces of Ireland and contained battalions of such famous Irish regiments as the Connaught Rangers, the Inniskilling Fusiliers, the Leinster Regiment and the Munster Fusiliers. Recruitment to the ranks brought in many thousands of ordinary Irishmen from various backgrounds. The officer class included middle-class Catholics, but it had a strong representation from both the Anglo-Irish social class and the regular British officer corps of the pre-wartime era. The Division trained in Ireland and the south of England before leaving for Gallipoli.

The Dardanelles proved to be a disaster for the 10th as for almost every other army division that served there. It experienced the death of over 2,000 men in the spring and summer of 1915; the beaches of Suvla proved to be a killing ground in which Turkish gunfire, intense heat, poor medical assistance and doggedly inept British military strategy all played their part.[1] When it was withdrawn from Gallipoli in the summer of 1915, the Division was greatly depleted not only in numbers but in morale. The majority of fresh soldiers who were drafted into the 10th Divisional ranks were not Irish; none the less, the military cemeteries of Greece bear testimony to the many Irishmen, both new and veteran, who did suffer and die in a strange and almost forgotten campaign against the Bulgarian Army in southern Macedonia, from the moment that the Division arrived there in October 1915 until its departure for another theatre of war in 1917.

The Division was sent from the barren landscape of Gallipoli to the city of Salonica just as Bulgaria joined the Central Power Alliance. Soon the 10th was joined by a range of French and British forces, which, if they could not march up the road to Belgrade to rescue their ally Serbia from occupation, could at least prevent Bulgaria from seizing a strip of key Mediterranean coastline.

The Division experienced a much lower rate of casualties than hitherto during its time at Salonica; the battle of Kosturino, the Division's most costly engagement, had produced a 'mere' 300 deaths.[2] Although the Division spent a good deal of time outside the 'front line' or engaged in low-level encounters with the enemy, a study of how the men experienced the war in Macedonia adds to our knowledge of the wider Irish experience of the First World War, and to our evaluation of that war's current place in Irish public memory.

These soldiers' experiences confirm for us that the sense of waste and degradation so typical on the Western Front, and at Gallipoli, was also present in Macedonia. One very typical feature of soldiers' diaries is the comment that the conditions under which they were being made to serve exceeded both the aggression of the enemy, and his capacity to harm and annoy them. During the part of the campaign centred in the Struma Valley, in the summer months of 1915 and 1916, men of the 10th would be sent on 'marches of up to 25 miles in the heat', despite the fact that the temperature in the valley was rising to 114°F. With almost comic levels of inefficiency, the authorities would send woollen underwear to them just when the weather was warmest, and sun-helmets would arrive when the hot season was over.[3] Long marches in such conditions could prove fatal. In June 1916, men fainted 'in scores' on a route march to the Struma, and one young soldier died at the roadside. Yet, as a witness recalled, the officers continued to use 'Prussian-like tactics to stimulate the men who faint', and the following day's march was preceded by a 'severe lecture and threats'.[4]

Severe rain could at other times reduce the ground to a proverbial 'sea of mud'.[5] Heavy Balkan thunderstorms would leave trenches 'full of water' or 'fallen in'.[6] Rivers from the mountains could suddenly rise, and men on route-marches sometimes found themselves wading across the River Struma, with water reaching shoulder height and 'their only support being a rope secured to pickets on either side'.[7] Soldiers were often expected to survive the harsh winter conditions of 'the savage, almost trackless country' of the high Macedonian mountains.[8] Sometimes 'hailstones as big as sparrow's eggs' would come lashing down.[9]

However, it was when extreme conditions combined with intense military action that the Irish soldier in the Macedonian countryside experienced suffering comparable with the worst excesses of the Western Front. In its first military action – an attempt to stem the headlong Bulgarian advance into Serbian Macedonia – the Division occupied precipitous mountain positions, north of Salonica, in the midst of appalling winter conditions. On the unfamiliar mountains above Kosturino, they were forced to retreat from superior Bulgarian numbers, losing many men in the process, including not only 300 dead, but also nearly 800 wounded or taken prisoner.[10]

Men's clothing froze as the temperature plummeted. Sodden greatcoats 'split like wood when attempts were made to bang garments back into shape'.[11] Men were told not to lie down at night to avoid the deadly coma of advanced exposure.[12] Amidst all this potentially fatal discomfort, in the disorienting mists and blizzards, the Bulgarians attacked. One shell landed in a group of Dublin Fusiliers, killing nine and wounding a dozen. But some of the most deadly Bulgarian attacks were by bayonet-charge. Men bled to death and were swiftly buried 'behind the trench-line', beneath the gathering snow.[13] The retreat was over 'rough stones and rocks' and perilous passes where 'water oozing out' of the hill formed a 'solid block of ice' in places.[14] Resting and sheltering from the enemy was of no particular relief; on the long retreat from Kosturino 'men huddled together on the lee side of rocks ... hardened men wept that their numbed fingers could not untie the frozen knots of their pack-loads ... the rocky ground, splintering on impact, intensified a hundredfold the killing power of their high-explosive shells'.[15]

As for the injured, there was the purgatory of being carried back by pack mule, 'over uncertain paths where a false step on the uneven ground would very often have meant certain death'.[16] Many soldiers, in later years, could still hear how men had 'shrieked with pain' at every jolt on the road back from the battlefield.[17] When the nursing staff finally had a chance to tend to these soldiers, the effects of frostbite were seen to be as bad as those of more customary injuries. One nurse, caring for the victims of Kosturino, found that a man's toes had fallen off when she opened his dressing in the hospital.[18]

The families of the men who had died soon received news of their bereavement. These were families in every part of Ireland: Patrick Kearney of Kingstown, Co. Dublin had died of wounds on 4 December 1915; James Malley of Newport, Co. Mayo, had been killed in action on 7 December, and Wesley Breakley of Portadown, Co. Armagh, had died on the same day, possibly as a result of the effects of exposure.[19]

These stories of death and destruction mirror the experiences of Irish soldiers everywhere in the war. For many soldiers in the 10th the daily routines of army life had also to be endured with the same kind of bitter frustration as on the Western Front, especially on a regional front line such as the one in the Struma Valley where so much time was spent on long, tactical 'stand-offs' with the enemy, in a zone of conflict that no one believed to be of any ultimate importance for final victory.

Soldiers noted the endless failures of conception and organisation in Macedonia as they did elsewhere in the Great War. They resented the way in which hundreds of thousands of Entente troops seemed to be incarcerated in the increasingly fortified 'birdcage' of Salonica – surely a hugely overplayed military measure to keep that city out of the hands of the enemy. But what was particularly galling was the long litany of incompetence that often accompanied the details of the military operation. Hardly any artillery arrived with the Division in Greece in the first few weeks and there had been virtually no provender for the mules and horses.[20] When telegraph wires were first laid along mountain roads, they were constantly broken. There were inaccurate maps.[21] In July 1916, much of the British artillery's ammunition was found to be unserviceable due to the effect of the extreme heat on the fuses.[22] Sometimes tents for the Division arrived without tent-poles.[23] When the first motor ambulances arrived in Greece, they were badly damaged as a result of being driven by untrained soldiers. Left out in blizzards, these vehicles developed cracked pipes and cylinders.[24]

Even after the general standard of organisation began to improve, for long periods throughout 1916 men found themselves engaged as 'navvies' in the arduous business of fortifying Salonica, in a marathon of trench-digging, quarrying, wiring and road-building. This was the experience that ultimately influenced the soldiers to claim that their Salonica campaign had been 'tedious and unrewarding',[25] a judgement reinforced by 'long hours of dismal guard duty, at isolated points of habitation, in a world of goat-herds and grasshoppers'.[26]

Fortunately for many men in this division, there was no access to the worst perspectives that some officers, war-correspondents and other observers could obtain on the indifference of the high command to the plight of the ordinary soldier. When the 10th Division participated in an onslaught on three key Macedonian villages held by Bulgarian troops in the autumn of 1916, General Sarrail, the French commander, was invited to join a group of other Greek, British and French guests and assorted official journalists, to watch the event from a nearby ridge. The party had the luxury of a band to play a musical accompaniment, and some rather fine coloured tents for shelter. To one cynical observer, 'never did a battle look so like a chase-game'. Nearby, stood the Corps commander, at a 'deal table' covered in maps, whilst on another hillock a short distance away was 'a battery of telescopes of all calibres' which were directed 'to different points of the valley below'.[27]

For many men in the 10th Division, once the episodic ordeal of battle was over for another spell, there was recourse to the usual personal strategies for dealing with stress and boredom. The occasional foray into Salonica, armed with a pocketful of drachmas, became a much safer experience once Greece was showing signs of siding 'properly' with the Allies. The seafront contained an intriguing mix of cafés, shops and brothels.[28]

For some soldiers, the arrival of mail from home became a matter of huge importance, especially when the mail-service was so much less efficient and speedy than in France and Flanders.[29] For many soldiers, there was a kind of diversion in watching the more exotic aspects of modern warfare unfold before their eyes: there were regular air-battles, featuring such figures as Germany's Balkan flying ace, Immelmann, in his red biplane; there was the spectacular shooting down of the occasional Zeppelin, whose gas-filled envelope would explode in a fiery ball against the night sky; there was the sight of scores of vessels negotiating the submarine-nets that surrounded Salonica's busy harbour; and there was, of course, the muffled sound of gunfire from the not-so-distant front line in the mountains.[30]

Some men in this, as in any other, division took refuge in faith. Yet even a Salvation Army background and constant evangelical prayerfulness could not prevent one medical orderly in the division from meditating with increased bitterness on the futilities of war: 'after breakfast ... church parade ... when the guns could be heard in the distance, sending forth messages of destruction and mutilation while we wait to receive blessing divine from a God of peace'.[31] For this particular man, some of the most distressing incidents involved needless and accidental injury or death, as when an officer in the division was killed in 'a bomb practice'. He witnessed how another soldier had his 'thigh-bone shattered, having been mistaken for a Bulgar and shot by his own corporal'. Eventually, when dealing with one wounded soldier in the Struma Valley in late May, 1917, this same young orderly would look at 'a wound 3 inches in diameter ... all the ligaments and tissues blown to atoms', and write in his diary shortly afterwards: 'what a useless sacrifice of poor men's lives ... it is as well people at home do not know these facts, or they would certainly rise against the unnecessary waste of manpower'.[32] By August 1917, he was attending a service to mark the anniversary of the beginning of the war and 'boiling' throughout it, with barely subdued anger. In his diary he wrote: 'We are upholding England as a righteous nation fighting a holy war. Demonising Germany in all things', to which he added the terse and dismissive comment – 'Hypocrisy'.[33]

For some, alcohol presented an all-too-easy refuge. A corporal in the Munster Fusiliers who was taken to hospital in December 1915 with alcoholic poisoning, was not the only 'drunk' in the division. Local 'koniac' was readily available and proved to be potent.[34] On St Patrick's Day, 1917, it seemed to some that there were scarcely a 'dozen sober men in the camp'.[35] For some, of course, the refuge of a relationship maintained by letter with a loved one at home was the greatest consolation. 'My own darling,' wrote one officer in the division to his girl in Ireland, 'your love just keeps me going ... thoughts of the future help me to face each day more easily ... we shall be happy some day ... it is hard to be away from you for so long ... how I worship you.'[36]

Yet for some, the strain – particularly at times of engagement with the enemy – was all too much to bear. Several soldiers faced courts martial for a variety of misdemeanours in Macedonia. Penal servitude was the usual punishment. However, one soldier paid the ultimate price for indiscipline in the face of the enemy. Private Patrick Joseph Downey, a 20-year-old from Limerick who served in 10th Division with a battalion of the Leinster Regiment, was shot two days after Christmas, 1915 for refusal to obey orders whilst at the battle of Kosturino. As one observer in another battalion put it: 'the authorities believe this is necessary for the recovery of discipline which is supposed to have weakened in the division'.[37]

Even though the shooting of Private Downey shocked many, the repercussions were no different from those in other cases of indiscipline and punishment in the British Army. There was private anger and resentment, but 'the gun had spoken' and the primacy of discipline would seem to have been established. But for many in the 10th Division, as in other army units – in Salonica, as elsewhere – an incident such as the shooting of Downey merely added deeply to the sense of being completely and utterly unappreciated. As one officer would later note at the end of the Division's Balkan campaign in 1917: 'Not one single officer of GHQ or Salonica staff came down to the quay to wish them bon voyage and good luck' as they were boarding ship for Alexandria.[38] This sentiment of bitter disappointment with one's superiors, and with those who 'ran' the war was something that made the Irish soldiers of Salonica typical of 'Tommies' everywhere.

Yet in other respects the experiences of the men in Macedonia were quite unusual. Soldiers in the Salonica Force were endlessly intrigued by the area's more exotic qualities, and because the Balkan campaign had a slower pace, they had some time for observation and reflection and the occasional chance to explore the region's characteristics more fully. The 10th Division came face-to-face with an array of foreign races in a way that troops fighting in France scarcely could (although divisional veterans would certainly also recall their first exotic journey from Ireland to the cosmopolitanism of Alexandria and the Dardanelles). In Salonica itself, men might encounter Greeks, Turks, Jews, Albanians, Serbs, French, Italians, and indeed both British and French imperial troops from a range of other far-off places. If men were ill or injured, nurses and staff from Toronto might look after them in No. 4 Canadian Base Hospital.[39]

The city's facilities included such delights as Floca's Café, where officers might sit in cane chairs whilst eating ices, and gazing out towards distant Mount Olympus. The music-hall near the White Tower was a lively venue, outside which raucous local women waited for the ordinary soldier's custom.[40] Many men would be intrigued by such colourful sights as the bottles of leeches for sale outside apothecary's shops.[41] Some were fascinated by the Greek funeral customs, which saw the body of the corpse exposed to public view. Other soldiers were interested in the crumbling mystery of the city's ancient walls and its minarets.[42]

Despite having to fight in it, the men were sometimes 'captivated' by the upland Macedonian landscape. For whole months at a time, there was a vista of snow-capped peaks, which were occasionally bathed in 'glittering sunshine'.[43] One officer wrote, in a moment of respite at Kosturino, of how 'the sun rose in a glorious sunburst on a sheet of cloud over Lake Doiran far below us'.[44] The onset of spring could bring a range of remarkable local natural glories. There were 'dazzling butterflies', and one 10th Divisional officer made a collection of them in his bivouac.[45] Soldiers living at such exotic locations as 'Jungle Island Bridge' on the River Struma, soon became acquainted with the local tortoises.[46] Those who camped near Lake Doiran became all too well acquainted with the ceaseless chorus of hundreds of frogs.[47] Other animals which fascinated soldiers included the snakes, the more venomous of which necessitated a supply of antidotes, kept with each regimental unit.[48] The fierce Macedonian sheepdogs and the gigantic storks were other sources of interest.[49] One Irish officer became famous for adopting a bear cub called Meriqua, for which a collar and lead were fashioned, but which was eventually shot dead by a sentry after it escaped from captivity.[50]

Indeed this was a war where officers sometimes went woodcock shooting or played makeshift tennis at the small port of Stavros, near the mouth of the Struma. It was a war in which each division had its own vegetable garden, its own locally made Greek cigarettes, and special beer brewed at a local brewery.[51] It was a war where delicious fresh fish from Lake Doiran occasionally supplemented the soldiers' more mundane diet, and where men could sometimes 'stuff themselves with wild cherries' or wild strawberries, while on patrol in some of the more lush parts of the region.[52] And it was a war where, on a day off in Salonica, men could, if they wished, walk to the top of a nearby mountain and see a vista of 'range after range of hills' and distant rivers 'snaking through green valleys'.[53] Involvement in the Salonica campaign was accompanied by unusual compensations, and by an occasional sense of release and 'overview', denied to men crammed into dugouts below ground-level, a few miles east of the English Channel.

For most Irish soldiers, even the enemy they faced was an exotic and barely-understood figure. The 'Bulgar' was a far less predictable and rather less merciless opponent than the dreaded and much mythologised Hun. Accounts of the battle at Yenekoi in which the Division was involved in 1916, stress how the Bulgarians who tried to take the town back were led 'by an officer on a white charger', whilst on Rocky Peak, in the previous year, they had attacked 'with blowing of trumpets and beating of drums'. While the prolonged stalemate in the Struma Valley was taking place, the enemy did not fire from their heights on the British recreational football matches going on below.[54] This kind of generosity was no doubt made easier by the fact that no-man's-land in this vicinity was often up to eight miles wide![55] These highly dangerous but occasionally courteous 'Bulgars', in their olive green, mustard and grey uniforms, were known to be largely conscripts (unlike the Irish soldiers), and many of those who were captured or who were deserters seemed to be simple but skilled men, such as the soldier who ended up 'mending the watches of the 10th Divisional staff'.[56] Some of the Irish soldiers noted the 'opinskis', the native sandals of untanned leather, used by the Bulgarians for maximum ease and grip on the Macedonian hill-slopes.[57] Some soldiers were aware, however, that if the Bulgarians fought the British Army 'on civilised lines', they might well behave differently with more crucial and more adjacent enemies and that accordingly, 'atrocities were reserved by them for the Serbians who fell into their hands'.[58]

Surely the most distinctive and 'exotic' feature of the Irish Division's campaign was one which they would much rather have done without. That feature was malaria. During the months from July to October, 1916, for example, over 20,000 soldiers in the British Salonica Army fell victim to the disease. Almost 300 would die. The others would suffer regular recurrences throughout the war, and into the post-war years.[59]

The Struma Valley was known to be Europe's most malarial region, yet British Head Quarters in Egypt had ridiculed the idea of taking careful pre-emptive measures.[60] Now the Irish soldiers who had to patrol the mosquito-ridden swamps of that river valley found themselves prey to a disease that could strike with lightning rapidity. At the end of July 1916, 150 soldiers from the 10th Division alone were collapsing with it every day. Malaria, apart from the damage which it inflicted, also weakened resistance to other illnesses.[61] Although men were allowed to move most of their patrols to higher altitudes (above the river valley) in the later stages of the Struma venture, the benefits were (supposedly) limited by the fact that a 'hill mosquito' was among the dominant types in the area.[62] As for those small groups of soldiers left behind to maintain a minimum patrol in the lowest part of the river valley, they slept on wooden platforms to lift them a few feet above the swampy ground where the mosquitoes swarmed. For them an attack of the disease was almost inevitable.

Those who were lucky enough to be evacuated would find themselves hospitalised in the relative ease of the malarial wards on the southern outskirts of Salonica, looking out over the bay toward the estuary of the River Vardar.[63] But for many, malaria meant a brush with death and it often seemed that 'it was the younger men who seemed to get bowled over more easily'.[64] A man in an Inniskilling battalion noted how, one day in 1916, a fellow-soldier 'left camp late in the afternoon for the ration-dump ... was seized with an attack of malaria ... an ambulance was summoned, he was taken to hospital, and evacuated to Malta and I never saw him again'.[65] Private William James Orr, another 'Inniskilling' from Newtown-cunningham in Co. Donegal, died of malaria on 20 September 1917. He was buried in Mikra military cemetery, to the south of Salonica, along with a number of other fellow-victims.[66]

The attempt to curtail the disease involved a huge range of stringent measures, including an intake of five grains of liquid quinine a day. Soldiers wore mosquito net veils over their faces, large protective gloves and special shorts with 'turn-ups' which could be opened out and tucked into the top of the puttees. Most hated of all the measures was the evil-smelling anti-mosquito jelly (paraffin based) which had to be smeared on the hands and face. Surely few soldiers in the entire war can have been less comfortable than those 10th Divisional sentries who were placed in tiny wattle-and-mud huts by the river, throughout the hot and humid summer months, draped in mosquito netting, doused in paraffin jelly, and with the foul taste of medicine still in their mouths from that morning's 'quinine parade'! Many hours of arduous toil were also required to canalise streams, cut long grass and drain swamps in an effort to lessen the mosquito plague. Ultimately, as one senior officer was to put it, 'the mosquito net was as important as the rifle' in the Macedonian campaign.[67]

However, for the Irish historian, the discomforts of malaria are not the most interesting marks of service in the Balkans, even though they are perhaps the most distinctive. Men here were to experience Balkan political, cultural and military conflict in a way that sets them apart from the 'Tommy' who did all his soldiering in France or Flanders. The soldiers in Macedonia found themselves on a front where the structure of enmity and alliance was always less than stable.

They became particularly aware of the mixed sentiments of the Greeks, who, having occupied Salonica after the recent Balkan Wars, now found themselves forced to allow their new city to play host to a growing army of 'foreign troops', including the 10th Division. Although the Greeks would later join the Entente alliance, and indeed Greek dislike of the Bulgarians was never in doubt, their reliability was certainly open to question, as when they handed over the forts in the Rupel Pass to Bulgaria, in May 1916, thereby rendering necessary the strong defence of the Struma Valley with its route south to the Mediterranean Sea.[68]

Greece, still officially neutral in 1915, had permitted Central Powers consulates to survive and indeed flourish in Salonica, thereby making it possible, before the eyes of all the allied soldiers, for a thriving spy network to exist. These soldiers also became aware of a growing dispute inside Greece itself. The Royalist forces, many of whom sided with Germany, clashed with the followers of the charismatic politician, Venizelos, who sympathised with the Entente. Men of the 10th observed the quelling of the attempted royalist coup in the city, and 'witnessed the disarmed Greek royalist troops being marched to the docks by French coloured troops'.[69] Indeed not only were the Greeks divided in their loyalties, they also showed individual soldiers in the British Army few personal favours: 'not only were we disliked by them, but they spared no pains to impress us with their enmity'.[70]

Soldiers became very aware that Macedonia, although officially Greek, was very much a patchwork of peoples. They noted with fascination the vibrant Turkish quarter, and they encountered Salonica's thriving Jewish population. The Turks were evidence of Macedonia's recent status as part of the Ottoman Empire and the Salonica Jews were a distinctive people who, since their forced migration from Spain centuries previously, had spoken a form of Spanish in the streets and marketplaces of their adopted city. Salonica provided a vista of 'mingled costume' and 'kaleidoscopic pageantry' from all across the Balkans and the Middle East.[71] For one soldier there was the particular fascination of the 'highly coloured bloomers' of many of the civilians and the 'short Spartan skirts' and the 'tasselled cap' of the Greek soldiers.[72] For another soldier it was the Babel of incomprehensible tongues that intrigued him, a diversity replicated inside the army itself, where notice-boards outside military churches were inscribed in six languages.[73]

Wariness, in the midst of this ethnic melting-pot, was crucial. For some soldiers in the division, the place seemed full of 'cut-throats and ruffians'. In the Turkish quarter in particular, loaded rifles and fixed bayonets were often the order of the day.[74] One man with the divisional signal corps would later recall how 'several men of the division found eternal rest with a knife-thrust in their ribs'.[75] There was also a range of other Balkan nationalities vying for attention in the cosmopolitan city of Salonica. As one war correspondent would observe, 'the Essad Pasha whom the Entente recognised as President of Albania, is living at Salonica, with his flag, a black star on a red ground, flying over his house as the residence of the President of Albania'.[76]

However, for many soldiers, there was a much deeper and highly chastening vision to be gained of the ongoing local history of enmity, expulsion, annexation and migration which had, already, during the two Balkan Wars of 1912/1913, dislodged some half a million people from their homes.[77] Thus, when the 10th Division made its first march to Lake Doiran in 1915, it did not march through a landscape in which war was a new experience. And the vista of war by Lake Doiran was indeed a sorry one. A 10th Divisional soldier saw 'a heart-rending sight ... thin, half-clad, starved women and children with sore bare feet' who were making their way down the mountain roads from the Bulgarian invader. This soldier could see how 'husbands drove little skeletons of donkeys loaded with all their belongings, consisting of a few old tins and spare clothing'. To his horror, he noted how 'some lay down and died' at the side of the road, exhausted by their journey over the freezing mountain passes. And as he would explain in his diary, this war of civilians and refugees was all the more shocking for being something 'not hitherto experienced [by] the 10th'.[78]

In war-torn villages in the vicinity of Lake Doiran, where Turk, Greek, Serb and Bulgarian had fought for years over the right to each mile of territory, soldiers experienced 'the moans of unmilked half-starved cattle, starved cats, dogs and chickens, with bones protruding ... and empty houses that contained furniture and little antiques'. Inevitably, in every wrecked village 'the tower of the church had suffered from shells, also many houses'.[79] Doiran town had already been sacked during the Balkan Wars, and had been occupied and re-occupied in turn. The wrecked shop-fronts had names painted and re-painted in rival Latin and Cyrillic scripts.[80]

Some soldiers endeavoured to assist the refugees from faraway villages whom they found by the roadsides: 'the fellows sacrificed their issue of cocoa to stragglers who, absolutely exhausted, had dropped helpless at the wayside'.[81] For those local Serb or Greek inhabitants who had 'stayed put' in their houses, the 10th Division was at least a temporary ally against further attacks by the enemy. Some of these women 'threw flowers from windows and balconies' to the soldiers.[82] Even when lodged in the army camp on the edge of Salonica, witnesses saw the roads to the big city being filled with a pathetic mix of 'every type of Balkan refugee ... in every conceivable costume ... the weirdest mix of orientalism and modernism ... a Homburg hat, umbrellas, lounge jackets, all mixed with broad sashes, baggy braided pantaloons, sandals and fezzes'.[83]

The sense of playing a part in a much more enduring and local war than that anticipated when first they were summoned to fight the Kaiser, must have overtaken men of the 10th Division when they found themselves occupying trenches in the Rendina Gorge, recently used in the war of 1912 by the Greeks against the Turks.[84] The unfamiliar, volatile and often improvised nature of Balkan allegiances must have been impressed upon the men of the Munster Fusilier battalion who encountered an enemy deserter, near Keupri, in November 1916, who told them that he had fought with the Turkish forces in 'the last war' and when captured by the Serbs, had fought on their side. Then, 'when this war started I fought with The Serbs against The Bulgars and when they took me prisoner I joined them against the British'.[85]

However, it was to those men of the Division who were taken prisoner by the Bulgarians that the fullest view of Balkan animosities presented itself. Amidst their own desolation and squalor, in which disease, hunger and abuse by prison guards played a major part, they were none the less in a better condition than the Serbian prisoners who shared incarceration with them. Some one hundred men of the division, having been captured in the winter of 1915, in the ill-fated Kosturino battle, were among numerous British soldiers who eventually found themselves in a large prisoner of war camp at Philippopolis.

In this grim institution, 'The Servians used to be flogged unmercifully ... one day three of them tried to get away ... and were recaptured and ordered 50 strokes with the usual thick stick ... the poor wretches screamed and wriggled ... two of them died the following day.' But in this camp such scenes were commonplace, and 'Serbs died in scores ... they dug holes just outside the camp and flung them in indiscriminately ... many being left by the graveside overnight to be half-eaten next morning by rats and the wild-dogs. Many who we saw who were not quite dead, and were carried out for burial and when we mentioned it to the Bulgars, they only laughed and said "dead soon".'[86] The Irish prisoners who survived to tell the tale were met by the British troops who poured through Bulgaria just after the final, victorious campaign in 1918, hearing, as they went, regular stories from Serbs and Macedonians of Bulgarian atrocities, including mutilation, torture and massacre.[87]

For some, the Serbs remained the gallant victims of the Balkans – as they had been at the start of the war, and the pro-Serb sentiments of one English soldier in another section of the Salonica Expeditionary Force no doubt rang true for members of the 10th Division: 'their country on the map had ceased to exist, their wives and children were at the mercy of the Austrian or Bulgarian invader'.[88]

The historian Henry Harris would later speculate, in referring to the 10th Division's first winter campaign in the Balkans, that there would have been a particular aptness in a special sympathy for Serbia in Irish ranks: 'if ever there had been an operation in the "cause of small nations" that Irishmen could have sought, it was that advance into Serbia on the road to Belgrade'.[89] There is, however, little evidence that such special Hiberno-Serbian parallels mattered in a division whose special sense of Irishness was so depleted and altered by Gallipoli, and in an ethnic melting-pot so complex as Macedonia. And although the proximity of Serb patients in hospital beds just a few hundred yards from the British malarial wards of Mikra would have generated a sense of sympathy and shared affliction, such encounters as did occur at these times may only have increased the sense of the fundamental otherness of these Balkan allies. One witness recorded how Serb voices were sometimes raised in songs about their own homeland but that sometimes they used to sing 'It's a Long Way to Tipperary', 'according to their own idea and with curious effect' as they 'embellished it and polished it ... till it was almost unrecognisable and somewhat like an old canticle'.[90]

Indeed an enduring impression that one receives from the Balkan experiences of the 10th Division is of soldiers making an encounter with the mysterious strangeness of that part of Europe which was, by tradition, most mingled with the Orient. Some soldiers in the Division recorded that they were bringing 'order' to the place, and initiating a 'revolution for orientalism ... the streets being cleaner than they have been for centuries'.[91] For some soldiers the 'fecklessness' and 'backwardness' of the Orient were everywhere in evidence. They saw women working harder than their menfolk who 'sat about gambling and drinking from morn till night'.[92] Some soldiers in the 10th Division, when entering abandoned mosques and Orthodox churches, were drawn to wonder about 'the crude manner [in which] these Macedonian inhabitants worship their Supreme Being'.[93] Several Irish officers kept referring to the region in highly colonial terms, looking on the locals as 'the natives' and noting how the military methods used were 'very similar to those used in the Indian Frontier'.[94] Others saw the landscape as 'something Biblical, with fishing nets spread out to dry ... wandering flocks of sheep ... old shepherds'.[95] At times it seemed to other soldiers that in Macedonia the men had lived 'a Robinson Crusoe life' and that it was only in leaving Salonica by boat that at last they were 'on the road to civilisation'.[96] Other witnesses were, however, aware that ancient civilisations had existed in this part of Europe. Some officers noted that Alexander had fought his battles where they now dug their trenches. Many soldiers knew enough to recognise that in particular parts of Macedonia, the Division was following in the footsteps of St Paul when he embarked on his first missionary journey to Europe.[97]

If there is a good record of how Irish soldiers perceived the Balkan region, there is less evidence of how these men pondered upon the political conflicts of their own homeland. Soldiers' correspondence is understandably scanty in such matters, due both to the prospect of censorship and the relative isolation from detailed, honest Irish political news in a zone almost entirely without home leave. One of the Division's officers, having heard of the Easter Rising, claimed in correspondence that he was too disgusted to even think about it, never mind write about it.[98] Amongst those in the ranks who would have had nationalist sympathies, only one significant record seems to survive of Macedonian 'home thoughts from abroad'. That record is in the form of a poem by Francis Ledwidge, a former Irish Volunteer, serving with the 5th Inniskilling Battalion. It was written before the watershed of Easter 1916, and contains a reflection – from the distant vantage-point of mountains near Kosturino – on the prospects for Irish national renewal:

Serbia, 1915

Beside the lake of Doiran
I watched the night fade, star by star
And sudden glories of the dawn
Shine on the muddy ranks of war.

At night my dreams of that fair land
Were full of Ireland's old regret,
And when the morning filled the sky
I wondered could we save her yet.

Far up the cloudy hills, the roads
Wound wearily into the morn.
I only saw with inner eye
A poor old woman all forlorn.[99]

Ledwidge's wistful, 'Balkan' variation on the popular politico-cultural symbolism of 'the old woman of Ireland' who is awaiting transformation into youth and beauty, is interesting for just how little Balkan content it actually contains. The 'soft-focus' landscape of the poem, although particularised by a place-name, has scarcely any specific Macedonian topographical features and could quite as easily be the hills of Wicklow or Donegal as those of Serbian Macedonia. More poignantly, the trails of actual flesh-and-blood refugees who were making their way along Doiran's muddy roads are completely absent. The old Balkan women who – as we have seen in other 10th Divisional accounts – were often dying at the side of the Macedonian mountain roads, just at this very time and in this very place, are occluded by Ledwidge's 'poor old woman' of Ireland. The poem is mystical and withdrawn. There is no relationship drawn between the cultural dilemmas of Irishman and Serb and no awareness suggested of the painful territorial conflicts always involved in 'national renewal'; conflicts evident in the town of Doiran, with its shop signs painted and repainted in Bulgarian and Serbian scripts.

Although we know from his correspondence that he was aware of the civilian refugees, and indeed treated some of them with real personal compassion,[100] Ledwidge's poetic contemplation of Irish national renewal within a Balkan landscape ignores their plight. It illustrates that the perceptual limitations which soldiers in the 10th Division brought to the Balkans were not simply those of its Anglo-Irishmen who might have been steeped in British Imperialist ideology. An Irish nationalist viewpoint could produce its own kind of introspection and its own kind of blatant distancing process from the sharp regional and national rivalries that were so patently on view. And these rivalries were, after all, not entirely without instructive parallels to those internal Irish conflicts which had been re-emerging during the Home Rule crisis and which would eventually blow the Irish version of a unified and resurgent nation so badly off-course.

The Irish soldier in Macedonia in the First World War was, then, a participant in a very different conflict from that witnessed on other fronts. Although the suffering endured was considerable, the distress was not on the epic scale so characteristic of this war. Indeed there were certain compensations in being in such a low-key and 'unusual' theatre of war rather than the vast mechanised slaughterhouse of the Western Front or the recently endured purgatory of Gallipoli. However, the soldier of the Salonica Force did, in a sense, 'dip his toe' into a sea of conflict, which between 1912 and 1923 would send two and a half million refugees back and forward across the region, as the Ottoman, Romanov, and Hapsburg empires dissolved, and the 'small nations' of South Eastern Europe found themselves caught up in hazardous dreams of national expansion or bitter arguments over the rights of recalcitrant minorities, with none more implicated than Greece itself, whose war for an expanded Hellenic union died in an apocalypse of mutual massacre and expulsion during the Graeco-Turkish war of the 1920s.

These were the very Balkan conflicts that in Sarajevo in 1914 actually ignited a world war, and they would be the conflicts that plagued the peoples of South Eastern Europe all through the century, culminating in the debacle of Kosovo in 1999, when once again Irishmen in the uniforms of the British Army would participate in the affairs of the region, although, this time, they opposed the Serbs who had once been their allies.

Clearly, the 'Salonica experience' is far less rooted in the psyche of Ireland than the darker and bigger experiences of the Somme, Ypres and Gallipoli. And it is understandable that, in the process of latter-day reclamation of the half-buried hurts of the Great War, a 'Peace Tower' should be located at Messines, on a site where Irish nationalist and unionist fought side by side on the Western Front. This commemorative monument was officially unveiled on November 11 1998 in a ceremony involving Queen Elizabeth II and the Irish President Mary McAleese, and was the result of a reconciliatory Irish cross-border project that stressed the need to incorporate into modern public memory the shared experiences of those battlefields which were an equally dire place for all Irish soldiers and their families, irrespective of their political allegiances.[101]

However it may be instructive to view Ireland's participation in the war not just from the viewpoint of Messines – where Irish internal enmities seem capable of being transcended, within the latter-day Western European recognition of the shared damage of 'the trenches' – but from a viewpoint such as the Mikra military cemetery in the vicinity of Salonica, where numerous Irish soldiers lie buried. These soldiers include Private Downey from Limerick, shot 'by his own side' for failure to obey orders during a virtually forgotten battle with young conscripts from Bulgaria, for a corner of Macedonia claimed by Serb, Turk, Bulgarian and Greek. Next to the cemetery lie many Greeks of Russian origin, in a graveyard dedicated to those refugees who fled to Macedonia after the turmoil generated by the Bolshevik revolution of 1917. And, in the centre of Salonica, the streets that in 1915 echoed to the sound of the town's thriving Jewish Community, now bear witness to the absence of Macedonia's proud Jewish heritage, destroyed in Auschwitz, during the years of the Nazi occupation.

Thus, from the viewpoint of Mikra, the war neither started in 1914, nor ended in 1918. Those Irish soldiers, from the 10th and from other divisions who lie buried in the Balkans, are to be found in a part of Eastern Europe where, in a sense, the grass never grew over the trenches, and where the vicious, totalitarian ideologies of Soviet Communism and Nazism and the more local, Balkan variants on extreme nationalism have left a region of Europe with an ongoing legacy of pain and conflict (a legacy that was, arguably, made even more toxic by various, recent, botched international military interventions).

There is a comforting myth of Peace and Reconciliation that operates in modern Irish politics, in which public exorcism of unwelcome Irish sectarian discord is conducted within the powerful master-discourse of 'Remembrance', which construes the 'Irish conflict' as being, like the Great War, a story of one of modernity's horrific but now negotiable wrong-turnings. Irish Premier, Bertie Ahern, when making a public pronouncement about the opening of the Messines monument in November 1998, spoke favourably of the reconciliatory ethos of the ceremony and then added the following comment: 'as the twentieth century draws to a close, we hope that we will never again see the bloody conflict between nations that scarred the battlefields of Europe over so many centuries'.[102] Significantly, the ceremony in Messines occurred in the presence of the King of Belgium, and during the same day Queen Elizabeth met with French President Jacques Chirac, for a joint French/British commemoration service. The hoped-for closure of the Irish political conflict was being situated within the context of modern European fraternity, a project which was endorsed by a commentator in one Irish newspaper of the time:

> I can think of no more eloquent symbol of reconciliation, of the laying of troubled spirits to rest and of the hope for a peaceful future, then the unveiling of an Irish memorial to our war-dead, North and South, by the president of Ireland, (a northern nationalist and self-proclaimed bridge-builder), the British Queen and the Belgian monarch, representing our common European past and future.[103]

The 10th Division's Irish Balkan war-dead cannot be so readily inscribed into this eloquent story of reconciliation. The (quite unlikely) establishment of an Irish 'Peace Park' at Mikra, in the Balkans would be destined to offer a very different lesson from the one currently hoped for at Messines. The Balkans, unlike Flanders, is a region where the 'troubled spirits' of the past do not give the impression of having been laid to rest, and where blithe optimism about a universally fraternal European future is less than wise. A visitor who gazes from the Mikra gravestones toward the adjacent Greek–Russian refugee graveyard will then look out across the city of Salonica, where Hitler's 'final solution' exterminated an ancient Jewry. The visitor can then look out over the ethnically cleansed and re-cleansed Macedonian hills, in the direction of the road to Belgrade, on which British forces waged war as recently as 1999. This visitor to Mikra might then be tempted toward the unwelcome thought that national and cultural antagonisms are fundamental to European regional affairs and that ideology can speedily turn those antagonisms into reasons for the cold and cruel abuse of power. The intelligent observer who stands thus at Mikra might well conclude that hatred, and its political uses, prospered all through the twentieth century because of the ways that Europeans continue to engage in the construction of identity, the legitimisation of aggression and sheer ideological hubris.

The establishment of the Irish tower at Messines is not to be scorned as an empty project. However, the Irish conflict, mired as it is in years of intimate distrust, cannot readily be ameliorated by the invocation of a distant armistice, when European militarism, rather than ending with a bugle call on November 11 1918, is, in a very real sense, still going on.

Notes

1 T. Johnstone, *Orange, Green and Khaki: The Story of the Irish Regiments in the Great War, 1914–18* (Dublin, Gill and Macmillan, 1992), p. 152, and H. Harris, *The Irish Regiments in the First World War* (Cork, Mercier Press, 1968), pp. 17–23.

2 Johnstone, *Orange, Green and Khaki*, p. 186.

3 A. Palmer, *The Gardeners of Salonika* (London, Deutsch, 1965), p. 65.

4 IWM, 96/29/1, J. McIlwaine, War Diary, 5/6 June.

5 F. W. E. Johnson, *A Short Record of the Services and Experiences of the 5th Battalion, Royal Irish Fusiliers in the Great War* (1919), p. 15.

6 RIFM, War Diaries of the 5th/6th Battalions, Royal Irish Fusiliers, 13–17 May 1916.

7 Johnson, *A Short Record*, p. 22.

8 C. Falls and A. F. Beck, *Military Operations: Macedonia*, vol. 1 (London, H. M. Stationery Office, 1933), p. 64.

9 *Ibid.*

10 Johnstone, *Orange, Green and Khaki*, p. 186.

11 M. Cunliffe, *The Royal Irish Fusiliers, 1793–1968* (Oxford, Oxford University Press, 1970), p. 328.

12 Harris, *Irish Regiments*, p. 61.

13 G. W. Price, *The Story of the Salonika Army* (London, 1918), p. 46.

14 Cunliffe, *Royal Irish Fusiliers*, p. 329, and 5th/6th Royal Irish Fusiliers War Diaries, 9 December 1915.

15 Johnson, *A Short Record*, 19.

16 *Ibid.*, p. 19, and J. J. Kennedy, *History of the 5th (Service) Battalion, Royal Inniskilling Fusiliers in the Great War*; a collection of items from *The Sprig of Shillelagh* (Londonderry, 1915–18), p. 169.

17 Kennedy, *History of the 5th*, p. 169.

18 IWM, 90/10/1, J. Patterson, 12 December, Pocket Diaries.

19 *Soldiers Dead in the Great War* (London, 1921) Records of the Irish Rifles.

20 Johnstone, *Orange, Green and Khaki*, pp. 163 and 173.

21 Falls and Beck, *Military Operations*, p. 273.

22 *Ibid.*

23 Harris, *Irish Regiments*, p. 66.

24 W. D. Macpherson, *Medical Services, European War, 1914–1918*, vol. 4 (London, 1931), pp. 78–9.

25 Cunliffe, *Royal Irish Fusiliers*, p. 332.

26 Palmer, *The Gardeners*, p. 142.

27 Price, *Salonika Army*, p. 165.

28 W. D. Mather, *Muckydonia, 1917–19: Being the Adventures of a One-Time Pioneer in Macedonia and Bulgaria During the First World War* (Illfracombe, Stockwell, 1979), pp. 160–1.

29 Johnson, *A Short Record*, pp. 24–5.
30 *The Mosquito* (journal of the Salonika Ex-Servicemen's Association) vol. 17, p. 34 and vol. 28, p. 82, and A. J. Mann, *The Salonkia Front* (London, A. & C. Black, 1920), pp. 10–25.
31 IWM, P 305, W. Knott, War Diary, 9 October 1916.
32 *Ibid.*, May–June 1917.
33 *Ibid.*, 5 August 1916.
34 McIlwaine, War Diary, 6 October 1915.
35 Knott, War Diary 17 March 1917.
36 IWM, CON SHELF, T. Sherwood, 1 June 1916.
37 A. Babington, *For the Sake of Example: Capital Courts-Martial, 1914–20* (London, Lee Cooper in association with Secker and Warburg, 1983), pp. 42–3; McIlwaine, War Diary, 27 December 1915; Soldiers Died (records of the Leinster Regiment); and Commonwealth War Graves Commission, *Records of the Commonwealth War Graves Commission* (London, 1989), (records of British military cemeteries in Greece).
38 Johnstone, *Orange, Green and Khaki*, p. 268.
39 *The Mosquito*, vol. 17, pp. 38–9.
40 Mann, *Salonika Front*, pp. 12–13 and 23.
41 *The Mosquito*, vol. 54, p. 51.
42 *Ibid.*, vol. 45, p. 57.
43 Knott, War Diary, 11 October 1916.
44 Johnstone, *Orange, Green and Khaki*, p. 179.
45 *Ibid.*, p. 267 and 5th/6th Royal Irish Fusiliers War Diaries, 23 March 1916.
46 Price, *Salonika Army*, p. 280.
47 Palmer, *The Gardeners*, p. 121.
48 Macpherson, *Medical Services*, p. 112.
49 Mann, *Salonika Front*, p. 155, and *The Mosquito*, vol. 56, p. 121.
50 *The Mosquito*, vol. 94, pp. 52–4.
51 Palmer, *The Gardeners*, p. 143, and Falls and Beck, *Military Operations*, pp. 270–1.
52 Kennedy, *History of the 5th, p. 143, and Knott, War Diary, 12 and 13 June 1916.*
53 Knott, War Diary, 30 January 1916.
54 5th/6th Royal Irish Fusiliers War Diaries, 7 December 1916.
55 F. E. Whitton, *History of the Prince of Wales's Leinster Regiment* (Aldershot, 1926), p. 29.
56 Price, *Salonika Army*, p. 45.
57 *Ibid.*
58 F. Fox, *The Royal Inniskilling Fusiliers in the World War* (London, Constable & Co., 1928), p. 208.
59 Johnstone, *Orange, Green and Khaki*, p. 260.
60 *Ibid.*
61 Macpherson, *Medical Services*, p. 326.
62 Falls and Beck, *Military Operations*, p. 144.
63 Macpherson, *Medical Services*, p. 98.
64 Whitton, *Prince of Wales*, p. 290.
65 Kennedy, *History of the 5th,* p. 260.
66 Commonwealth War Graves Commission, *Records of the Commonwealth War Graves Commission* (London, 1989), G5.
67 S. McCance, *History of the Royal Munster Fusiliers* (Aldershot, Gale and Polden, 1927), p. 185, and Falls and Beck, *Military Operations* (vol. 2), p. 7.
68 Johnstone, *Orange, Green and Khaki*, p. 261.
69 McIlwaine, War Diary, 16 September 1916.
70 *Ibid.*, 8 December, 1915.
71 Mann, *Salonkia Front*, p. 13.

72 *The Mosquito*, vol. 59, pp. 80–6.
73 *Ibid.*
74 Whitton, *Prince of Wales*, p. 276.
75 *The Mosquito*, vol. 28, p. 81.
76 Price, *Salonika Army*, p. 294.
77 T. Judah, *The Serbs: History, Myths and the Destruction of Yugoslavia* (New Haven and London, Yale University Press, 1997), p. 88.
78 Knott, War Diary, 10 November 1915.
79 *Ibid.*, 9 November 1915.
80 *The Mosquito*, vol. 17, p. 386.
81 Knott, War Diary, 18 November 1915.
82 McIlwaine, War Diary, 8 November 1915.
83 IWM, 92/36/1, R. J. Bailey, March 1916.
84 McIlwaine, War Diary, 12 January 1916.
85 McCance, *Royal Munster Fusiliers*, p. 184.
86 IWM, 14/26/27, T. J. Simpson, War Diary, p. 14; 84/1/1/, pp. 26–7.
87 IWM, 87/10/1, J. Sellors, War Diary, p. 60.
88 Mann, *Salonika Front*, pp. 124 and 160.
89 Harris, *Irish Regiments*, p. 67.
90 I. Hutton, *With a Woman's Unit in Serbia, Selonika and Sebasatopol* (London, Williams, 1928), p. 77.
91 Knott, War Diary, 18 December 1915.
92 *Ibid.*, 7 September 1915.
93 *Ibid.*, 15 April 1916.
94 W. Trimble, *The Story of the 6th Royal Inniskilling Fusiliers* (Enniskillen, n.d.), p. 30, and Kennedy, *History of the 5th*, p. 69.
95 Knott, War Diary, 18 March 1916.
96 *Ibid.*, 30 August 1917.
97 *The Mosquito*, vol. 50, p. 45.
98 Sherwood, 1 June 1916.
99 L. O'Mara (ed.), *F. Ledwidge: the Complete Poems* (Newbridge, Goldsmith Press, 1997), p. 216.
100 A. Curtayne, *Francis Ledwidge* (London, Martin Brian and O'Keeffe, 1972), p. 140.
101 *Belfast Telegraph*, 11 November 1998.
102 *Ibid.*
103 *Ibid.*

10

'That party politics should divide our tents': nationalism, unionism and the First World War.[1]

D. G. BOYCE

Consider Captain Blackadder, when Blackadder went forth. Here was a comedy set in the Great War, with Captain Blackadder and Lieutenant George coping as best they could with the follies and absurdities of the General Staff. Despite the fact that it was set in a war which ended nearly eighty years ago, a television audience, consisting almost entirely of people whose memories do not stretch back that far, could instantly identify with the image of the Great War projected in the programme: moustachioed, past-their-time generals and field marshals whose chief aim was, as Blackadder put it, to launch costly offensives that would move General Haig's drinks cabinet a few yards nearer to Berlin. The script writers could take much for granted; they could assume that the audience possessed some general, if hazy, notion of the war, of its character, with even some knowledge of the battle between desk-wallahs and soldiers.

The point here is that there is in Great Britain still a kind of folk memory of the war; and the incongruity between the war the soldiers fought, and the war the generals fought, offers scope for comedy, since incongruity is one of the prime ingredients of humour. But here I come to the different perception of that war in Ireland. It is not a conflict that helps bind a nation together through some kind of folk memory; it is not a conflict where courage and self-sacrifice could be honoured even if folk memory has it (as it has in England) that these qualities were expended in brave, but tragic, endeavour.[2] Or at least, that memory does not act uniformly throughout Ireland. It is divisive; it is a subject of controversy; it even arouses bitter debate. There is no consensus about the war. This can be illustrated in the words of Dr Hearty, Archbishop of Cashel and Emly, unveiling a Celtic Cross on 22 December 1922:

> They were men who freely gave their lives in defence of their hearths and homes. To these men we are paying a nation's tribute of respect. To their memory we here raised this glorious monument. Their names will never be forgotten and that memory will help to hand on to future days the memory of men who did not fear the common foe.

This tribute of respect was not to the Irish soldiers of 1914–18, but to those men of the East, Mid and West Limerick Brigade, 'killed in action against the British in the war of 1920–1921'.[3]

Well, does that matter? Yes it does. In 1966 two Irish anniversaries were celebrated, that of the 1916 Rising in Dublin, a Republican rising to throw off British rule and arouse the nation from its political inertia; and the anniversary of the battle of the Somme, in July 1916, which, as will be seen, Ulster Protestants have always taken as a key symbolic event in their emergence as a distinct people with a special history, one almost guided by providence. The celebrations provoked controversy, and the preparations for the Somme anniversary caused rancorous divisions among nationalists and unionists in Ulster, even in 1966 when the 'golden age', however illusory, of the Terence O'Neill premiership was still shedding some of its glow. But as always with historical anniversaries, the dog (as Sherlock Holmes remarked) that did not bark is as important as the dog that did bark. The Somme anniversary went by with no mention, no commendation in the Republic of Ireland. That piece of history was extracted from the public mind. National amnesia held firm. The many thousands of Irish soldiers who fought in the Great War were forgotten, their cause and motives ignored, and the whole concept behind that great commitment – that Ireland would take her place as a Home Rule government in the United Kingdom, and as a nation equal with the other nations of the British empire – was regarded as almost a form of treason. The thirteen rebels executed by the British after the Rising were remembered; the thousands who died in France and Gallipoli were not. Thus the Great War, and especially the Somme battle, was captured by unionists for the unionist tradition; it contributed to the unionist myth, that between 1910 and 1921 there emerged in the north of Ireland a solid, united self-reliant, and successful Ulster movement, which made good its claim to statehood, if not nationhood, and whose claim was sealed in blood: the blood of the men at the Somme.

Ulster is full of barking dogs, but travelling throughout Ireland, the observer will note some discordant objects, some odd juxtapositions. As he or she approaches the strongly republican town of Dundalk, near the Northern Ireland border, he or she will spot a war memorial to the men who died for freedom: not in 1916, nor in the war of independence of 1919–21, but in the war of 1914–18. A similar monument stands in the strongly nationalist town of Newry. A memorial is to be found in Cork city, a short distance away from one to nationalist heroes of the struggle against Britain. Yet, until recently, Irish history text-books were silent about the reason why they were there at all. Indeed the question of why was not asked, irrespective of the answer that might be given. An empathy exercise in a school history pack asked pupils to imagine that they were runners for the Irish Volunteers in the Post Office in 1916; no one thought of asking pupils to empathise with a runner in the trenches in France in 1914–18.

The Great War was a crucial episode in the history of modern Ireland. When it broke out, in August 1914, Ireland and indeed Great Britain appeared to be on the brink of civil war, as the Liberal government sought to impose Home Rule on the Protestants of Ireland, an attempt resisted by the British Conservative party, and by the unionists of Ireland, and especially Ulster. Ulster unionists relied, not only on the British Conservative party but on their own strength, as they saw it, and especially on the Ulster Volunteer Force (UVF), a military organisation created to defend unionist Ulster against Home Rule. This organisation was armed from April 1914, thanks to a gun running episode worthy of a great espionage novel; and what made the predicament more ominous was the fact that the Irish nationalists, who supported Home Rule, founded a counter organisation, the Irish Volunteers. This did not have the sanction of the leader of the Irish Parliamentary Party and movement, John Redmond; but he was able to use his influence to take control of it. Nevertheless, there was the probability of a clash between the UVF and the Irish Volunteers; the British army and the UVF; the British army and the Irish Volunteers; and even mutiny in the British army, as the Curragh incident revealed in March 1914, when officers of the third cavalry brigade vowed to refuse orders rather than coerce Ulster into Home Rule. This crisis shook all the assumptions about the non-political British army tradition to the core. In the Asquith papers there are maps: maps coloured green and orange, striped, dotted, crossed, as the Liberals sought some way out of the impasse; no wonder Asquith greeted the outbreak of war with a heartfelt sigh of relief. Nothing, not even European war, could be as bad as the Irish tangle.

And his hope seemed justified. The war brought the same rush of enthusiasm in Ireland as it did in Great Britain. Some historians are inclined to doubt this, to point out that there was resentment in both parts of Ireland at the Liberals' policy in August–September 1914. They placed Home Rule on the statute book thus offending the Ulster and Irish unionists; they suspended its operation thus offending nationalists. Certainly, Sir Edward Carson for the unionists, and Redmond for the nationalists offered at first a cautious response. Carson would only send his UVF to fight for Britain if the British government played fair with the unionists (it did not); Redmond offered the IVF, but only to defend the shores of Ireland (against what, or whom? cynics asked). But both men soon found themselves committed to the war in full. Carson, as a highly patriotic man, could not but advise the UVF to fight in France; Redmond, now seeing the chance to demonstrate Ireland's true nature, and win for himself the affection of the British people, made a famous speech at Woodenbridge, Co. Wicklow, on 20 September, in which he urged the Irish Volunteers to go 'wherever the firing line extends'. But before this, on 2 September, William O'Brien, the maverick home ruler, and Maurice Healy, urged nationalists in Cork to enlist.[4] And there is no doubt that the general public, nationalist and unionist, responded, as everyone did in the early months of the war, with a naïve enthusiasm for war that now seems almost incomprehensible. Three Irish divisions were formed: the 10th and 16th Irish (almost exclusively Catholic) and the 36th Ulster (almost to a man Protestant). They were trained, shipped to France or Gallipoli, and duly met their fate.

A new era; a new hope. The sending of these divisions to France created – perhaps – new possibilities for the political development of Ireland. Surely if men fought and died together, then – as Redmond believed – the history of Ireland, that history of strife and division, would be forgotten. There would be a new atmosphere – a reality of comradeship and war, in which new and lasting bonds of friendship would be forged. The Irish nationalist party had shown sympathy to the enemies of England in her last great struggle, the Boer War, but, as the contemporary song went:

> You used to call us traitors, when we were agitators,
> But you can't call us traitors now.

When recruits for the Royal Munster Fusiliers left in August 1914 for the regimental depot in Tralee, they were seen off by enthusiastic crowds singing 'Rule Britannia' and 'A Nation Once Again' at Limerick station.[5] When the first Irish Victoria Cross was won, by Guardsman Michael O'Leary, his rapturous reception in Dublin was only surpassed by that in the British newspaper *Press*, with such statements as: 'How Michael O'Leary, V.C., kills eight Germans and takes two barricades'; 'The wonderful story of Michael O'Leary, V.C.' – a phenomenon which Michael MacDonagh, compiler of *The Irish at the Front*, ascribed to his name 'which sounds so musically, and so irresistibly suggests the romance and dare-devildom of the Irish race'.[6]

Soldiers are traditionally regarded as different from politicians. They are above politics; at least the rank and file are. Irishmen had served in the Victorian army in large numbers, the peak period being after the great famine, when thousands of Irishmen left Ireland to emigrate to Great Britain, and found the army a convenient employer. These were long term, long service, hard professional soldiers, and though they might indeed sing rebel songs as they marched through Bombay or Calcutta, they were men with only one real home: their regiment. But the new armies of 1914–16 were different: they were peoples' armies, citizens' armies, volunteers. Precise figures of the number of Irishmen who volunteered between 1914 and 1918 are hard to get, but among various calculations, one authority suggests some 116,972, of whom about 65,000 were Roman Catholics and 53,000 Protestants.[7]

This religious breakdown is not without significance, if only because nationalist and unionist MPs vied with each other in parliament in contrasting their side's recruitment figures with the other side.[8] It affected the character and identity of the Irish Divisions. The 36th Ulster Division was noted for its solidly unionist sentiments. J. L. Stewart-Moore, who in September 1914 enlisted in the 12th Battalion of the Royal Irish Rifles (mainly recruited in Belfast) found that his company was drawn from various parts of County Antrim. The vast majority were 'working class lads who had left school at the age of twelve and had never been away from home before, never slept out of the family bed'. They were all UVF men with a basic training. Stewart had been a student at Trinity College, Dublin, where religion and politics were discussed; but now

> I found myself in a camp of four thousand men where no such debates were possible because everybody thought exactly alike; Protestant fervour was at its height ... the tents were decorated, many of them, with Union Jacks and Orange emblems and at night the overflowing enthusiasm of the men found its outlet in song. For the first week or so I went to sleep every night to the strains of Orange ditties such as:
>
> > 'Come back to Ireland those who are over the sea
> > Come back to Ireland and fight for liberty.
> > They are flying the flag, the harp without a crown
> > So come back to Ireland and keep popery down.'

On 12 July 1915 the same officer was woken by a skirl of bagpipes, and saw the whole battalion, less the officers, on the parade ground 'led by a soldier representing King William, in khaki, and of course riding a white horse'.[9] Captain Cyril Falls, who served with the Division, and was himself an Ulsterman, and who later held the Chichele Professorship of the History of War in Oxford University, noted what he called the 'old covenanting spirit, the old sense of the alliance of "Bible and Sword"', 'reborn' in these men. He bore personal witness to the 'not uncommon' experience of finding a man 'sitting on the fire-step of a front-line trench, reading one of the small copies of the New Testament which were issued to the troops by the people at home'.[10]

The Protestant character of the Ulster Division had its counterpart in the Roman Catholic character of the 10th and 16th Irish Divisions, into which Northern Catholic nationalists were recruited also. Whereas Cyril Falls's Protestant Ulstermen were 'sometimes a little startled and pained at first on finding a countryside so liberally bespeckled with shrines and crucifixes',[11] nationalist writers liked to stress the sincere Catholic piety of the Irish Divisions. For example, Henry Harrison, in an article entitled 'The other half million' (a title chosen to highlight the contrast between the numbers of Irish soldiers in the British army as against the 1,500 who turned out in the Easter

Rising of 1916, but with numbers inflated by including those of Irish descent living in Great Britain) wrote of the 'Irish Guards marching through a French village, instinctively baring their heads to an old priest as they pass, and he, openly surprised, gives them his blessing'.[12] A ballad entitled 'The Munster Fusiliers', sold at Cork Quay, ran:

> When marching up through Belgium sure we thought of days of old,
> The cruel sights that met your eyes would make your blood run cold.
> To see the ruined convents and the Holy Nuns in tears
> By God on high, revenge or die, cried the Munster Fusiliers.[13]

The war was seen by John Redmond as a means of securing Ireland's place in the British Empire, of gaining Home Rule for Ireland, and of making Ireland the South Africa of the British Isles, presided over by himself, as the new Smuts or Botha: a restive and even rebellious nation now demonstrating its loyalty to the British Empire. The reality was less clear-cut. Lord Kitchener was not against Irish nationalist recruitment, but he preferred recruits to enlist in the regular army battalions rather than forming, as Redmond wanted, special Irish brigades. The Ulster Volunteers were given a more positive response and in early September they were being constituted as a special UVF based Division.[14] There was also the class consciousness characteristic of the military at this time. Lieutenant-General Sir Lawrence Parsons, commander of the 16th Irish Division, wrote contemptuously of applicants for commissions who 'write their applications in red or green ink on a blank bill-head of a village shop. These are the class most successfully weeded out by the enlisting ordeal, as they think it beneath their dignity to enlist as "Common" soldiers to be herded off with "riff-raff"'.[15] And while nationalists spoke glowingly of the fact that Irishmen of all shades of political opinion were joining in the great common enterprise, H. J. Tennant (Liberal Under-Secretary of State for War) thought it necessary to bring to Parsons's attention the fact that 'certain men enlisted in the Connaught Rangers and the Leinster regiment are about to be sent to the Royal Inniskilling Fusiliers', and while he was reluctant to interfere or to raise political considerations,

> in Ireland it seems impossible to proceed without impinging upon sensibilities which are closely allied to such considerations. And I venture to suggest to you that to send men who enlisted to serve among their friends and sympathisers to Regiments where the predominating sentiment is diametrically opposed to their prepossessions and ideas is to run a considerable risk.[16]

Parsons replied on 27 February 1915 that, fortunately, the military necessity to have all battalions of equal strength enabled him to collect the scattered friends which previously he was compelled to divide, adding, rather sardonically, that he could not tell what the 'predominating political sentiment' in the 7th and 8th battalions of the Royal Inniskilling Fusiliers happened to be, 'as in the army no return of political faiths is required. The largely predominating religious faith is Roman Catholic, which perhaps gives a clue to the others'.[17] Tennant was relieved that there need be no fear that Parsons would 'try to force INVs and UVFs into each other's arms', thus avoiding 'what I feared might be a calamity'.[18]

What were the British army's Irish soldiers in France to achieve? What did Ireland's new armies join up to fight for? Some joined for financial reasons: one contemporary described recruits as 'mainly the poor people from the towns, who had nothing much to lose anyway ... The labouring people were awful poor in those days. I think most of them went for the excitement of it all. It was better than staying here.'[19] Some joined as 'Pals' battalions', as they did elsewhere in the British Isles: the Irish Rugby Football Union's company of the 7th Royal Dublin Fusiliers, for example.[20] Some joined because their fathers had soldiered in the Boer War or their grandfathers in the Crimean War. But there was always a special political dimension to the new Catholic, as well as the new Protestant, armies.

Redmond argued that Irish nationalism was being vindicated in the war; that the war was a sacrifice that would tell the British and the world that Ireland was at last a nation, for 'no people can be said to have rightly proved their nationhood and their power to maintain it until they have demonstrated their military prowess'.[21] In his *Irish at the Front*, Michael MacDonagh told tales of Irish gallantry and loyalty to the British cause to endeavour to prove that Ireland was indeed worthy of taking her place among the nations of the British empire. In *Trench Pictures from France*, published in 1917, Major William Redmond, John Redmond's brother, described, in a chapter called 'The Square of Empire', how officers from all the nations of the empire gathered in a 'fair sized French town', representing as they did 'almost all parts of the world-wide empire of Britain and constituting, so to speak, an informal but very cheery Imperial military conference at tea'.[22] In 1937 Henry Harrison, the veteran Irish Home Rule MP, wrote a book arguing Ireland's case in the Anglo-Irish conference on economic and political matters that was then about to take place in London between de Valera's and Neville Chamberlain's governments. He devoted a chapter to extolling Ireland's contribution to the war effort, taking pains to compare the Catholic and Protestant contributions, quoting *The Times*'s (rather stereotyped) description of the Irish Catholic soldiers as 'the finest missile troops that we possess' and complaining about anti-Irish propaganda that 'sought and still seeks to suppress Ireland's magnificent part in the war effort'.[23]

It was also an essential point of nationalist interpretation of the war to stress that in the trenches, the political differences between nationalist and unionist, Ulsterman and Irishman, quickly vanished; that, as William Redmond put it in his *Trench Pictures from France,*

> These young men came from the North of Ireland and from the South, with the famous Irish regiments ... they professed different creeds; they held different views on politics and public affairs; but they were knitted and welded into one by a common cause. They fought side by side for their country, they died side by side ...[24]

In his last speech in the House of Commons in March 1917, shortly before his own death, Redmond made an emotional appeal for this brotherhood of death to be transformed into one of political life. Bitter mistakes had been made; but in the face of a war that was threatening civilisation, 'are we still to continue in Ireland our conflicts and our arguments and disputes about the merits of the Stuarts, about the Battle of the Boyne and the rest?'. He told how one Catholic officer who served with the Ulster Division admitted that 'it had dawned upon him that they certainly were Irishmen and were not Englishmen or Scotsmen'.[25] Privately he wrote in a more sombre vein to Lady Parsons: 'You and the General can understand how unhappy I am about the Irish question. Alas! Poor Ireland!' [26]

Surviving records do seem to suggest that indeed the war did have some impact on mutual prejudice and perception, though not always for the best. One English officer, who had transferred from the Guards to the Connaught Rangers, wrote:

> It is like living in a new world to be amongst these Irishmen, so great is the contrast between their natural characteristics and those of the men I have come from. They are, I should imagine, difficult to drive but easy to lead. They are intensely religious, loyal to their officers ... they are easily made happy. Perhaps they are easily depressed. [27]

The idea of the simple, but good-hearted, Irishman, is a stereotype, and revealed that the officer of the Guards had confirmed, rather than altered, his prejudices.[28] In the course of my own researches an elderly lady told me that her father, who had served at Gallipoli, found that the Irish soldiers were the best in the British army – provided they were led by Englishmen.

But there emerges from such evidence as I have come across a picture of men rubbing shoulders with other men whose existence they had hardly acknowledged, apart from some vague notion of what the 'other side' might be like. Bryan Cooper, a southern Protestant and unionist, wrote from his experience of the Gallipoli landings:

> The bond of common service and common sacrifice proved so strong and endur-
> ing that Catholic and Protestant, unionist and nationalist, lived and fought and

died side by side like brothers. Little was spoken concerning the points on which we differed, and once we had tacitly agreed to let the past be buried we found thousands of points on which we agreed. To an Englishman this no doubt seems natural, for beneath all superficial disagreements the English do possess a nature in common and look on things from the same point of view, but in Ireland up to the present things have been very different.[29]

Captain Noel Drury, a member of the Trinity College Dublin officers' training corps, now in the Dublin Fusiliers, found himself obliged to attend Roman Catholic worship on St Patrick's Day:

> Good Presbyterians like myself paraded and marched off to the tunes of the 'Boys of Wexford' and 'A Nation Once Again' and went off to chapel for the first, and perhaps, the only time in our lives. What a change the war has brought over things to be sure. If anyone had told me a year ago that I would have marched off to a Roman Catholic chapel to a rebel tune, I would have said they were potty to say the least of it. It was rather disconcerting to find myself standing up and sitting down at the wrong time through ignorance of the ritual but nobody seemed to mind.[30]

A Belfastman and a Protestant, C. A. Brett, joined the 56th Battalion the Connaught Rangers, with more than 700 recruits from the Falls Road, and found himself joining a protest against the serving of boiled chestnuts instead of potatoes, which naturally evoked much furious protest from an Irish Regiment.[31] When the Guards officer and gentleman, Rowland Fielding, Commander-in-Chief of the 6th Connaught Rangers, was watching a football match between his men and soldiers of the 36th Ulster Division, he overheard a 'wag on the Ulster side' to say 'I wonder if we shall get into trouble for fraternising with the enemy'. And when he heard of the death of Willie Redmond, Fielding wrote to his wife:

> How one's ideas change! And how war makes one loathe the party politics that condone and even approve when his opponents revile such a man as this! I classify him with Stephen Gwynn, and Harrison – all three men – Irish nationalists, too, whom you and I, in our Tory schooling, have been brought up to regard as anathema! What effect will his death have in Ireland? I wonder, will he be a saint or a traitor? I hope and pray it may teach all – North as well as South – something of the larger side of their duty to the Empire.[32]

The news of the Easter Rising was greeted by the Irish soldiers in France with a mixture of incredulity and shame; the efforts of Sir Roger Casement to recruit an 'Irish Brigade' in the service of Germany from Irish Prisoners of War, and to encourage desertion from the front, were met with scorn and derision. The Dublin Fusilier officer, Noel Drury (albeit a Presbyterian), probably expressed the mood of his comrades accurately enough when he wrote in his diary on 29 April 1916 that:

> We got the most astounding news on the 27th that a rebellion has broken out in
> Ireland. Isn't it awful. Goodness knows what they think they are going to gain by
> it. It's a regular stab in the back for our fellows out there, who don't know how
> their people at home are. I don't know how we will be able to hold our heads up
> here ... as we are sure to be looked upon with suspicion. The men are mad about
> it all, but don't understand who is mixed up in the affair. I am sure Germany is at
> the bottom somehow.[33]

But there were signs of political division as well: in November 1917 some
soldiers of the Royal Munster Fusiliers held an informal meeting in an Irish
town, declaring that they were 'as good Irishmen and nationalists as any Sinn
Féiners. Though they fought for England against the Hun, and would
continue to fight till the war was won, their interest in their country was just
as "SF" as anyone else'.[34] On another occasion in the same year a Royal
Munster Fusilier officer proposed a toast at Christmas dinner in the
Tipperary depot: 'More sacred to many of us than any King, Ireland a
nation'. When this struggle was decided, 'there was another coming'.[35]

The unreal world of the trenches did not have any permanent impact on
the fundamentals of political divisions in Ireland. Even as these Irishmen,
Ulstermen and Englishmen were taking tentative steps towards each other,
the UVF Headquarters Council was seeking recruits to keep the organisation
alive in Ulster, and this same organisation formed the basis of the Ulster
Special Constabulary who played a significant and at times controversial role
in the troubles of 1920–23. Subsequently unionists liked to claim that their
soldiers loyally supported the British cause, while Roman Catholics stayed at
home; and claimed also that 'Ulster will strike for England, and England will
not forget'.[36]

But, in case England did forget, Ulster unionists were determined to
keep the Ulster Division, based as it was on the UVF, together as a coherent unit, for, if ever Home Rule were to be imposed on Ireland, then they
would be in a position to oppose all attempts to force the Bill upon unionist Ulster. The UVF continued to recruit to its ranks in order to supply the
Ulster Division with reinforcements; and money was raised to support prisoners and those invalided out of the war. Sir Edward Carson underlined
the message when he said in a speech at Bangor, Co. Down, in 1915:

> Some nations must go down in this war. We are not going down ... There
> seems to be more joy in political circles of a particular character over one
> nationalist that enlisted than over a whole Ulster Division ... I was told over
> and over again that I had started regiments of rebels ... I always boasted that
> I was a chief rebel myself ... Yes, we have 17,000 rebels in camp now. God
> bless the rebels! These men who served in the trenches have given us breathing

time. How are we taking advantage of it? Today we may be able to do something; tomorrow the time may have passed ... we are not a harum scarum lot of people gathered from here, there and everywhere. No, we are all brothers. They are our own Volunteers; they are men of our own religion. They are men of our own way of thinking; they are men of the great Ulster tradition.[37]

In 1918 Sir Edward Carson told the House of Commons that 'As I passed through Belfast a short time ago a woman in the streets roared out, "I have lost three children, Sir Edward, in the war. Are you going to get Home Rule?"' Were the Ulster unionists the people to be sacrificed for government policy?[38]

When Captain Cyril Falls wrote his *History of the 36th (Ulster) Division* in 1922, he spoke of the 'very special significance' of the date of the Somme Battle (1 July in the old calendar – thus the 12th in the new[39]). This was the anniversary of the battle of the Boyne in 1690, and now 'the sons of the victors in that battle, after eight generations, fought the great fight ... A stirring in their blood bore witness to the silent call of their ancestors'.[40]

The spirit of the charge was caught in a celebrated painting, copies of which were exhibited in unionist shop windows from 1 July, by J. Prinsep Beadle entitled 'The Attack by the Ulster Division'. As it happens, the young man at the centrepiece of the picture was not an Ulsterman at all, but what one contemporary, J. L. Stewart-Moore, described as 'fresh from an English public school'. When Stewart-Moore saw the young soldier depicted on an Orange banner, some twenty years later, he mused on what the young man, with his English background, would have made of it.[41]

At least 5,000 men of the Ulster Division were casualties of the attack, about half of them killed in action. Sir Henry Wilson unveiled the memorial to the Ulster Division's sacrifice at Thiepval, in November 1921; a memorial modelled on that of Helen's Tower in the Clandeboye estate in Co. Down, where Tennyson's lines, written in memory of the Marquis of Dufferin, were etched:

> Helen's Tower here I stand,
> Dominant over sea and land;
> Son's love built me, and I hold
> Mother's love in lettered gold.

But at Thiepval, for the words 'Mother's love' there was inscribed instead 'Ulster's Love'. Mother, Ulster; Ulster, Mother – the dedication of love, son to mother, son to Ulster, is fused, and a national myth is born.[42]

Remembering that heroic charge, and that war, became an integral part of Ulster unionist thinking and mythology. Orange banners depicted the battle; and the gable ends of houses in loyalist streets in the north today depict it, with the words, 'betrayed'.[43] Ulster unionist MPs recall it when they want to make a point, that a sacrifice was made, but is now in danger of being forgotten. Under pressure, under political pressure, such sentiments are remade and refashioned and come to the surface again and again.

How did nationalist Ireland respond to the commitment of its regiments in the war? It might seem that the question is hardly worth asking: and that the words of Tom Kettle, Irish Home Rule MP, British officer, and devout Catholic, sum up the predicament of the Irish soldier after the Easter Rising of 1916, when the gap between soldiers at the front, and public opinion at home, first began to appear. In July 1916, as he prepared for his return to duty, a young boy noted that, as he wrapped his puttees round his feet, Kettle looked tired; and while the grown ups talked about the Rising, Kettle admitted sadly: 'These men will go down in history as heroes and martyrs, and I will go down – if I go down at all – as a bloody British officer'.[44]

The war was soon perceived as the wrong war, fought in the wrong place, and against the wrong foe – a view which became political orthodoxy as Sinn Féin won a victory over the Home Rule party in the general election of December 1918, and was set in tablets of stone when, after three years of terror and counter-terror, the Irish Free State was established on the ruins of the British administration. Irish ex-servicemen were not on the whole subject to vendettas, though some did suffer at the hands both of the Black and Tans[45] (recruited by the British government to fight the war against the IRA) and the IRA itself. Nor did they seek to form a special political group, though some of them joined the IRA. Most of them inclined towards Labour and socialist politics.[46] Their urban recruiting origin in any case rendered them marginal in an Ireland where the countryside has, at least until very recent times, shaped the character of Irish politics.

Ex-servicemen, and their cause, simply sank into political oblivion, as nationalists applied a sort of field dressing, in the shape of a national amnesia, to the Great War experience. Yet it cannot be assumed that this process was instantly successful or uncontroversial.

Between 1919 and 1931 armistice day was celebrated throughout southern Ireland. Mass for the war dead was said in every Roman Catholic church in Dublin, though a discordant note was struck when students from Trinity College Dublin confronted those from University College, with 'God Save the King' met by the republican anthem 'A Soldier's Song'.[47] The *Irish Times* reported in November 1922 that the poppy sellers in Grafton Street, Dublin, were 'literally besieged ... Stocks were cleared and replenished time and time again'. In 1929 thousands of veterans marched in Phoenix Park, and a representative of the Free State government laid a wreath. 'God save the King' was sung.[48] From 1933 no government representative attended the ceremonies, for by now Eamon de Valera's Fianna Fáil government was in office, and Fianna Fáil was, after all, the Republican party; but the Irish High Commissioner in London attended the wreath laying ceremony at the cenotaph until the Second World War.[49] A turning point came (or, rather did not come) in 1939 when de Valera agreed to preside over the unveiling of a national war memorial at Islandbridge, Co. Dublin. This memorial was built by a mixture of public subscription and state funding, and was designed by Edward Lutyens. It was at the centre of a controversy in 1934, when the government proposed appointing as caretaker an ex-soldier who had been implicated in the mutiny of the Connaught Rangers in India in 1920. The Irish branch of the British Legion reminded de Valera that this was not a 'Free State memorial' but an all-Ireland one. In the event, de Valera changed his mind when, in April 1939, it seemed that military conscription might be introduced into Northern Ireland. There were those in the Fianna Fáil party who believed that:

> Such a ceremony could be treated as symbolical of the unification of all elements of the country under an agreed democratic constitution. The gesture could hardly fail to create a good impression beyond the border and upon British public opinion.[50]

The gesture was not made; and the interpretation of Ireland's place in the war, if offered at all, was couched from the beginning in certain specific terms: not as part of the social, military and political history of the British Isles, nor as an attempt by Irish nationalists to defend the rights of their small nation, but as a great mistake, a profound betrayal, one that could only be compensated for by Irish neutrality in the Second World War. Northern Ireland, by contrast, participated in that war, and this served to widen yet further the gap between the two communities' perception of themselves, their history and their destiny (despite the fact that many thousands of southern Irishmen joined the British army). When the Ulster writer Sam McAughtry returned to the north from his military service in 1945 he was approached by a friend who offered him an application form to join the Ulster Special Constabulary. When he replied that he had had enough of fighting, his friend answered: 'That's in case there's a real war'.[51]

But the First World War, together with many other Irish historical controversies, has been receiving increased attention from historians (both professional and non-professional), and also from literary men and women. I now want to conclude by considering their impact on the interpretation of this piece of past history which is also inseparable from present politics.

Academic research on the subject is now beginning to appear in articles and books; and some of the popular assumptions about the war are being revised or challenged. Among the grievances handed down to post-war generations were: that the 36th Ulster Division was given its own special flag and emblem (a Red Hand of Ulster), but the 10th and 16th were refused any special recognition; that there were hardly any Roman Catholic officers, because the War Office had a prejudice against them; that the contribution of the Irish soldiers to the Gallipoli landings was ignored in official despatches. Some of these complaints have not stood up to the test of historical investigation. General Sir Lawrence Parsons, commander of the 16th Division, was simply not interested in national emblems, for, as a professional, he objected to any variation in the emblems of old and historic Irish regiments. There were more Roman Catholic officers than critics alleged, but the problem lay outside the prejudice of the British, and was attributable to the fact that few Catholic schools had Officer Training Corps organisations: those which did, like the Jesuit schools, produced an officer class. Lord Kitchener, who was accused of failing to sanction a special Irish Divisional badge, did in fact sanction one, and also sanctioned the gift of an Irish wolfhound to Redmond as a mascot for an Irish regiment. John Redmond's son, Archer Redmond, was secured a commission in the army, though not without some delay, due to Parsons' desire that he bring 100 recruits with him. Parsons always maintained cordial relations with nationalists.[52] On the other hand, there was a tendency, when things went wrong at the front, to emphasise the inexperience of non-regular soldiers, of contingents from Ireland (and Australia) and to overlook their particular contribution when things went right.[53] Irish soldiers were credited with dash and courage, but not with field craft; yet the Ulster Division's initial success on the first day of the Somme was attributable to their policy of ignoring the text-book, and fighting in an intelligent and self-reliant way.[54]

The whole social, political and military contribution to the war effort, and the impact of the war on Irish society, is now the subject of some important new work. The Trinity College Dublin History Workshop has produced a book setting out some of the results of recent research. Important PhD theses have been written. Two new studies of the Irish regiments have been published.[55] A selection of letters written by men of the 36th Ulster Division has appeared, allowing men of the Division to tell their own story in their own words. Veterans were allowed to challenge some long cherished stories, for example that the men wore their Orange sashes on the first day of the Somme:

> What nonsense is stuck onto the story ... Certainly Major Gaffikin waved an orange handkerchief, but orange was the colour of our battalion. If he had said (and if anybody could have heard him), 'Come on boys, this is the first of July!' – how many would have known the Boyne was fought on the first of July? I don't know why they plaster such incidents on our battle. Nothing was further from my mind than the Boyne on the Somme.[56]

Philip Orr, the editor of this anthology, not only contributed to the 'Everyman at War' approach to war studies; he was bold enough to declare that men of the Division did break ranks and run (and who can blame them?), and to declare that 'Ulstermen's natural fire and aggression' were not the reason for the

Division's initial success; this lay in the more mundane, but militarily significant fact that the Ulster HQ decided to send the Division into no man's land
before the artillery bombardment lifted, and they got to their objective before
the Germans could prepare to meet them with machine gun fire – as happened
also with the 18th Division.[57]

But an exploration of the place of the Great War in national memory – or,
I should say, national memories – cannot be confined to the history archives
alone. That war, more than any other, has been the subject of a deep and
sustained literary exploration, one indeed that has properly earned the criticism of military historians as having shaped only too vividly the mental
picture we have of the war – so much so that the idea of loss, sacrifice and
useless slaughter caused someone to observe in a television debate on public
schools that the British class system had 'lost us the Great War'. But whether
we like it or not, history and literature are inseparable, at least in Ireland. As
Thomas Flanagan has observed, literary works seek to recover, for whatever
reasons, a past or a version of the past, and nearly always of some specific
past.[58]

There is no Irish equivalent of the classic and deeply influential literary
output that followed the Great War in Britain. W. B. Yeats in his 'Easter
1916' captured the mood of self-sacrifice that inspired the rising in Dublin;
but he wrote one poem dealing directly with the war – 'The Irish Airman
Foresees his Death' – which is also a poem about the Anglo-Irish predicament in the twentieth century.

When the southern unionists witnessed the outbreak of the Great War in
August 1914 they hoped that the goodwill shown by nationalists towards the
British war effort might yet create a new atmosphere in which the rancour
generated by the crisis over the third Home Rule Bill would evaporate. 'For
the Southern unionists this was their finest hour,' writes their historian R. B.
MacDowell. They were able to throw themselves wholeheartedly into
serving the empire in a time of peril, proudly sharing the fears, hopes and
sacrifices of their fellow-subjects in Great Britain.[59] The 1916 Rising
outraged them, as a stab in the back; but even more alarming was the British
government response, which hardly changed until 1921, to seek a settlement
of the crisis in the shape of Home Rule for the south and west of Ireland, and
the partition of Ulster counties (six or nine as the case might be) from the rest
of Ireland, thus throwing southern unionists to the wolves. The question of
whether or not to seek accommodation with nationalists in order to avoid
the calamity of partition, or to stand for the Union entire to avoid the same
calamity, split the southern unionists in 1918–19, and they now faced 'a
political abyss'.[60]

It was against the fraught political background that Yeats wrote his poem,
'An Irish Airman'. The poem can, with a certain exaggeration, be described
as a sectarian work; it reflects the southern unionist perspective and that

alone. The Irish airman Major Robert Gregory, Lady Gregory's only son,[61] faces the fact that he has to ask himself questions that no Englishman need ask himself: What is his country? Where should his allegiance lie? The Irish airman cannot identify with the country of his birth, Ireland; nor can he completely identify with the country on whose side he fights in this war, England.

> I know that I shall meet my fate
> Somewhere among the clouds above;
> Those that I fight I do not hate
> Those that I guard I do not love.[62]

Yeats' 'lonely impulse of delight' shows his rejection of all public purpose. The Irish airman's country is Kiltartan Cross, his countrymen Kiltartan's poor.

> No likely end could bring them loss
> Or leave them happier than before.

For the airman

> Nor law, nor duty bade me fight,
> Nor public men, nor cheering crowds,
> A lonely impulse of delight
> Drove to this tumult in the clouds;
>
> I balanced all, brought all to mind,
> The years to come seem waste of breath,
> A waste of breath the years behind
> In balance with this life, this death. [63]

In Ireland, Yeats wrote, the assumption was that the heroic act was the act of some man at the moment when he was least himself, most completely the crowd; but the heroic act

> as it descends through tradition, is an act done because a man is himself, because, being himself, he can ask nothing of other men but room amid remembered tragedies; a sacrifice of himself to himself, so little may he bargain, of the moment to the moment ... So lonely is that ancient act, so great the pathos of its joy.

The Irish airman delights in that loneliness: of the sky in whose space he fights; in the anonymity of the conflict (the enemy he does not hate); because he is detached from the *nationalist* idea of the Irish nation, his identity is one of locality, local place, a pre-national Ireland. He is also detached from the crowd, from the cheers of the crowd, the public men. The Anglo-Irishman is comforted by his act, an act of remembering a great tradition of heroic sacrifice, like that of the great Celtic chieftain Cuchulainn, 'room amid remembered tragedies'. This offers a route of escape from the Anglo-Irish predicament; the heroic act expresses southern Irish Protestant patriotism, 'hesitating' but with its 'own nobility, its own heroism'.[64] Thus does war and the combat that is its essence offer a means of self-expression for the Anglo-Irishman, and a means of escape from the uncomfortable context of his divided loyalties. In 1948 – and not until then – Yeats' second poem on this subject was published. Lying dormant for nearly thirty years because Yeats feared it would offend Gregory's family, it referred to one of the worst incidents of the Black and Tan war of 1920–21, when a member of that notorious force fired from a moving vehicle and killed a young woman sitting with her child in her lap. Yeats wrote bitterly of the airman Robert Gregory:

> Some nineteen German planes, they say,
> You had brought down before you died.
> We called it a good death. Today
> Can ghost or man be satisfied?
> Although your last exciting year
> Outweighed all other years, you said,
> Though battle joy may be so dear
> A memory, even to the dead,
> It chases other thoughts away,
> Yet rise from your Italian tomb,
> Flit to Kiltartan cross and stay
> Till certain second thoughts have come
> Upon the cause you served, that we
> Imagined such a fine affair:
> Half-drunk or whole-mad soldiery
> Are murdering your tenants there.
> Men that revere your father yet
> Are shot at on the open plain.
> Where may new-married women sit
> And suckle children now? Armed men
> May murder them in passing by
> Nor law nor parliament take heed.[65]

These two poems must be read together: for their merging of two wars – the Great War and the Irish War of Independence – again explains the reason why remembering the former could not create the common folk memory that it did in Great Britain:

> Close your ears with dust and lie
> Among the other cheated dead.

Ireland did have her own soldier-poet: Francis Ledwidge, a young nationalist from County Monaghan, an Irish Volunteer, who originally opposed the Irish Volunteers joining the British army, but who enlisted in the Royal Inniskilling Fusiliers in October 1914, and who was killed in July 1917. Ledwidge was at one and the same time a British soldier and an Irish nationalist. Ledwidge's duality was marked in the version of his poems published in 1918 which described him as a 'Poet of the Insurrection' and as a 'war poet'.[66] His poems are evocative, gentle, and poignant, filled with a deep love of the Irish countryside, utterly devoid of hatred or violence, but expressing an underlying sense of the moral rightness of his decision to enter the war: he had, 'a soldier's heart'. But he was made aware of the way in which Irish politics had divided him from his comrades in the British army. Ledwidge was friends with a Belfast Protestant, Bob Christie, who mused ironically that, after the Easter Rising, 'the trouble that Frank was now heading for was due to his talk. Need I say that there was no right or wrong in any opinion expressed unless it was one hundred per cent loyal'. It was in vain that Ledwidge appealed to Bob Christie in May 1916, 'do our sympathies not go to Cathleen ni Houlihan? Poor MacDonagh and Pearse were two of my best friends, and now they are dead, shot by England'.[67]

What provoked a renewed interest – or, rather, the first interest – in Ireland and the Great War amongst writers was, I think, the troubles that engulfed the north of Ireland from the late 1960s. These provoked new explorations of Irishness, and the Great War was now perceived, rightly if belatedly, as central to the forging of Irish identities. The central place of the Somme in Ulster unionist ideology has been mentioned. But the literary explorations ranged widely, and in many respects fruitfully.

Jennifer Johnston is a novelist who has been widely praised in Dublin and London. She did not begin to write until her late thirties, but soon won various literary prizes. Her novel, published in 1974, *How many Miles to Babylon?* is set in the time of the Great War in France. Johnston manages to be both a republican in politics and a southern Irish Protestant, and her novels explore the predicament of the southern Protestant minority, of the Anglo-Irish 'big-house' society. 'I am focusing on a dwindling way of thinking about Ireland,' she said in 1984. 'I would also like to feel ... that there's a bridge being built there because I think that there are such fantastic misunderstandings ... The two cultures in Ireland cannot live without each other.' Her decision to write a novel about the Great War was inspired, as she herself put it, 'as a metaphor for what is presently happening. I was trying to write about human relationships with the undercurrent of violence'. She was also aware that

> The First World War seemed to be happening on everybody's back door ... every single person in Ireland must have lost someone in the war ... I think a rather sad thing has happened in Ireland about that war. Those men and what they did,

without understanding what was happening at all, have now been turned into some sort of treachery. When they were making the film *How many Miles to Babylon?* They had a hundred Irish soldiers marching around Co. Wicklow, dressed up in British uniforms, looking like all the photographs you've seen of those kids going out to the Somme. I was talking to some of them, and I asked if any of their grandfathers fought in World War I. There was a very long silence while they all looked at me, and then one of them said, 'Yes, my grandfather was a Connaught Ranger'. Another said, 'I had a great uncle', and somebody else said he had somebody in it. Suddenly you realised that they wouldn't admit it to each other. Of course they all had connections with the Great War. It didn't mean that their grandfathers were worse or better Irishmen. It meant that they were, in their own way, small heroes.[68]

Johnston's novel is concerned with what she agreed was the lack of ability of people, not merely to understand but to make implicit bonds with each other and with Irish dimensions of this theme. She explores the relationship between the son of Anglo-Irish gentry, Frederick Moore, and a stable boy, Jerry Crowe. Frederick's father is something of a home ruler, endowed with a love of the land and a strong sense of his own Irishness (or at least his non-Englishness), yet the family live in fundamental isolation from their Catholic neighbours: they are neighbours yet strangers. Frederick's isolation is felt the more keenly because he finds little affection from his mother, and his father is unable to convey the affection that he feels for his son. When war breaks out, Jerry and his boyhood friend, Fred, enlist in the army, but for very different reasons: Jerry to learn the trade of war, the better to use it to fight for Irish independence; Fred because his mother reveals that his father is not his real father at all. Their friendship comforts them at the front, despite their differences in rank, religion and class. Jerry protests that in the new independent Ireland, 'We need each other, though. Your kind and mine. You'll see'.[69] This sense of identity is reinforced by the attitude of their commanding officer, Major Glendinning, an Englishman who has, to his eternal shame, been posted to an Irish regiment. 'You are all amateurs,' he complains, 'I will make you professionals ... I never asked for a bunch of damn bog Irish. I must make the best of it.'[70] The closeness of the bond between Roman Catholic, peasant Sinn Féiner, and gentry Anglo-Irishman is symbolised in two acts: firstly, Jerry removes Fred's shoes and bathes his painful swollen feet. Shortly afterwards, Jerry temporarily deserts, to find out what has happened to his father, also a British soldier: to help him if he is wounded or to secure his mother's pension rights if he is dead. When Jerry returns and is arrested, Glendinning orders Fred to take charge of the firing party which will execute the deserter. Fred's act of self sacrifice is a fatal one: he uses his revolver to shoot his friend, thus sparing him the ignominy of the firing squad, knowing that he, Fred, is also sacrificing his life. And so he awaits the firing squad: 'they will never understand'.[71]

The novel explores how the mutual estrangement of Jerry and Fred is symbolic of the estrangement between the Anglo-Irish and the Catholic Irish, how this has damaged Ireland, and each other. Yet they are, or could be, united by two bonds: love of the land, and mutual, individual concern that transcends political and religious division. Both men sacrifice their political (in Jerry's case) and social (in Fred's case) beliefs for friendship; both find their common Irishness in the trenches, and in opposition to the uncomprehending Major Glendinning. The novel leaves key questions unanswered: would this mutual sympathy have survived a return to Ireland? Would Jerry's projected 'war of liberation' – one, he admits, where 'every town, every village will be the front line'[72] – have spared Frederick or his ancestral home? In what way could their very different social circles be reconciled? Was it only in death that they were not divided?

As Dr Edna Longley points out, English writers who concern themselves with the past, such as Thomas Hardy, see the pastness of the past; Irish writers are more aware of its irreversible presentness. The Ulster poet, Michael Longley, contrasts the glory and swagger of the Ulster Division at the Somme – 'wilder than the Gurkhas' – with his father's slow death as a result of wounds received in the war:

> He said – lead traces flaring till they hurt –
> I am dying for King and Country, slowly.

Longley then considers the violence in contemporary Ulster, a hole in the corner, casual violence inflicted by a 'shivering boy' on a bus conductor (who was to be a witness at the trial of a Republican):

> Before they could turn the television down
> Or tidy away the supper dishes.
> To the children, to a bewildered wife,
> I think, 'Sorry Missus' was what he said.[73]

Ulster, Ireland, reared on memories of glorious violence, nationalist, unionist, now finds itself reliving the war in contemporary politics.

Likewise, Frank McGuinness in his play, *Observe the Sons of Ulster Marching Towards the Somme*, chooses a theme which as an Ulster Catholic he could not respond to with instinctive sympathy, but which enabled him to explain how a character in his drama could say 'I love my Ulster' with as much difficulty as McGuinness himself felt in articulating these words.[74] This enables him to explore this vital moment in the construction of one of the sustaining myths of unionist history.

The first part of the play is entitled 'Remembrance'. Kenneth Pyper, now an old man, still sees the ghosts of the soldiers with whom he went to war, and the use of ghosts is itself significant – the past returns to haunt, to disturb – it will not go away. Pyper is in fact the most cynical, detached, and – as he thinks – untypical of the Ulster Protestants with whom he finds himself as a young man, a difference reinforced by his homosexuality. Yet the shared experience of the Somme and the horror of war, mean that as the best educated, most powerful of the men, he finds himself becoming, almost against his will, their leader and their comforter. Before the Somme, on its very dawn, two of the soldiers have a mock reconstruction of the Battle of the Boyne. Millen, who has been chosen to play King James' horse, asks plaintively, 'Why do we have to be King James? He has to get beaten.' McIlwaine replies, 'Because somebody has to be King James. And, anyway, you're only his horse.' Says Millen, 'This is not a fair fight', to which Anderson remarks, 'What fight is ever fair? Are you right? Let battle commence. And remember, King James, we know the result, you know the result, keep to the result.'[75]

But seconds before the real battle the soldiers' prejudices are elevated above mere prejudice. Pyper, the cynic, the outsider, reminds the men of their homeland. The river Somme, which the men can smell, 'is bringing us home', says Pyper. 'We're not in France. We're home. We're on our own territory. We're fighting for home. This river is ours. This land's ours. We've come home.'

Anderson hands Pyper an Orange sash to wear. 'It's not mine', says Pyper. 'It is now. It's a gift. From us.' Pyper takes it. He has embraced his destiny. The men sing a hymn. And Pyper says a last prayer:[76]

> Save us. Save our country. Destroy our enemies at home and on this field of battle. Let this day at the Somme be as glorious in the memory of Ulster as that day at the Boyne, when you scattered our enemies. Lead us back from this exile. To Derry. To the Foyle. To Belfast and the Lagan. To Armagh. To Tyrone. To the Bann and its banks, To Erne and its islands. Protect them. Protect us. Protect me. Let us fight bravely. Let us win gloriously. Lord, look down on us. Spare us. I love – Observe the sons of Ulster marching towards the Somme. I love their lives. I love my own life. I love my home. I love my Ulster.

The chant, taken up by all the men, turns into a battle cry.[77] But a cry to what end? To Pyper's loneliness, his ghosts. His home has grown cold; the province has grown lonely. Pyper fought to maintain what they fought for, but he only believed because the men who died taught him. Yet he is not at peace. The Temple of the Lord is ransacked in modern Ulster.[78]

Ulster's culture has trapped these men, even the cynical Pyper. In the end, he is the most trapped. He is still trapped as an old man, yet the play is not merely a lesson for Ulstermen or anyone else about the blind alley that loyalties can lead a man towards. It gives a clear and moving illustration of their humanity, their fear, and the desperation of their fate. The soldiers' rancorous sectarianism is lifted above rancour by their discovery of themselves, of each other, by their pairing and bonding, and by their energy. The play is full of energy, and wit, and seems to say – this event can lead you inwards as it does Pyper; but can not the love he develops for his comrades lead outwards? And the play is outward-looking in another way. It leads the audience to explore traditions with which they may not sympathise, may not even understand. It has no lessons to preach, no sermons; only an invitation to examine a very complex, absorbing, rebarbative, but vibrant culture.

Asking questions of a culture is an essential part of the historian and the imaginative writer alike. Seamus Heaney poses some questions in his poem, 'In Memoriam, Francis Ledwidge', the Catholic soldier I have already referred to, who fought for Irish freedom in a khaki uniform, who was on leave when the 1916 Rising broke out, and who wrote a poem in memory of the rebels who were executed by men wearing the same khaki uniforms as himself. Heaney begins his poem by recalling a figure cast in bronze, a war memorial, which meant little to him as he walked hand in hand with his aunt along Portstewart promenade; but now he recalls Ledwidge,

> in your Tommy's uniform.
> A haunted Catholic face, pallid and brave,
> Ghosting the trenches with a bloom of hawthorn
> Or silence cored from a Boyne passage grave.

Heaney touches, though he does not resolve, the paradox of the Catholic soldier:

> 'To be called a British soldier while my country
> Has no place among nations ...' You were rent
> By shrapnel six weeks later. 'I am sorry
> That party politics should divide our tents.'

Here is the enigma; but Heaney cannot construct anything upon it, it is a 'dead enigma', one in which 'all the strains criss-cross in useless equilibrium'.

> And as the wind tunes through this vigilant bronze
> I hear again the sure confusing drum.

Ledwidge, unlike the men this bronze statue commemorates, was no 'true blue', but, Heaney ends grimly 'all of you consort now underground'.[79] Only in death are unionist and nationalist not divided. Ledwidge, British soldier, Irish patriot, fighting to free nations. Not like other British soldiers, for Ledwidge's nation is not free; yet anxious that party politics should not stand in the way of what he, and his like, sought: the winning of Home Rule, the recasting of the Anglo-Irish relationship, and yet the ending of the deep quarrel with Ulster unionists. Here is a set of contradictions: the bronze soldier, solid, harsh, the bloom of hawthorn on a trench; the Catholic face, the British army uniform. In an essay, Heaney sees Ledwidge 'conflicting elements in the Irish inheritance which continue to be repressed or unresolved'. There is, he says, still minimal public acknowledgement in Ireland of the part played by Irish soldiers in the First World War, although their devotion to the ideal of independence was passionate in its day. Heaney then adds an interesting observation: 'We do now see the development of a corresponding unwillingness to acknowledge the heroic aspect of the 1916 Rising.'[80]

Heaney might have taken this important point further, for it raises the question of the impact of these two seminal events on the making of modern Ireland. The 1916 rebels fought, as they saw it, for a united and free Ireland, promising to cherish all the children of the nation equally. Yet it is commonly acknowledged by historians at least that their Rising further exacerbated the divisions within Ireland between unionist and nationalist. There is no doubt about their bravery and determination in engaging in battle with the British army (though some of the units fighting the rebels were also Irish). Indeed, the spectacle of Irishman fighting Irishman was an ominous portent.[81] The 36th Ulster Division, and the 10th and 16th Irish Divisions might likewise be seen as fighting in a common cause, and one that would unite the nation; but their unionism and nationalism were not softened by war (though individual soldiers could appreciate each other's common humanity and predicament). As Jane Leonard points out, the question of commemoration in southern Ireland fluctuated with the political temperature since 1969: events such as the IRA hunger strikes necessitated a lower profile; the IRA bombing of the Enniskillen Remembrance Day ceremony in 1987 caused a revival of sympathy for the Irish war dead, and poppy sales were resumed in certain parts of counties Dublin and Wicklow.[82] And there has been since 1993 a definite move towards using the Great War dead as a means of healing up the wounds of the contemporary Northern Ireland conflict. In 1993 the Irish President, Mary Robinson, attended the Remembrance Day service in St Patrick's Cathedral; in July 1994 the Fianna Fáil leader, Bertie Ahern, declared the Islandbridge memorial park formally open and complete. Finally in November 1998, a memorial to all the Irish dead was opened in Flanders, overlooking Messines Ridge, in the shape of an Irish round tower, with the new President, Mary McAleese (an Ulster Catholic) attending, and with a clear message that the war should be a cause of unity, not division 'redeeming', the President said, 'of the memory' of the Irish who died in the First World War. [83]

But this, though laudable, shifts the ground from the motives of the men of the Great War, who fought for 'Ireland' or 'Ulster', for a Home Rule Ireland, or for an Ireland located firmly in the United Kingdom. The Irish soldiers of the Great War were, then, pursuing a course of action as divisive in its own way as that of the 1916 rebels. And the political interpretation of the battle of the Somme, contrasted as it was with the disloyalty of the 1916 rebels, deepened those divisions: now that 'Ulster' had made her blood sacrifice, she had proved herself a kind of nation, or at least a people, with a distinctive character and political destiny. But the exigency of the contemporary peace process in Northern Ireland has reinterpreted this Great War experience. The beat of the 'sure, confusing drum' might encourage contemporary Ireland to march to a different tempo. However, the echo of that other seminal Great War military event, the Easter Rising, another sure confusing drum, still seems to defy such a conciliatory interpretation.

Notes

1 An earlier version of this paper is '*The Sure Confusing Drum*': *Ireland and the First World War* (University of Wales, Swansea, 1993). I am grateful to the University for permission to reprint much of this version.

2 For a criticism of this 'folk-history' see B. Bond (ed.), *The First World War and British Military History* (Oxford, Oxford University Press, 1991), pp. 268–9 and 284–6.

3 M. O'Callaghan, 'Language or religion: the quest for identity in the Irish Free State, 1922–32' (MA thesis, National University of Ireland, University College Dublin, 1981), p. 1.

4 M. Staunton, 'The Royal Munster Fusiliers in the Great War, 1914–19' (MA thesis, National University of Ireland, University College Dublin, 1986), p. 59. For Redmond's speech see D. Gwynn, *John Redmond's Last Years* (London, Arnold, 1919), pp. 154–5.

5 Staunton, 'Royal Munster Fusiliers', p. 23.

6 M. MacDonagh, *The Irish at the Front* (London, Hodder and Stoughton, 1916), pp. 154–8.

7 P. Callan, 'Voluntary Recruitment for the British Army in Ireland during the First World War' (PhD thesis, National University of Ireland, University College Dublin, 1984), p. 385. But see K. Jeffery, *Ireland and the Great War* (Cambridge, Cambridge University Press, 2000), p. 7 for a different and larger, number.

8 Callan, p. 68.

9 NAM, Ms. 7704–6, J. L. Stewart-Moore, Random recollections recalled by J. L. Stewart-Moore, part II, The Great War, 1914–18.

10 C. Falls, *The History of the 36th Ulster Division* (Belfast, M'Caw, Stevenson & Orr, 1922), pp. 16–17. For further examples see P. Orr, *The Road to the Somme* (Belfast, Blackstaff Press, 1987), pp. 57, 67 and 125.

11 Falls, *History of the 36th Ulster Division*, p. 23.

12 H. Harris, 'The other half million', in O. Dudley Edwards and F. Pyle (eds) *1916: The Easter Rising* (London, MacGibbon and Kee, 1968), pp. 101–15 and 103.

13 Staunton, 'Royal Munster Fusiliers', Appendix 1.

14 D. Fitzpatrick, 'Militarism in Ireland, 1900–1922', in T. Bartlett and K. Jeffery (eds) *A Military History of Ireland* (Cambridge, Cambridge University Press, 1996), pp. 379–406 and 386–8.

15 NLI, Ms. 21,278, Parsons to the Secretary of State, War Office, 29 November 1914, p. 8.

16 NLI, Ms. 21,278, H. J. Tennant to Parsons, 11 February 1915, p. 18.

17 NLI, Ms. 21,278, Parsons to Tennant, 27 February 1915, p. 25.

18 NLI, Ms. 21,2778, Tennant to Parsons, 8 March 1915, p. 29.

19 D. Fitzpatrick, *Ireland and the First World War* (Dublin, Trinity College, 1986), p. 16. See

also Jeffery, *Ireland and the Great War*, pp. 8–12, and T. P. Dooley, *Irishmen or English Soldiers? The Times and World of a Catholic Irish Man* (Liverpool, Liverpool University Press, 1995), ch. 4.

20 J. Leonard, 'Lest we forget', in Fitzpatrick, *Ireland and the First World War*, p. 60.

21 MacDonagh, *The Irish at the Front*, p. 13.

22 W. Redmond, *Trench Pictures from France* (London, Andrew Melrose, August 1917 [reprinted September 1917]), pp. 139–47.

23 H. Harrison, *Ireland and the British Empire, 1937: Conflict or Conciliation* (London, Robert Hale, 1937), pp. 20–36.

24 Redmond, *Trench Pictures from France*, p. 69.

25 *Ibid.*, pp. 178–80.

26 NLI, Ms. 21,278, Redmond to Lady Parsons, 16 March 1917, p. 93a.

27 NAM, R. Fielding, Letters to a Wife (London, 1929), p. 121.

28 For a discussion of the English perception and stereotype of the Irish soldiers in the Great War see T. Denman, 'The Catholic Irish soldier in the First World War: the "racial environment"', in *Irish Historical Studies*, vol. 27 (November, 1991), pp. 354–61.

29 Quoted in P. Buckland, *The Anglo-Irish and the New Ireland, 1885–1922* (Dublin, Gill and Macmillan, 1972), p. 47.

30 NAM, Ms. 7670–61–1, N. E. Drury, My War Diary, 1914–1918.

31 NAM, Ms. 7608–40, Recollections of C. A. Brett.

32 Fielding, Letters to a Wife, pp. 169–70 and 191–2.

33 NAM, Ms. 7607–69–2, N. E. Drury, My War Diary, 1914–1918; *The Times*, 17 May 1916 (Press cutting in the NAM, Ms. 5809–27–8); Staunton, 'Royal Munster Fusiliers', pp. 200, 229 and 231–2, Jeffery, *Ireland and the Great War*, pp. 54–5.

34 Staunton, 'Royal Munster Fusiliers', pp. 201–2.

35 *Ibid.*

36 Orr, *Road to the Somme*, p. 54.

37 I. Colvin, *The Life of Lord Carson* (London, Victor Gollancz, 1936), p. 41. See also General Richardson, Commander of the UVF, who referred to 'thoroughly well trained men' who would 'return to the attack and relegate Home Rule to the devil' (Gwynn, *John Redmond's Last Days*, p. 163).

38 *Ibid.*, p. 342.

39 In 1582 Pope Gregory XIII put right an error in the Julian calendar, caused by the failure to calculate accurately the period taken by the earth to go round the sun. On 24 February 1582, Gregory ordered that the day after 4 October should be recast as 15 October, i.e. eleven days were added. Therefore, 1 July was 12 July if the eleven 'missing' days are added – a whimsical point, and one sitting oddly with the Ulster Protestant tradition, which had no great respect for the doings of popes.

40 Falls, *History of the 36th Ulster Division*, p. 51.

41 NAM, Ms. 7704–76, Recollections of J. L. Stewart-Moore.

42 Orr, *Road to the Somme*, pp. 219–22.

43 B. Rolston, *Politics and Painting: Murals and Conflict in Northern Ireland* (New Jersey, London and Ontario, Associated University Press, 1991), pp. 32–3 and 44–5.

44 J. B. Lyons, *The Enigma of Tom Kettle: Irish Nationalist, Essayist, Poet and British Soldier, 1880–1916* (Dublin, Glendale Press, 1983), pp. 292–3.

45 Harrison, *Ireland and the British Empire*, p. 30.

46 Staunton, 'Royal Munster Fusiliersr', pp. 293–304.

47 J. Leonard, 'The twinge of memory: Armistice day and Remembrance Sunday in Dublin since 1919', in R. English and G. Walker (eds), *Unionism in Modern Ireland: New Perspectives on Politics and Culture* (London, Macmillan, 1996), pp. 99–114 and p.101.

48 *Irish Times*, 13 November 1922, 12 November 1929 and 13 November 1933.

49 Leonard, 'The twinge of memory', p. 105.

50 Leonard, 'Lest we forget', pp. 64–7. For a full discussion on the long and tortuous process of the making of the Islandbridge memorial see Jeffery, *Ireland and the Great War*, pp. 113–23.

51 Quoted in M. Goldring, *Belfast: From Loyalty to Rebellion* (London, Lawrence and Wishart, 1991), p. 97.

52 NLI, Ms. 21,278, H. J. Tennant to Parsons, 5 February 1915, p. 17; Ms. 21, 278, Denis Gwynn to Mrs M. D. Robertson, n.d., p. 122.

53 For Australia see A. Thomson, 'History and "Betrayal": the Anzac controversy', in *History Today*, vol. 43 (January 1993), pp. 8–11. For the Gallipoli controversy as it affected Ireland see P. Maume, *The Long Gestation: Irish Nationalist Life, 1891–1918* (Dublin, Gill and MacMillan, 1999), p. 154.

54 P. Simkins, 'Everyman at war: recent interpretations of the front line experience' in Bond, *The First World War*, p. 302.

55 T. Denman, *Ireland's Unknown Soldiers: The 16th (Irish) Division in the Great War* (Dublin, Irish Academic Press, 1992); Tom Johnstone, *Orange, Green and Khaki: The Story of the Irish Regiments in the Great War, 1914–18* (Dublin, Gill and MacMillan, 1992).

56 Orr, *Road to the Somme*, p. 225. But the Great War Museum at Albert has an Ulster Division display showing soldiers of the Division wearing Orange Order sashes.

57 *Ibid.*, pp. 180 and 200–1.

58 T. Flanagan, 'Contrasting fables in the year of the French', in A. S. Eyler and R. E. Garrett (eds), *The Uses of the Past; Essays on Irish Culture* (Newark and London, University of Delaware Press, 1988), p. 13.

59 R. B. Macdowell, *Crisis and Decline: The Fate of the Southern Unionists* (Dublin, Lilliput Press, 1997), p. 53.

60 *Ibid.*, p. 66.

61 Robert Gregory (1881–1918), was shot down over Italy on 23 January 1918. He was 'a man noted for the versatility of his gifts', and Yeats saw him as 'a model of human perfection, a personification of youth and talent and largeness of being': Albright (ed.), *The Poems*, notes on pp. 551–2.

62 W. B. Yeats, *Collected Poems*, (London, 1990), p. 152.

63 Albright, pp. 184–5.

64 T. Webb (ed.), *W. B. Yeats: Selected Poetry* (London, Penguin Books, 1991), pp. 256–7.

65 Albright, *The Poems*, pp. 555–6.

66 A. Curtayne, *Francis Ledwidge: A Life of the Poet* (London, Martin Brian and O'Keefe, 1972), p.159; Jeffery, *Ireland and the Great War*, p. 105.

67 *Ibid.*, p. 151.

68 Interview in the *Irish Literary Supplement*, vol. 3 (Fall, 1984), pp. 25–7.

69 J. Johnston, *How many Miles to Babylon?* (London, Penguin edition, 1974), p. 111.

70 *Ibid.*, p. 92.

71 *Ibid.*, p. 156.

72 *Ibid.*, p. 111. For an analysis of Irish war writing see Jeffery, *Ireland and the Great War*, pp. 95–106.

73 E. Longley, 'When did you last see your father? Perceptions of the past in Northern Irish writing, 1965–1985', in M. Kenneally (ed.), *Cultural Contexts and Literary Idioms in Contemporary Irish Literature* (Gerrards Cross, Colin Smythe, 1988), pp. 88–95.

74 Quoted in H. Lojek, 'Difference without indifference: the drama of Frank McGuinness and Anne Devlin', in *Éire-Ireland*, vol. 25 (Summer 1990), p. 58.

75 F. McGuinness, *Observe the Sons of Ulster Marching Towards the Somme* (London, Faber and Faber, 1990), p. 70.

76 *Ibid.*, pp. 73–4.
77 *Ibid.*, pp. 79–80.
78 *Ibid.*, p. 80.
79 P. Muldoon (ed.), *The Faber Book of Contemporary Irish Poetry* (London, Faber, 1986), pp. 262–4.
80 S. Heaney, 'Introduction' in Curtayne, *Francis Ledwidge*, pp. 19–20.
81 Fitzpatrick, 'Militarism in Ireland', p. 394.
82 Leonard, 'The twinge of memory', pp. 107–9.
83 *The Times*, 9 October 1998; Jeffery, *Ireland and the Great War*, pp. 139–42. Andrew Lockhart, a Donegal Protestant, is buried at the foot of the tower.

Index